JOYCE CARY AND THE DIMENSIONS OF ORDER

Joyce Cary and the Dimensions of Order

Michael J C Echeruo

Professor of English Literature
University of Ibadan, Nigeria

BOOKS
10 East 53d St., New York 10022
(a division of Harper & Row Publishers, Inc.)

First published 1979 by
THE MACMILLAN PRESS LTD
London and Basingstoke

Published in the U.S.A. 1979 by
HARPER & ROW PUBLISHERS, INC.
BARNES & NOBLE IMPORT DIVISION

Printed in Great Britain

Library of Congress Cataloging in Publication Data

Echeruo, Michael J C
Joyce Cary and the dimensions of order.

Bibliography: p.
Includes index.
1. Cary, Joyce, 1888–1957 — Criticism and interpre-
tation. I. Title.
PR6005.A77Z647 1979   823$'$.9$'$12   78-9857
ISBN 0-06-491875-0

For
Rose Nkeonyere Echeruo

Contents

Acknowledgements

The author and publishers wish to thank the Joyce Cary Estate for permission to quote from the works of Joyce Cary, copyright the Joyce Cary Estate.

Preface

Joyce Cary was essentially and perhaps inevitably a genius of irregular competence. The first phase of his career (1932–39) was devoted to an attempt, as it were, to write his African experience out of his system. The novels that resulted from his tours of duty as a District Officer in the Nigerian Colonial Service (1913–19) and which form the subject of my earlier book, *Joyce Cary and the Novel of Africa* (Longman, 1973), were experimental: Cary was still trying to 'educate' himself and to find a way of relating his philosophy of life to his experience of the foreign African scene, and he was still battling with the problem of finding a narrative device to embody his ideas. In his four novels of Africa, Cary adopted the third person omniscient narrative point of view which allowed him to identify occasionally with particular African characters—Aissa, Obai, Elizabeth and Johnson. However, Cary was anxious not to lose a controlling hand on the events of the novels as they concern his European characters, whose presence in Africa is the occasion for the novels themselves.

The novels studied in this book belong to a later phase, to the two major periods of Cary's writing career (1940–44; 1952–55) when he appeared to have fully resolved the philosophical doubts of his earlier years and found his own narrative style. The first of these two periods begins with *Charley Is My Darling* (1940), Cary's first novel of Europe and the first to win him real recognition in the serious press. It ends with *The Horse's Mouth* (1944), the last novel of what is usually called simply the 'First Trilogy' but ought to be recognised as the 'Existentialist Trilogy'. Between this and the second phase we have nearly a decade during which, though he published his two unevenly executed novels of womanhood (*The Moonlight*, 1946 and *A Fearful Joy*, 1949), Cary was actually preparing for and working on the novels of his 'second' or 'Political Trilogy', the last novel of which (*Not Honour More*) was published in 1955.

In referring to these years as 'periods' and 'phases', it is not being suggested that Cary's philosophical and aesthetic contentions are only to be found in these major novels; the argument is rather that only in them was Cary able to combine philosophy and art, able to sustain a philosophical argument in fully and beautifully realised works of prose fiction.

Ibadan, Nigeria   M. J. C. E.
December 1977

1 Ideas

After the excitement of the last ten years or so, it is time perhaps to return to Joyce Cary and the ideas which, so he believed, made his fiction possible and worthwhile.[1] Joyce Cary is certainly not one of England's greatest novelists, and we do not find in his work the larger-than-life tales or the immense and grand issues which are usually associated with immortal fiction. Curiously enough, though, Cary continues to intrigue his readers by the hints his novels give of the seriousness and relevance of what he has to say, the essential truth of the sense-of-life with which he surrounds his characters and—which is almost distinctive with him—the almost abstract nature of the ideas which interested him.

What we have, therefore, is the curious situation in which Joyce Cary, who read philosophy seriously and tried to be exact in his use of it in his fiction, seems to us less 'profound' in his statement of his philosophy than other artists who had a more generalised interest in some philosophers but a more 'impressive' application of the relevant ideas in their fiction. What the Notebooks and Diaries now at the Bodleian Library of Oxford University attest to is Joyce Cary's consistent and sincere interest in abstract philosophy; the contrast they establish is with Cary's novels themselves in which speculative thought, as such, is hardly ever adequately represented, and even then at a level where it is totally indistinguishable from mere feeling.[2] Thus, the Joyce Cary who devoted several pages in his notebooks to rephrasing Plato, Kant, Tolstoy and Croce refused to create a correspondent character in his fiction to prosecute a similar interest. No wonder, then, that many of his critics, including the most sympathetic and provocative ones among them, have somehow come to believe not only that Cary's ideas, *qua* ideas, are no more than a 'species of captivating but disquieting philosophical and moral largesse' but that to approach him at all is to be concerned 'inescapably, if not woefully, with his failure, by and large, to interest the best minds of our time'.[3]

I think it is possible to see why this impression is unjustified both in relation to Cary's ideas and to his achievement as a philosophical novelist. Indeed, Cary found his feet as a novelist quite late in life, not so much because he lacked the technical competence to write well, but because, as he himself put it, he lacked a proper education for his role as a writer. What he needed was 'a new education in ethics, in history, in philosophy'. From 1920, when he returned finally from his tour of duty in the Nigerian Colonial Service, to 1932, when *Aissa Saved*, his first novel, was published, Cary devoted himself to acquiring that education.

> Although I did not know it, how could I, my mind was split . . . And until I had made a reconciliation I could not even write dialogue. I had no religion, no integrated ideas of the world. I believed vaguely in God and I believed vaguely in science, but I had never seen the need to reconcile the mechanism of the scientific idea and the free creative soul of the world.[4]

METAPHYSICS

To understand Cary's ideas and appreciate the argument of his novels, therefore, we need to reflect on the implications of this statement. For Cary seems to be saying that this opposition of Science to God and of Mechanism to Freedom constituted his most important source of spiritual and intellectual uncertainty. If, indeed, he was able to write fiction only after he had resolved this conflict—'made a reconciliation', as he put it—then Cary's specific conclusions in his individual novels and in his other writings would in some important way be related to that original dichotomy between Spirit and Matter, between Necessity and Freedom. It is not, therefore, simply a matter of recognising the place of the imagination or the recurrence of the ideas of freedom in Cary's work as his critics have sometimes tended to do, but of giving these ideas their full philosophical status and of accepting that a total world-view is derivable from them. It is certainly one implication of Cary's own statement that he believed the reconciliation he sought would resolve the philosophical and aesthetic problems which he would encounter in writing fiction.

Fortunately, it is not difficult to place Cary's task in relation to the ideas of earlier philosophers, especially Kant. Indeed the problem which Cary was trying to resolve for himself was the same that Kant encountered when he wanted to reconcile the *necessity* of classical philosophy with the idea of the *freedom of the self* enjoined by the practical reason. As Copleston has put it, Kant's philosophy was an 'original attempt to solve the problem of reconciling the two realms of necessity and freedom, not by reducing the one to the other, but by finding their meeting-point in the moral consciousness of man'.[5] This reconciliation is, in fact, derived from the empirical philosophy of Hume as revolutionised by the transcendental criticism of Kant. In so far as man's existence is subject to time-conditions, Kant argued, his actions form part of the mechanical system of Nature and are determined by antecedent causes. That is *necessity* or mechanism. Rebelling, however, against empiricist mechanism, Kant argued that 'the very same subject, being on the other hand conscious of himself as a thing-in-itself, considers his existence also in so far as determinable only through laws which he gives himself through reason'.[6] Kant's solution came in the form of a paradox:

It does not involve a contradiction to assert on the one hand that the will, in the phenomenal realm (of visible action), necessarily obeys the laws of nature, and to this extent is not free; and on the other hand, that, as belonging to a thing-in-itself, it is not subject to such laws and accordingly is free.[7]

Cary phrases his in a similar vein:

The creative soul needs the machine, as the living world needs fixed character, or it could not exist at all. It would be merely an idea. But by a paradox we have to accept, part of this fixed character is the free mind, the creative imagination, in everlasting conflict with facts, including its own machinery, its own tools.[8]

In Kant, then, Cary found his own answer to those 'scientific' philosophies—of Darwin, Nietzsche, Spengler, Freud and Marx—which were, in a sense, parallel to the Newtonian 'mechanism' of Kant's time. Man needed a 'spirit' to counteract the supremacy of matter; a transcendental 'God' to challenge the material God of the scientists. Moreover, God may be dead, in the sense, according to

Nietzsche, that Science has triumphed and made Providence unnecessary. But a universe without a unifying principle parallel to the moral will of man, or to God, would be a meaningless and absurd one. In Kant, Cary found a philosophy in which the 'truths' of human freedom and the existence of God, though not scientifically demonstrable, are introduced as 'implications' of the moral nature of man.[9] When Cary was asked by the *Paris Review* interviewers whether he was a 'determinist', he answered pointedly:

> Everyone but a lunatic has reason for what he does. Yes, in this sense I am a determinist. But I believe, with Kant, that the mind is self-determined . . . Of course, anyone can deny the freedom of the mind. He can argue that our ideas are conditioned. But anyone who argues so must not stop there. He must deny all freedom and say that the world is simply an elaborate kind of clock. He must be a behaviourist. There is no alternative, in logic, between behaviorism, mechanism, and the personal God who is the soul of beauty, love and truth.[10]

In a way, Cary's novels are his own way of giving expression to this philosophical position within the framework of art. Cary was himself very reluctant to embrace the title of 'philosophical novelist'. 'I have been called a metaphisical novelist, and if that means that I have a fairly comprehensive idea of the world I'm writing about, I suppose that's true'.[11] And also: 'I do not care for philosophers in books. They are always bores'.[12] But these statements do not amount to a rejection of philosophy. As Cary himself put it, his novels aim at a kind of truth which 'is not to be grasped, any more than any other kind of reality, by the brain alone, in contemplation, but only by a combination [of] thought and feeling'.[13] Whereas the philosopher's job is to 'make sense of life to the mind', it is the novelist's to make sense of it 'to the senses'.[14] Yet, in *Art and Reality*, in reflecting on 'the mind – body gap which all idealist philosophers and mechanists are eager to get rid of', Cary argues that 'even to our experience', this gap is not 'fixed' but 'varies from individual to individual and continually shifts'. And again: 'The individual mind appears to itself cut off from the general real except in so far as it can intuit that real'.[15] In these statements, Cary is clearly offering a significant alternative proposition to both the idealists and the mechanists. If these propositions also inform the fiction, they will not appear explicitly in an occasional situation or dialogue, or directly as independent disputations, but will condition the interpretation of situation, character and even structure.

The important point, then, in any serious study of Joyce Cary's thought and fiction, is to determine the relevance of his ideas, as ideas, to the specific life of the individual novels, as novels. There are difficulties in such an effort. Walter Allen, for example, has pointed out that a man may have the 'profoundest, most comprehensive and wisest views on the nature of things and still, when he attempts fiction, be a very poor novelist'.[16] There is danger, therefore, in making too much of the abstract philosophies of novelists. But there is an equally serious danger in totally failing to come to terms with a novelist's ideas on the assumption that it cannot 'matter much' whether those ideas are 'deep or superficial'.[17] We remember in this connection how F. R. Leavis dismissed *Tristram Shandy* as an 'irresponsible' and 'trifling' work. Early in that novel, in fact, Sterne spoke of those 'strong combinations of ideas, [which] the sagacious Locke, who certainly understood the nature of these things better than most men, affirms to have produced more wry actions than all other sources of prejudice whatsoever'.[18] But Leavis was not disposed to undertake a patient consideration of the possible import of Sterne's indirection and jocularity. For though it is true that to know of *Tristram Shandy's* connections with Locke's thought is not therefore to determine the quality of Sterne's use of Locke, the knowledge is at least a safeguard against regarding the novel as blatantly irresponsible. It has now been demonstrated that, far from being an irresponsible and trifling book, *Tristram Shandy* is a subtle and positive contribution, within the framework of fiction, to the current of thought initiated by Locke's refutation of the concept of innate ideas.[19] As novelist, Sterne was able to create characters and situations, and to represent life; as thinker, he was also able, through that life, to comment on the implications of Locke's analysis of ideas and his attempt to determine the significance of words. 'Exploiting Locke's own scepticism to a point where, as analytic method, even his limited rationalism is undermined, Tristram/Sterne invents the dramatic situations implicit in these conflicts of personal apprehension'.[20]

Just as the jocularity and indirection of *Tristram Shandy* become responsible when read in the proper light of Locke and philosophy, so also do we come to appreciate the intellectual seriousness of Cary's novels even when his characters are very unintellectual. For Cary's heroes live in the experiential, not the cerebral world; their task is to live in the world, not to analyse it. They are sensible and sensitive, but they are not engaged in an intellectual search for the significance of their lives. Because Cary's characters are of this sort, the impression is often created that their concerns are synonymous with Cary's, as if the intellectual capacity of the novelist and the quality of the fiction depend on the intellectual vitality of the hero. With some novelists, James Joyce and Viriginia Woolf, for example, the intellectual quality of the fiction is the product of the intellectual sophistication of the protagonists. Virginia Woolf's heroines—outside of Mrs Dalloway— are naturally inclined, because of their sensitivity to what may be called the moods of the intellect, to sustained and dramatic extensions of mind. Virginia Woolf felt required to create such heroines in protest against the intellectual placidity of the novel in her time, and against what Cary himself calls 'the statistical abstractions of the sociological school'.[21] Similarly, Joyce's concern in the *Portrait of the Artist as a Young Man*, as Miss Van Ghent has pointed out, is with the 'associative patterns' arising in Stephen's mind. Joyce is concerned with these patterns 'as they show the dialectical process by which a world-shape evolves in the mind. This process is conducted in the absolute solitude of the inside of the skull'.[22] The result is an intellectually taut, immensely erudite but witty biography of the artist's evolution. There is in this case, as in that of Virginia Woolf, a close connection between the ostensible in-tellectual quality of a novel and the intellectual disposition of its protagonists. This is not the only source of intellectual strength in these novels, obviously. But it encourges their readers to feel that if the hero of the novel is an intellectual, the ostensible or overt intellectual character of the novel will be stronger than if, for example, he is an inveterate and inarticulate sensibilist.[23]

In assessing the quality of thought in Cary's novels, we will need to use this understanding. For Cary's first-person narrators, indeed all his characters, are not even remotely the kind of intellectual that Stephen is. Cary seems to prefer to derive the philosophical vitality of his fiction not from the intellectual stature of his characters but from the nature of their situation. The argument of *Herself Surprised* is not the less important for the novel being narrated by a character immensely less cultivated and thoughtful than the narrators of *To Be a Pilgrim* and *The Horse's Mouth*. Nor, because he is an intelligent student of Spinoza, is Plantie (of *The Horse's Mouth*) more significant in Cary's drama of the problem of evil than the disinherited and inarticulate Obai of *An American Visitor*, to use an extreme example from one of Cary's early novels.

Cary's non-intellectualism is, fortunately, functional. Sterne's Tristram implored his readers that if he 'should seem sometimes to put on a fool's cap with a bell to it', they should bear with him and 'rather courteously give [him] credit for a little more wisdom than appears upon [his] outside'.[24] Cary does not make a similarly explicit plea for his characters, but he implies an equally extenuating argument. In *Except the Lord*, he speaks of the 'mystery' of the human mind, and of 'the mighty and everlasting pressure of the soul seeking by ways unseen and often unsuspected, its own good, freedom and enlightenment'.[25] In the Preface to *Castle Corner*, he says that his characters are 'conceived with those springs of action which seemed [to him] most important in all character, working out their fates in a world charged throughout with individuality, and the consequences of that inescapable freedom'.[26] In a world under 'pressure' and endowed with 'inescapable freedom', the individual intellect can make only a puny contribution towards bringing order and meaning to its own gross ineptitude. Intellectual power has of necessity to be imposed on the character and his action by the organizing power of art. It becomes the burden of fiction to present a drama of life which would supply a sustaining intellectual meaning to a frankly non-intellectual world.

This relative unimportance of the intellect in his characters is also a positive and predictable consequence of Cary's philosophical view of human existence, his belief in the freedom, isolation and creativeness of the individual. This belief, as would be expected, attaches greater importance to the power of the creative imagination than to that of the analytical intellect. In one of his conversations with Lord David Cecil, Cary argues that life is 'primarily experience'. The free individual has his own 'complex of personal feelings', and these feelings arise 'in the first place out of universal Nature'. 'Each man uses his mind and his imagination to create a world satisfactory to himself'. This creation is the individual's attempt to satisfy 'his feelings, his affections, his ambitions, his hopes and fears and so on'.[27] Cary understands this process of 'satisfaction' in Kant's transcendental rather than Hume's mechanical terms. Adopting Kierkegaard's views (themselves derived from Kant),[28] Cary argues that man 'has to create' (or satisfy his feelings and ambitions) 'because he is isolated'. He is 'free, and therefore isolated—the two things go together, you can't have one without the other'.[29]

From this conviction arises one of the most central ideas of Cary's thought and his fiction—the idea of the cherished self-created universe.

> The world loves its own creation, which is its life. Not merely the artist, but every man and woman, begins from childhood to create for himself a world to which, as creator, he is deeply attached . . . He creates them in his imagination, and lives in them. Deprived of them, or even any large part of them, he would wither and die.[30]

This idea is related in many ways to contemporary existentialist thinking and is the source of both Cary's sense of human tragedy and his worship of human freedom. First, the self-created universe is an isolated and private universe—and has to be. 'We are alone in our worlds', Cary states. 'We can sympathize with each other, be fond of each other, but we can never completely understand each other. We are not only different in character and mind, we don't know how far this difference goes'.[31] What men have in common is a shared predicament, not a common identity. Each man, as both Kierkegaard and Sartre would argue, is isolated and at the same time 'condemned to be free'.[32]

Secondly, however 'wrong' the individual's created universe may be, it can only be the 'light' one for him, in an existentialist sense. Hume lent indirect support to this view. 'Nothing is more usual in philosophy, and even in common life, than to talk of the combat of passion and reason, to give the preference to reason, and assert that men are only so far virtuous as they conform themselves to its dictates . . . [but] nothing can oppose or retard the impulse of passion, but a contrary impulse'.[33] Cary agrees. Men 'live by their feelings and desires', not because they are 'completely selfish'—for 'passions are often regardless of self'—but because men will accept only those ideas that enable 'emotions formerly in conflict, therefore frustrated' to 'find complete satisfaction'.[34] Explaining his acceptance of Kierkegaard, Cary reiterates this supremacy of the self-created world: 'you've got to find out what people *believe*, what is pushing them on . . . And of course it's a matter, too, of the simpler emotional drives—like ambition and love'.[35]

What Cary is emphasising here is the vivacity and autonomy of the private idea of the world as a motive to action for the individual. The 'self-confidence of the Marxist convert' may be 'unjustified', Cary claims, but it is real and powerful, and (for him) valid.

> The neurotic and frustrated muddlehead of a month ago, uncertain and bewildered in every contact, in every relation, has become completely sure of himself and full of eagerness to realise this world that he has now found, to realize himself, to enjoy himself, in that world . . . He does not accept any fact that would injure his new faith, in which alone he finds his way in life.[36]

What is worth emphasising in this idea of the 'privacy' of self-created worlds is that the vivacity of such worlds is not equivalent to their 'truth', and that to record the integrity of each private world is not so much to recommend that idea of the world as to affirm the commitment which gives it power.

This attitude to the private world easily lends support to the complaint that Cary is what is loosely called a 'relativist' and a 'reluctant sage'.[37] This is unfortunate. For example, Cary opens *Art and Reality* with the simple statement that it is 'an attempt to examine the relation of the artist with the world as it seems to him and to see what he does with it'.[38] And again: 'I should perhaps repeat here that this picture of things, as I give it, is not intended for an absolute truth; no one can know what it is'.[39] This simplicity in phrasing can be misleading because both statements are precisely worded formulations of the purpose and method of his essay. Moreover, his meticulous specification of its limitations is demanded by the very philosophical assumptions on which he was trying to build his aesthetics. His claim is, in fact, the simple Kantian one that what we call 'truth' is essentially only a postulate, our attempt to comprehend the reality outside us, as perceived and organised by our particular minds and feelings. What Cary seeks to make clear in those qualifications, therefore, is that all knowledge, all truth is, by definition, *limited*, since the human mind cannot escape from its natural limitations, even in imagination.[40] 'The individual mind appears to itself as cut off from the general real except in so far as it can intuit that real'.[41]

As one would except, this view is a modification of Hume through Kant. Hume argued that

> . . . nothing is ever present to the mind but perceptions, and since all ideas are derived from something antecedently present to the

mind, it follows that it is impossible for us so much as to conceive or form an idea of anything specifically different from ideas and impressions. Let us fix our attention out of ourselves as much as possible; let us chase our imagination to the heavens, or to the utmost limits of the universe; we never really advance a step beyond ourselves, nor can we conceive any kind of existence, but those perceptions which have appeared in that narrow compass. This is the universe of the imagination, nor have we any idea but what is there produced.[42]

Kant confessed that this sceptical philosophy roused him from his 'dogmatic slumber' and induced him to make the crucial 'discovery' that there must be certain *a priori* synthetic forms or moulds in the human mind to give order to the abundance and apparent disorder of perceived phenomena. The conjunction of Hume and Kant first enables Cary to reject such dogmatism as seemed to conflict with the empirical evidence of nature, and secondly leads him to a recognition of the tremendous capacity and need of the human mind to create a transcending order for itself.

A connection is easily seen between this philosophical position and that 'conflict between order and freedom, between the static and the dynamic'[43] which most commentators admit is 'central' to Cary's work. What are the origins and consequences of this conflict in so far as the world of social and public affairs is concerned? This is an important question because the actual world in which the characters of Cary's novels live is shot through and through with the problems of order and freedom and the judgments which we make of their lives and of Cary's achievement depend on our understanding of the issues at stake. When it is realised that, in a very obvious sense, order and freedom are the standard issues in all politics, popularly understood, the need becomes greater to determine in what exact sense Cary's concern with order is to be taken. It then becomes clear that Cary's real interest is not in politics as such, nor in government (in the sense of 'law and order') but in the management of metaphysical and human order.

POLITICS

Cary's view of politics, accordingly, derives immediately from that idea of the self's consciousness of its own identity already referred to.

It is not a commonplace view, nor is it one accepted by all philosophers. Hume, for example, denied the existence of such an identity. 'Self or person is not any one impression, but that to which our several impressions and ideas are suppos'd to have a reference. If any impression gives rise to the idea of self, that impression must continue invariably the same, thro' the whole course of our lives; since self is suppos'd to exist after that manner. But there is no impression constant and invariable'.[44] Because Hume considered man's 'consciousness' as no more than 'a bundle of different perceptions, which succeed each other with an inconceivable rapidity, and are in a perpetual flux and movement',[45] he postulated that we 'may imagine we feel a liberty within ourselves; but a spectator can commonly infer our actions from our motives and character; and even where he cannot, he concludes in general, that he might, were he perfectly acquainted with every circumstance of our situation and temper'.[46] The 'freedom' of the individual is accordingly merely the minimal '*power of acting or not acting, according to* THE DETERMINATION OF THE WILL; that is, if we choose to remain at rest, we may; if we choose to move, we also may. Now this hypothetical liberty is universally allowed to belong to everyone who is not a prisoner and in chains. Here then is no subject of dispute'.[47]

This doctrine—a doctrine of Necessity—did not allow room for what Cary calls 'purposive action',[48] and Hume himself was soon to find his own position inadequate: 'upon a more strict review of the section concerning *personal identity*, I find myself in . . . a labyrinth'.[49] Kant tried to find a solution to the problem. He agreed with Hume that we are conscious of Self—that is, the empirical ego which is perceived introspectively only in its successive states— only because we are conscious of non-self. In the *Critique of Pure Reason*, he argued that a man's consciousness of his own existence is at the same time an immediate consciousness of the existence of other things outside him.[50] To establish the necessity for this personal identity, Kant maintained that the will of a rational being must regard itself as independent and continuous. That is, the will of a rational being cannot be a will of its own in any meaningful sense except under the idea of its own identity and freedom.[51] Hence the idea of personal identity and that of personal freedom become imperative, though they cannot be *proved* to exist. Every time a man said, 'I ought to do so-and-so', Kant argued, he assumed that he had a real independent power.[52]

That, at any rate, was how Cary understood Kant's position on the subject. 'This argument', Cary comments, 'is important in metaphysics and in the theory of liberty'.[53] According to this thinking, the sense of individual identity and freedom is closely linked with and indistinguishable from the sense of free-will or autonomy of the self as a self-determined agent. 'Thus', says Cary, 'we know that we have liberty exactly as we know that we are ourselves. A man who said, "But I am not a self, I am nobody" may fairly be asked, "Who, then is giving this opinion and what is it worth?"'[54]

Taken strictly, even this resolution of the metaphysical problem is somewhat inconclusive. As Edward Caird has pointed out in his study of Kant:

> The consciousness of freedom or self-determination in the individual, *i.e.*, of the consciousness of his being the author of his own actions and responsible to himself independently of all circumstances, must always, appear a paradox so long as, and in so far as, the individual, in whom such a consciousness is awakened, regards anything or being to which he is related as purely external to himself, and acting on him from without. Hence for the individual, the consciousness of freedom must be a contradiction, unless he can regard himself as identified with a principle which, while it realises itself through his particular individuality and that of others, binds them all to each other as members of real freedom, a freedom which is not merely the negation of limits, but of which such limits have become an expression.[55]

Even so, it is important to understand this metaphysical premise because we would otherwise be inclined to see Cary's views on liberty and politics as a mere expression of what a critic has called that permissiveness or relativism to which 'we all do formal obeisance'.[56] Instead, Cary's liberalism is the application to human relations of a metaphysical (Kantian) conclusion. 'The idea of freedom makes me a member of an intelligible world, in consequence of which, supposing that I were nothing else, all my actions *would* always conform to the autonomy of the will'.[57] The identity of the individual and his moral 'responsibility' for his own actions presume a capacity to 'will' to act or not to act without any apparent determination from outside. Cary calls this capacity 'power'; true liberty consists in this 'free power of action', and 'the feeling' of this power, Cary claims, is 'as old as self-consciousness itself', and 'the source of the idea of liberty'.[58]

Cary's view of liberal politics was obviously influenced by the current thinking before and immediately after the First World War, and had its connections in latter-day English liberalism.[59] A Liberal, Cary was regarded at one time as an advocate of old-fashioned nineteenth-century *laissez-faire*.[60] We ought, nevertheless, to insist that Cary's liberalism is one consequence of a philosophical view of man. In fact, Cary speaks of liberalism in two senses. In one sense he means the freedom of the will in man, the 'creative' power which comes from man's consciousness of himself as a virtually self-determined actor. In a second sense, he speaks of the liberty which comes from the availability of those conditions which give this innate power an unrestricted scope for full realisation. This second sense coincides with progressive English liberal thought in many respects. But Cary's conception of liberty goes beyond it, and involves that innate potential in man which is inseparable from consciousness itself. In this sense, Cary's liberty is primarily metaphysical. His theory of politics arises from it and Cary did not hesitate to claim that his *Power in Men* was propounding a 'new state theory'.

Andrew Wright recognised this when he claimed that Cary was building a whole political theory on 'the theological conception of moral freedom—especially a power to act'.[61] This philosophy of human nature and human order is crucial to whatever else Cary says about freedom and politics and explains the importance he attaches to the concepts of 'creativeness' and 'power' when used of men and states. Human freedom is 'creative' because the difference between a creature with only instinct and a man with reason and will is that 'the former is limited to a tribal or collective action. Its liberty is only to repeat'.[62] Man is different: He 'realizes for himself his instinctive desires, what we call his nature, by the use of independent judgment. That is his means and his only means of development'.[63] Here again, Cary's meaning is best appreciated through its origins in Kant's idea of the self-determined individual with a moral nature. Kant found in the autonomy of the will the 'sole principle of all moral laws and of the corresponding duties'.[64] This moral potential distinguishes man from beast and makes him a 'creator' in his own right, the originator of self-determined purposive action. This liberty, Cary says, 'is creation in the act . . .

Whether man recognizes it for what it is or calls it what it is not, it is always at work. It is real in the strictest and profoundest sense'.[65]

Because the state cannot claim this same self-determining identity, it cannot share in the special prerogative of self-consciousness (which is freedom) or in the power of self-realisation. Accordingly, Cary finds the age-old arguments about the relative powers of the individual and of the state beside the point. 'The unique unit of every state, the most civilized as well as the most primitive, is the individual. He is real and everything else in the social order is derived and conditional'.[66] Cary also acknowledges the 'power' of the state, but argues that a 'man's power is different *in kind* from state power . . . The power in man is real, but the power of a nation is derived'. State power is, in fact, 'the creation of men'.[67] Accordingly the only justifiable end of political philosophy is its ability to help in providing a formula for a state 'organized to give power to man' beyond dictatorship and anarchy.[68] Moreover, the nineteenth-century norm of liberty as the absence of restraint did not face the realities of a world of inevitable conflict. It somehow assumed that the forces which had determined man's evolution to his present condition would also determine a safe and friction-free path for orderly social organisation in the future. Cary finds this view 'utterly discredited' both by history and by the metaphysics of creative and destructive freedom. First, 'a dead man feels the weight of no law. By the old definition of liberty, he is the freest man in the world. In fact he has no liberty at all. Liberty is not an absence but a power'[69]. Secondly, the idea of either a 'dialectal advance' or of an 'automatic progress' is only 'a fantasy . . . There is no automatic principle or dialectic which will produce, by its own certain and unaided operation, a golden age of security and peace'.[70]

Because of this emphasis on freedom and power, Cary's politics is that of individual 'men-in-action'. 'In any political question, I first ask, how does this affect the real men on the ground, the people in their private lives'.[71] And again: 'the real question of politics underlying all other temporary questions, is not, how shall the world be ruled'.[72] Such a foundation for political conduct enabled Cary to include almost all forms of human action within the sphere of 'politics'. Cary's task in his fiction, therefore, is to insist on the complication of public and the private worlds in the actual living human being. In consequence, also, Cary's men are all seeking some 'political' world where they can realise their dream of a convenient and (at the same time) orderly world. When he was asked in 1931 by the Liberal Committee to write a book about politics, Cary recalls, he at first refused. 'I had forgotten politics. I was deep in other studies, in philosophy, history, and letters'. But when he was offered a free hand ('to write what I liked'), he began to consider politics. 'I found to my surprise, and I am afraid, the surprise of the Committee, that the philosophy, since it dealt with realities, led, logically, to a new state theory'.[73] In other words, Cary found that the realities of life were illuminated by his study of philosophy, and that the philosophy led him 'logically' (that is, necessarily) to a theory of politics.

This interconnection, and the notion that his state theory was valid because it was grounded on 'realities', gave Cary his confidence in dealing with the interaction of power and public service and with its effect on individual human beings. It also gave him the confidence to attempt to project that philosophy in his fiction. In the novels, we find Cary returning to religious and private themes even when he tries to discuss public affairs of state. We also find his novels urging religious and familial resolutions to crises which would seem to demand a less personal and a more public determination. It is the scope of his view of politics that leads him to distinguish politics—in the wider sense of man's adjustment and readjustment of his needs to his environment—from the narrow sense of it as the mere struggle for public office or the harmonious governance of a given geographical unit. When he uses the term in the first sense, Cary calls it the most important power in man. In the second, narrow sense of the term, Cary is more cautious. Man, he says, 'is not a political or economic animal. He is moved by sympathies, tastes, faith, which have nothing to do with politics or cash, and he is ready to fight for them'.[74] The whole man, in other words, cannot be understood in terms of only a few of the many demands of his nature, even if those demands happen to be such important ones as 'politics' and cash. There are fears, passions, hopes and pleasures strong enough, he argues, to induce action patently in conflict even with those economic and political pressures. 'Religious wars, nationalist wars, what are now called wars of ideology are neither economic nor political, but ideal. They seek power to impose a rule of life not only upon the political and economic system of a people, but its thoughts, pleasures, its total being'.[75] This final dependence of even 'politics' and economics on the ideal—or, in Kierkegaard's sense, the irrational—desires of the individual human being means, of course, that 'political' action, in the two senses of the word, has to accommodate the somewhat independent demands of freedom and necessity. One demand is that for the non-rational needs and capacities of man, and the other, for the logical and desirable requirements of order.

The challenge of these demands, when applied to specific issues, or to a series of such issues which affect men's lives, constitutes the major dilemma of politics itself. Its untidiness and uncertainty, in fact, derive from the human element. In Cary's view, the alternative to determining the proper dimensions of order is disaster, either anarchical or despotic. Cary's political philosophy proposes a form of political order which can respond to both the calls of individual freedom and the common need for order. What Cary makes abundantly clear in his political writings is that no institutions which run directly against these basic ideas of human nature have a chance of survival. Without organisation, there would, of course, be nothing but chaos. Nevertheless, individual people have to be satisfied, if there is to be order, since without the individuals, 'there is no state, no people, no nation, no family, no organization, no politics'.[76] In his fiction, Cary dramatises the constant challenge in actual life of individual people seeking their own solution to these same 'political' problems. In *Power in Men* Cary suggests a philosophical norm to eliminate the weaknesses of political systems.[77] Cary calls it the 'norm of liberty'. 'Such a norm stands against man so: How far has he realized his native powers? And against the state: How far has it enabled men to realize their powers?' Such a norm will be 'independent of opinion'; it will be 'true liberty' because it will give power—'natural in man, collective in the state'. In theory and in practice, such a norm will involve 'organic cooperation between man and state'.[78] Cary calls the resulting liberty a 'power more subtle than thought; as persistent as nature, of which it is the life; as all-pervading as life of which it is spirit'.[79]

This worship of liberty is not an expression of cheap optimism. Such a view of it has, indeed, been responsible for that impression which Andrew Wright called the 'most harmful and inaccurate' which has been formed about Cary—that 'here at least in the twentieth century is something like the Browning of popular imagination, the happy Browning—hearty, superficial, myopic: a man whose work is like to give solace to old ladies'.[80] There is a faith in liberty and in man throughout Cary's work, but it is not simple, uncritical faith. It is, in fact, near-tragic faith, as much of his fiction reveals. According to Enid Starkie, Cary saw life as 'unjust and finally disappointing'. 'He understood . . . the pathos and tragedy of failure better than the glory of triumph'.[81] All politics, Cary claims in *Power in Men*, 'are real in this sense, that they deal with real people and their demands, with real situations, where there is suffering, ambition, passion, and anger'.[82] It is because of the importance, scope and the difficulty of this responsibility that Cary's politicians live a precarious and thankless life and enjoy his warmest sympathy. The burden of the ruler and the claims of liberty constitute the two dimensions of Cary's political order and correspond to the consequences of the diversity and individuality of human nature. This knowledge is fully behind his second ('political') trilogy. Life 'cannot avoid tension, and tragedy. They are in the nature of things, of a world in everlasting creation and therefore continuous change'. The task of the administrator or of any political system is not to try to eliminate this creative condition, which would be a vain effort, but to seek to mitigate its destructive consequences. 'To try to make the world safe for anyone is as hopeless a project (as dictators have often discovered) as to command that everyone shall think alike, or stop thinking altogether; that no one shall get old or sick; that storms shall stop blowing and earthquakes cease to crumple'.[83]

AESTHETICS

Cary's statement, just quoted, also has an important connection with the problem of aesthetic order. For just as it is a 'hopeless project' to try to 'make the world safe for anyone', so also is a perfect correlation between Art and Reality impossible. In both circumstances, nevertheless, the challenge remains. For the politican, it is how to save man from himself and for himself; for the artist, it is how to so represent reality that both its actual and its hypothetical characters are fully realised; so, in other words, that the inescapable disorder of actual reality is accurately represented in a work which remains nevertheless ordered and beautiful.

Art and Reality: Ways of the Creative Process (1958) is Cary's statement of this theory of art.[84] Cary's title and subtitle are indicative of the extent of his attachment to metaphysics and to art.[85] The title forces a dichotomy on the work—between the world which the artist 'intuits' and the work of art at which is his

'expression' of that intuition. The subtitle points to Cary's particular emphasis. It promises both a psychological and a metaphysical view of the artist as creator, his work as the created thing, and of
the process of this creation.

There is a clear advantage in Cary's approach. In his essay 'On
Art', Tolstoy pointed out the dangers in presuming an aesthetic idea
and writing on its basis without defence or elaboration. He wrote:

> In our time a man who wishes to follow art either takes a subject
> current at the time and praised by people who in his opinion are
> clever, and clothes it as best as he can in what is called artistic
> form; or he chooses a subject which gives him most opportunity to
> display his technical skill, and with toil and patience produces
> what he considers to be a work of art; or having received some
> chance impression he takes what caused that impression for his
> subject, imagining that it will yield a work of art since it
> happened to produce an impression on him.[86]

The consequence of this attitude to art, according to Tolstoy, is that
because 'with patience a technique can always be learnt', people
who 'are without any definition of what they themselves hold to be
art' invariably produce what is at best only pseudo-art. Tolstoy had
his own difficulties defining art, and the three criteria which he used
so vindictively against de Maupassant, Baudelaire and the *Symbolistes* are hardly a solution to the problem he saw so clearly. Yet
Tolstoy recognised that any proper definition of art would have to
consider 'the peculiarity of that activity, both in its origins in the
soul of the producer and in the peculiarity of its action on the souls of
the recipients'.[87]

Again Tolstoy was limited in his description of the process of
artistic creation. He recognised, as Cary does, that creation begins
with an individual's intuition. A man 'surmises or dimly feels
something that is perfectly new to him, which he has never heard
from anybody'. In an attempt to understand this intuition, to assure
himself of its 'real' existence, and to share the knowledge with
others, he is impelled into an intense exploration of the particulars of
his intuition. He 'directs his whole strength to the task of making his
discovery so clear that there cannot be the smallest doubt, either for
himself or other people, as to the existence of that which he
perceives'.[88] It is in this, Tolstoy concluded, 'that the activity of the
artist consists: and to this activity is related the feeling of the

recipient'.[89] But unlike Cary, Tolstoy did not address himself to the question of formal structures as an aspect of the experience or intuition being communicated by the artist. So immediately was he concerned with rejecting what he regarded as the obsessive craftmanship of the *Symbolistes* and with denouncing their 'eccentricity', 'lack of clearness' and 'premeditated obscurity'[90] that he virtually made the 'communication of feeling' the supreme character and end of art.

It is not necessary here to defend Tolstoy's alternative to the cult of mere craftmanship and mere technical skill. We need only point out that Cary's *Art and Reality*, like Tolstoy's essay which inspired it in many ways, begins with an account of the origins of artistic activity. Like Tolstoy, Cary's study indicates the limitations of mere technical skill, 'the false originality of the clever fellow who takes up a current fashion and gives it a new turn'.[91] Unlike Tolstoy, however, Cary attaches great importance to 'form' as an instrument of perception and expression, as the *species* ('appearance') under which the mind can see not only merely the data of experience but their relationships. Art, Cary argues, is not only communication, but also 'discovery'; not only the 'expression of a theme', but 'the exploration of technical limits'.[92]

Art and Reality has the advantage, also, of avoiding the restricting view of the role of art which compromised Tolstoy's aesthetics and made it a servant of his ethical convictions. Thus, whereas for Tolstoy, Art is simply a *useful* means of 'union among men, joining them together in the same feelings, and indispensable for the life and progress towards well-being of individuals and a humanity',[93] for Cary it is a *necessary* means of communication between men. Where Tolstoy emphasised the *utility* of art, Cary stresses the *necessity* for it, the fact that it is the only way by which men separated in mind (though united in feeling) can share not only facts of reality, but feelings about these facts; and not only share these facts and feelings, but also explore their limits and possibilities.[94]

This difference between Tolstoy and Cary is the product of Cary's philosophical bias. The empiricism of Hume enabled Cary to believe in a world of feeling, experience and intuition. Kantian philosophy provided him with the idea of *a priori* forms or categories by virtue of which he can postulate the possibility of an empirical reality arranged into formal systems that are pleasurable (that is, satisfying) to the mind. Together, both philosophies justified his idea of art as a simultaneous and complex expression of feelings as well as of concepts. 'All works of art' Cary argues, 'all ideas of life, all philosophies are "As if" ', which can, however, be 'checked with an objective reality'.[95] In a dramatic combination of Hume and Kant, Cary calls works of art 'propositions for truth' and argues that their truth 'can be decided by their correspondence (in logic and experience) with the real'.[96] Thus, Art is ordered by the mind according to the logic of consciousness; in an empiricist as well as an analytical sense, art is both an *experience* and a *postulate*. Because man's mode of experiencing external reality is constant and because his mind has the capacity for comprehending formal constructs and making them part of conscious experience, it is possible, in Cary's view, for the artist to create his work, and his readers to share in it.

Like many other aestheticians, Cary builds *Art and Reality* on the idea that the writer's intuition is the basis of all art. But unlike some of them he distinguishes 'intuition' from 'experience' which he equates with the ordinary sensory apprehension of an external reality. Intuition, Cary says, is not even an experience which 'surprises' the individual. It is 'truer' to say 'that it is the truth [which] comes upon him as a discovery' than that the artist *comes upon it*. For it is that apprehension of an aspect of reality over and above primary experience that constitutes the genuine artistic intuition. Monet's 'intuition' came when, as a young man, he 'suddenly saw the fields, not as solid flat objects covered with grass or useful crops and dotted with trees, but as colour in astonishing variety and subtlety of gradation'.[97]

This distinction between experience and intuition is a crucial one. It places the emphasis no longer on the photographic realism of experience but on its formal reorganisation. Intuition, thus, has its own kind of independent existence. It is true, of course, that Monet's new view of the same field is 'something independent of Monet himself'. In that sense, Cary argues, 'Monet had discovered a truth about the actual world'. But that discovery is also bound up with Monet's sensibility; and the particular relationship he 'saw' is the 'creation' of his own mind: in simple terms it is the child of the union of Monet and the field. In other words, Monet's intuition is the germ-of-art in the mind, a *fictional* (that is, created) insight into the *real* world.

Cary is empiricist enough to make Monet's experience of the fields the basis of his insight; but he depends on Kantian analysis for his view of the nature of intuition as independent of mere experience, and as therefore partaking of the qualities of all abstract and ideal entities. Monet's 'variety and subtlety' of colour gradations, Housman's sudden vision of his cherry tree 'before it had changed into just another tree in blossom' and Conrad's 'discovery' 'all at once' of what 'it meant to Jim to lose his honour'[98] are all versions of intuition. They transcend mere perception. Cary calls this transcendence a 'direct knowledge of the world as it is'. This, he says, 'is the primary knowledge of the artist and writer. This joy of discovery is his starting point'.[99]

This distinction between experience and intuition also enables us to understand Cary properly when he says that he begins his fiction not with an *idea* but with a *character in a situation*. He begins, in other words, with an intuition based on a particular reality, not with a formal idea arrived at independently of empirical experience. Like Housman's view of a particular cherry-tree, Cary's character-in-a-situation is the occasion for an intuition, or a discovery. In other words, the character-in-a-situation leads to, but is not, the truth of his intuition, his apprehension of a truth about a reality. Experience merely reproduces the customary forms of reality: it apprehends the world in the light of common day. Artistic intuition, however, is a perception of the same world in an ordered and significant light.

Cary further distinguishes artistic intuition from artistic *expression*. In intuition, the artist perceives a new truth, a new relationship between the elements of the external world. Art is his *expression* of this truth. Croce, whom Cary cites in *Art and Reality*, also made a distinction between intuition and perception. But he argued that the mind does not really 'intuit' until it has found the necessary means of expressing its 'intuition'. 'The spirit only intuits in making, forming, expressing'. Again: 'Intuitive activity possesses intuitions to the extent that it expresses them'.[100] Cary rejects this view because it would amount to saying that 'we can't know what we have intuited until we have named it, or given it a formal character'.[101] For him art (or expression) is the attempt of the discoverer to 'fix' his intuition, to transfer his intuition from the idea in his mind to the medium of words, stone or colour. The artist has 'somehow to translate an intuition from real objects into a formal and ideal arrangement of colours and shapes, which will still, mysteriously, fix and convey his sense of the unique quality, the magic of these objects in their private existence'.[102] The intuition itself is only 'a subconscious recognition of the real', like 'a flash between two electric poles'.[103]

This disagreement with Croce is fundamental. For to accept

Croce's identification of expression and intuition is to agree with him that all expression is necessarily beautiful. The ugly, Croce argued, 'is unsuccessful expression', and the only value of the term 'beautiful' in aesthetics is in its use to refer to '*successful expression*, or rather, *expression* and nothing more, because expression when it is not successful is not expression'.[104] Principally because of the Kantian strain in his thinking, Cary holds a different view.[105] Because, for him (as for Kant), intuition is not expression, and because the end of art is the adequate expression of intuition, Cary reserves the term 'beauty' for the *form* of adequate work, in so far as such a work is perceived without any conception of its utility. Beauty, that is, resides in the form of expression, not in the native intuition. 'In painting, sculpture, and in all the formative arts', Kant stated, 'the *delineation* is the essential thing; and here it is not what gratifies in sensation but what pleases by means of form that is fundamental for taste'.[106] Beauty 'properly is only concerned with form'.[107] Art is thus a formal construct. 'The form' 'which an artist devises to 'express and communicate his total meaning' will 'dictate his valuation of details'.[108] 'This selection, this tone, this emphasis is art'.[109]

The idea of form is essential to Cary's aesthetics because, for him, intuition is a private activity within the realm of personality. Because it is by its very nature evanescent, intuition can only be communicated through art. Taking off from Hume's view of the necessary isolation of men's minds, Cary argues that only art can work 'in the medium of common sympathies, commong feeling, universal reaction to colour, sound, form. It is the bridge between souls, meaning not only men's minds but their character and feeling. And it carries all the traffic'.[110] Men can share the meaning of art because they have what Cary says one can call 'a primitive equipment of aesthetic response'.[111] This equipment, and the capacity of the human mind to know and to reflect on that knowledge, make it possible for men to share their intuitions provided they can find forms 'capable of attaching to themselves the emotional supercharges' involved in the original intitution.[112] This view is, of course, derived from the Kantian notion that expressions of intuitions are either schemata or symbols, direct or indirect representations of a concept.[113] According to Kant, art is necessarily symbolic because only through the attachment of 'emotional supercharges' to aesthetic 'forms' is communication possible between men. Croce rejected this argument,[114] because he believed that expression is independent of imposed forms. Cary holds to the Kantian view that man cannot avoid the 'predicament of the free independent mind compelled to use language, symbols, for the communication of its ideas'.[115] Thus, Cary finds Lawrence's description of the Brangwen family in the first chapter of *The Rainbow* symbolic because it reveals an intuition of life as lived 'finally at the level of fundamental passion and fundamental needs, of an order of life not reducible to logic or rational judgment'.[116] Similarly, the straightforward scene in his own *Prisoner of Grace*, Cary says, is symbolic because it tries to record an 'experience fundamental to the book's meaning'.[117]

Cary was intensely aware of the role of the symbol in art. The great artist—Hardy is one of his examples—'breaks through the conceptual and habitual crust of everyday, where every activity has its common use and its conceptual label, where life wears the mask of a mechanical pursuit of material aims, of temporal appeasement', and reveals to us an essential insight into 'what makes life worth living'. Hardy accomplishes this 'by manipulation of the symbol, with all its defects. It is the only means available to him'.[118] The defects of the symbol are exactly those of any system: 'as a mere thing, it requires to have its associations renewed. It tends always to lose them and to sink into the empty object, the bare concept-label, the mechanical sign or gesture. The word becomes a word from a dictionary'.[119] With frequent and unrejuvenated use, the symbol freezes into a style and soon 'the public is seeing, not a revelation of the real, but a fine example of so-and-so with all his characteristic tricks'.[120] The 'trick' replaces the 'illumination' which, because it had long been made, now becomes 'common daylight'.

The defect of the symbol, as a system of communication, is that it is subject to the constant creative onslaught of the free mind; and the conflict between its fixed label and its changing associations is directly parallel to that in the artist between concept and intuition.[121] From this defect, escape is necessarily impossible, for the factors responsible for the limitations also provide it with its strength. The factors are the Kantian notions of a world of permanent reality, and the world-mind of constant change. 'Man', Cary says, 'can't change the elemental characters. If you could, the world would probably vanish into nothing. But because of their very permanence, you can assemble them into new forms . . . The creative soul needs the machine, as living world need a fixed character, or it could not exist at all. It would merely be an idea'.[122]

When Cary applies this paradox (his own word) to the symbol, it explains for him why, though all art is symbolic, some symbols are more powerfully realised than others. Here it is the metaphysical insight that clarifies the aesthetic paradox. The 'essential power' of the symbol, Cary asserts, 'resides' in its very defects. As 'label' or 'concept', it is invariably in association with feeling, which thus limits its purity as concept; as a 'consistent vehicle of emotion' it suffers from the tendency to sink back into a 'mere sign'.

> But since, however, unstable, it combines both elements, it is the only means by which it is possible to achieve any unity between the knowledge of fact and the feeling about the fact, the machine and the soul, the universal consistencies and the individual character so that they can be joined together in an ordered experience of the real which, one must suppose, includes them both in one total personal character of existence.[123]

Cary goes even further than this apologetic praise to urge that it is the very 'ambivalence of the symbol'—as concept and experience— that enables the artist 'as creator of meanings' to achieve the formal and experiential beauty of art: 'to bridge the gap between the individual idea and the universal realm of emotion, forming by art a personality which unites them both in a single active and rational will'.[124]

Cary also distinguishes sharply between symbol and allegory. Croce did so too. The symbol, Croce argued, cannot be separated from the thing symbolised; hence, allegory—the 'exposition of an abstract concept'—cannot legitimately have aesthetic significance.

> . . . given a statue of a beautiful woman, the sculptor can attach a label to the statue saying that it represents *Clemency* or *Goodness*. This allegory that arrives attached to a finished *work post festum* does not change the work of art. What then is it? It is an expression externally *added* to another expression . . . to the statue nothing but the single word: *Clemency* or *Goodness*.[125]

Cary, for his part, distinguishes the two for quite different reasons. In part, this difference can be linked with Cary's rejection of Croce's identification of intuition and expression. Beyond that, however, Cary argues that allegory is a fable, extrapolated from the complication of actual life, and used subsequently to argue a theme or a proposition in a world far more uncertain than that of the allegory. In symbolic art, we 'recognize fundamental human nature at work in (a) new setting'. It exists 'within a universal moral real'. As concept and experience, the symbol enables us to feel 'the revelation of a new formal beauty in [an] unexpected thing'.[126] Allegory, on the other hand, insists on arriving at the revelation without exploring or presenting the experience on which its intuition is founded.

Allegory is 'false' because 'it lays down categorical imperatives for conduct in a world of particular and unique events. It treats the world as a mechanism whereas it is a world of free souls'.[127] The symbol can serve the ends of art because it can bridge in the subconscious 'the gap between experience and thought, direct knowledge of the real and the reflective judgment'. Allegory actually destroys that bridge by 'dividing the reader into an emotional memory which is already losing its significance, and a conceptual judgment which is coldly analyzing and labelling a set of technical tricks'.[128] The philosophical foundation for this view has already been pointed out. Cary emphasises it specifically in his chapter on the 'Form of Allegory'. This 'matter of allegory', he says there, 'may seem too unimportant to be treated at length. But it is not so . . . We are asking how does a great writer overcome all the obstacles of conceptual judgment and the deceitful symbol to give us a truth about reality in the only way it can be given—to make us feel it'.[129]

The artist, Cary answers, 'has to create the work of art, by hard conceptual labour, and yet to convey an ordered whole of feeling'.[130] Because the rational mind, relying on its independence and its imagination, is 'capable of any fantasy and able, by the force of ideas, to impose an order of habitual reaction upon the feelings',[131] there is a temptation for it to regard its own intellectual victory as equivalent to the victory of the whole person, which it cannot be because the comprehension of beauty or of any other aesthetic virtue is not only conceptual but emotional. In its conceptual sense, for example, Beauty is (as Cary says) 'a relation', or the form of a suitable object, in so far as that object is perceived without any conception of its utility (as Kant claimed). In its subjective or emotional sense, however, Beauty (in Cary's phrase) is a 'feeling' and derives from that which, in general and necessarily, without reasoning, and without practical advantage, pleases. Kant's *Urteilskraft*, or Cary's 'artistic judgment'[132] combines these two processes. The limitation of allegory is the neglect of the subjective aspect of reality inherent in the conceptual character of allegory.

A story, nevertheless, is not life but art, and is subject 'to the limitations of art, in this case, to the logic of the subconscious, allotting by association a meaning to each character, to each development in a construction that is fundamentally As If'.[133] 'As If' is the crucial phrase. On the one hand it reminds us of the Kantian element in Cary's thinking, the conditional principle of '*als ob*' which Kant formulated at the end of the *Critique of Pure Reason*. It preserves the formal and independent existence of a work of art as an 'ideal order' (Cary's phrase) 'which remains an object of achievement'.[134] On the other hand, it presupposes an antecedent reality of which the work of art is in some sense analogous. Thus, art is not only an 'ideal order', it is one to be achieved by a writer 'in the world as he knows it'.[135] Quite clearly therefore, the true antithesis to Cary's 'realism' is not symbolism—which, we saw, is itself founded on reality—but allegory, which is weighted in favour of the conceptual, at the expense of the 'real'.

Given this redefinition, it is not difficult to see how relevant an understanding of Cary's 'realism' is to the evaluation of his kind of fiction. In the Preface to *Castle Corner*, Cary speaks of his difficulties in completing the projected novels of the series. The criticisms of *Castle Corner*, he tells us, made him wonder 'if I had found the right means of saying what I had to say'.[136] His difficulty was how to make life meaningful; that is, in his sense of the word, symbolic. 'I had to ask myself if anyone would notice that the book had any general meaning; if, in fact, it did mean anything; if the contrast of different characters, though all making their lives, seeking fulfilment of one kind or another, did not result in that very neutral tint which we find in the events of life.'[137] Cary phrases this problem in two other ways. 'What I had to ask', he writes in one instance, 'was if the pattern would come out from a mere tale of currents, winds, moons and rocks.'[138] In the second formulation, he asks: 'But how could a story which is strictly concerned with persons, answer universal *political* questions? Would not a reader say "So that's what happened to Jarvis, or Bridget (who became a rich woman in England, but a drunkard), or Cleve, because they were what they were"?'[139] The novel that would answer to Cary's requirements would obviously have to be both a realistic and a symbolic novel. It would have to give the facts of life and character (as, for example,

Trollope's novels do) and depend consequently on the social 'symbols' of hat, pipe and flag to communicate the immediacy of that kind or realism. It would *also* have to be symbolic in the sense that the details of that life, in Cary's arrangement of them, would have a significance beyond this immediate realism.

Judged by Cary's own criteria, then, *Castle Corner* was doomed to fail. First, Cary would not employ a frankly conceptual framework which, in the spirit of the allegory, could have proved his thesis by presuming it. Secondly, realism was not only his means, it was also his theme. Cary was not only intent on creating 'rounded' characters, but on showing exactly in what ways characters can be rounded. In other words, he was aiming at both a metaphysical and a political theme, at a general statement about the nature of being, and at a particular statement about a particular experience of being. He was not trying, as he claimed Tolstoy (in *The Ressurrection*) and Dostoievsky (in *The Brothers Karamazov*) did, to 'weave a spell', to state 'not the case, but a case'; to see 'everything from one angle', to create situations which would be ' "true" only for their own characters in that situation, carefully chosen and limited to drive home one moral slogan and excluding all the complex issues of real life'. He aimed at a realism which is at the same time capable of making a metaphysical statement about the nature of realism itself. He wanted to create characters

> . . . conceived with those springs of action which seemed to me most important in all characters, working out their fates in a world charged throughout with freedom and individuality, and the consequences of that inescapable freedom, where moral principles must be like those of an army on the march, inventive, flexible, for ever balanced between the immediate circumstances (this man's nature, this crisis) and on ultimate end (the good, the true, etc.) and a final judgement is final only in the sense that it is the best (however bad) solution of an immediate problem.[140]

Cary failed in the attempt. In his view, he failed not because he could not convey a sense of immediate life, but because he did not *also* convey a sense of the general meaning, the symbolic meaning. 'The better I drew my characters, the more they would fail as illustrations of general laws'.[141] Cary's failure in *Castle Corner*, as he himself admits, was both technical and philosophical. 'I had learnt enough to know that the same general theme can be expressed in many different forms, but I had not fully realized that the very virtue of art, of which the power is that it can give experience, on that same account, limits its scope in argument'.[142] Cary's best novels attest to his considerable mastery of these technical and philosophical difficulties, his ability in his best fiction to find characters and situations which both convey the vitality of daily life and the implications of his philosophical insight. With such a combination, Cary could convey the only kind of truth he considered possible through art—'truth in a context' which is 'made actual, complete and purposeful to our experience'.[143] 'Beauty is truth, truth beauty.' 'Has this statement any basis,' Cary asks.

> I suggest, with all diffidence, that it does mean something of importance; that when we recognise beauty in any ordered form of art, we are actually discovering new formal relations in a reality which is permanent and objective to ourselves . . . we are recognising aesthetic meaning in the character of the universe.[144]

How these philosophical attitudes affect Cary's fiction should, ultimately, be the primary concern of the critic, especially because of Cary's objection to the *roman a thèse* which, he says, fails to preserve the intriguing duality of freedom and necessity of actual life. This, in a sense, is the thought behind his one criticism of Hardy and Lawrence. Speaking of the scene at Stonehenge in Hardy's *Tess of the D'Urbervilles*, Cary says that Hardy there made a 'stage property' of his heroine. Like Lawrence, he claims, Hardy 'cannot bear the complacency, the self-satisfaction of the world'.[145] Cary's own willingness to confront and use this 'self-satisfaction' is one of the most distinguishing features of his fiction. His novels consequently do not seek to prove, but to be his philosophy. The result, fortunately, is a solid body of fiction having all the richness of imaginative and emotional life associated with the traditional, and especially the eighteenth-century and nineteenth-century novels; novels, moreover, in which (as in Tolstoy and Dickens), individual characters are fully realised with almost idiosyncratic vividness; but novels in which this realisation is always an instrument for an intellectual statement of a distinct and penetrating kind.

There is some irony in making these claims for Cary because it is perhaps true to say that no other artist of his generation has had so obsessive an involvement with his art (in theory and in practice) and yet remained, in himself, the non-artist. Malcolm Forster's biography of him, M. M. Mahood's account of Cary's life in Africa and of his habits of composition, and the copious notes, sketches and drafts now in the Bodleian Library of Oxford University, all attest to a normal—even commonplace—writer who nevertheless had an almost sacred conception of his calling as artist. Perhaps a sense of property and of propriety derived from his family background; perhaps an attachment to Victorian and Edwardian values analogous to those of Wilcher (in *To Be A Pilgrim*) prevented Cary from being the kind of modern artist he himself represented in Gulley Jimson of *The Horse's Mouth*. He was concerned neither with the social scene in C. P. Snow's contemporary and immediate sense nor with the inner man after Samuel Beckett's anguished and existential manner.[146] His concern was with a peculiar combination of the temporal and the existential, with history and the individual and with the interactions of time and the free self. For background, he used a world which stretches from the no-man's land between the demise of high Victorianism to the birth of the post-1918 world of Nazism, Fascism and international Communism. But the life of the self within those worlds is permanent, and is shown as transcending (though not avoiding) the circumstances of time and history.

2 Man in the Making

In his Preface to *Charley Is My Darling*, Cary says that the child is not 'equipped with the experience and judgment necessary to put the world of related ideas together for himself'.[1] In *Art and Reality*, he argues that there are constants in the physical, social and moral relations of the world which man cannot ignore. Because there is no other way of knowing these relations than through experience and 'education', Cary says that the actions of children are really only 'experiments' to test the limits of these constants; that is to say, the *dimensions of order*. Because there is a considerable difference in moral certainty and in the power of judgment between the infant and the adolescent, Cary studies the actual development of this faculty, the process whereby the non-moral universe of the newborn babe changes to the morally responsible world of the young adult. His novel thus becomes a study of man-in-the-making, a study of childhood and the growth of moral consciousness.

Cary also states in his Preface that the shaving of Charley's lousy head 'gave the boy a bad start',[2] of a kind among the children. In the novel itself the shaving makes Charley's head seem 'absurdly small, the ears project like a dog's' with the result that Charley 'is changed from a respectable looking young citizen in a brown suit, to something between the convict of history and the kind of street Arab represented in old comic papers'.[3] This physical disability is, however, made secondary to the resulting destruction of Charley's sense of assurance and, as it were, the loss of his sense of individual integrity. Because of this bad start, the other evacuees, who are also 'jostling for position among themselves', unite to jeer at him in an effort to challenge Charley's presumption to leadership among them. Cary moves behind both Charley's personal condition as expressed in his outward purposelessness and in the attitude of his fellow children to see the moral issues which this condition poses for Charley. The other children can sense the confused state of Charley's mind which the novel says is 'like a splitting up of the brain into senseless fragments'. (p. 40). Because of this confusion,

Charley has to resolve the problem responsible for his moral uncertainty before he can act confidently. He needs to understand the moral order responsible for the apparent connection between his suffering and the unhealthy condition of his head. Charley can see no logical connection between them and because of the resulting moral uncertainty, he is afflicted with the 'strange misery of not knowing what was the extent of his crime in being lousy, among a set of boys who, apparently, had never been lousy' (p. 40).

In this context, then, the shaving of Charley's lousy head can almost be seen to have the importance of a symbolic deprivation of power. Another kind of novelist might have sought to indicate this importance by making the symbolic possibilities of this event quite explicit. Cary avoids any such explicitness. What he offers, instead, is a deliberately straightforward description which has, nevertheless, all the implications of a symbolic rendering. Charley puts on his hat 'hastily, with a guilty and nervous gesture', and the children ('as if . . . for the first time') 'see him as he is, a frightened, breathless small boy' (p. 35). Cary's choice of method is, of course, dictated and, justified by the very argument of the novel which is, in part, that there can be no clearcut opposition of good to evil in the world of the adolescent. The conflict in *Charley Is My Darling* is not between Charley's Jehovah and a Dagon represented by the adult world. Miss Allchin is not Delilah. Charley's innocence is not set in opposition to the social injustice of the world because, as the novel presents the matter, evil and innocence cannot be located consistently and inevitably in youth or age, in individuals or institutions. Evil, for example, is a force which cannot be separated, either in its nature or in its manifestations, from the larger world of good and indifferent action, though it remains a distinct and actual part of the world.[4] The problem is in reconciling its existence with the possibility of a logical and universal notion of order. In *Charley Is My Darling*, evil is shown to be part of a universal condition which the 'uninstructed' judgment of childhood is incapable of seeing as compatible with a notion of the universal 'good'. Accordingly, because the moral environment in *Charley Is My Darling* rejects the existence of 'purposive' evil, it also precludes a moral agon, the dramatisation of a pitched conflict of good and evil.[5]

It is typically Cary to explore the dimensions of a moral order rather than dramatise the assumed incompatibility of its various components. *Charley Is My Darling* studies the circumstances and the modes of evil and good action in children, carefully avoiding the invocation of sociological or theological explanations which were bound to be too neat for a philosophically complex interrelationship. Similarly, Charley's desire for 'leadership' is not simply the astute power-lust of adulthood but rather a metaphysical state of mind; for, as the novel shows, even though he wants to be seen as leader and, for that reason, in an early scene of mischief, dares the bull, Charley is (like the other children) 'visibly terrified' and as 'solemn' as if he can hardly believe his 'own daring' (p. 25).[6]

What has happened, then, is that the particular mischief the children commit has no direct moral counterpart in the adult world. The letting of the bull out of the yard becomes not a purposive moral act on their part but the consequence of a struggle for 'power'. For example, when the other children challenge him to attempt this particular mischief, Charley asks for the key to the barn, believing they will not be able to produce it. When they are in fact able to produce it, he is 'taken aback'. And just because the 'crime' is not even a moral situation but an occasion for a contest of a different kind, the children are 'bored' when it is over. 'Their expressions resemble those of dogs, who having chased a cat across two streets, suddenly realize that they have lost their master' (p. 26). Charley would gladly have asked for a truce in the contest for power but for the unabashed admiration with which the gang greets him: 'Good ole Sinbad'. Charley cannot deny that this is his first felony. If he speaks the truth and says he 'has never before stolen anything except lumps of sugar or spoonfuls of jam', he will not be believed. But 'if he claims to be an old hand, a real thief', he 'will command their respect'. Moreover the other children 'are strangers and know nothing about his past', and this allows him the freedom to 'make for himself, whichever position he chooses' (p. 29). The circumstances of Charley's choice here make it clear that Cary's concern is with the nature of the child's 'moral' world, with the kind of competition which determines what is 'good' action.

But childhood is a process not a state. Two elements dominate the character of the change that does take place in the novel's world of childhood. One is the influence of a larger world of adult values; the other, the growth of the children's own understanding of the 'constants' of that adult world. Phyllis is more sympathetic than annoyed when she learns that the boys have broken into Wicken's barn. 'Like flies arn't they, for getting in everywhere?' (p. 21). She and Miss Allchin have the sympathy necessary to understand the nature of children. But it is also their responsibility to ensure that the children do not run foul of the legal and moral constants of adult world. Because they have both sympathy and responsibility, they adopt a protective and moralising attitude to the children which, though well-meant, in turn produces its own complications.

The children, for their part, are prepared to suppress their fears in order not to hurt those adults sympathetic to their cause. Hence though Charley is unhappy about having his head shaved, he is willing to compromise his integrity in an effort, as he sees it, to reciprocate the kindness of the adults.

'I hope you're not feeling too uncomfortable.'
'No, miss.'
'And you're not angry with us?'
'No, miss' (p. 30).

This act of accommodation points to the very close connection in the minds of children between their action—which they see as indifferent, and the good opinion of the adults—which they do not want to lose. When they plan to steal booze the children's first fear is not simply of being caught stealing, but rather of provoking the displeasure of the adult world. Even in the most elaborate of Charley's exploits, he is haunted with the fear of being caught. He knows he is 'taking absurd risks for very little return'. But, from his point of view, to do otherwise would be to cease to be himself or to be free. In that situation, Charley becomes *will-less*. 'He could look at reason, appreciate it, but he was obstinately prevented from making any use of it' (p. 215). When Ginger and Harry warn him of his recklessness, Charley only laughs.

'I ain't laughing at ya.'
'Wot you laughing at then?'
'I just laughing' (p. 215).

When Charley finally decides to steal it is not in order to challenge adult law or adult opinion, but because he is exploring the limits of the moral order and experiencing the consequences of doing so.

What is required, then, is a fusion of the two worlds and two moral codes: that of the adult world which the children know exists and which is first made apparent to them in their sense of guilt in hurting otherwise friendly adults, and the other, the world of adolescence which is fully independent of the larger world but has increasingly to seek an accommodation with the world of adulthood. This search for accommodation is to be seen in sometimes poignant, sometimes comic situations. When the children are called up for questioning after their Twyport adventure, their solidarity is impressive. Charley shows a 'most cheerful indifference', smiling at 'all Ginger's obstinate "Noes" ' (p. 142). Lina's only concern is that Charley 'will not be frightened or fail to do himself justice'. When summoned, Charley is 'so frightened' that he cannot think. Charley does not survive the close and clever questioning of the officer, and before too long he is filled with the 'depression of perplexity and the sense of failure' (p. 143). Nor, after this failure, does his 'total' confession save him from the punishment which infringement of adult law imposes. The novel argues, in effect, that it is in the very nature of the worlds of childhood and adult-life that communication should fail. The fault is neither in Charley and in Lina, nor in the police officers, but in the separate, juxtaposed but unfused moral worlds of childhood and adulthood. In such circumstances, the intense feelings of the one party, deeply rooted in the moral order of its generation, seeks in vain to justify itself to the equally intense and even sympathetic feelings of the other.

One such situation develops during that admonitory interview when Miss Allchin seeks to combine her liking for Charley with her responsibility for his conduct. The scene, as Robert Bloom has pointed out, is 'a dramatization of the distance between child and adult moral comprehension'.[7] But the meaning of that interview extends beyond the insight of its moment; it is part of a continuing effort of the two orders to fuse into one. One of the elements of adult moral order which Miss Allchin assumes in her argument is the evil will: 'I didn't think you were like that . . . It's so cruel and mean—and you don't seem to care a bit' (p. 272). But as the novel says, Charley's will is, in fact, like 'a tunnel of glass set on an incline, down which [Charley] was flying' (p. 215). Miss Allchin does not see this. Equating the evil act with the evil will, she imputes wickedness to Charley's soul. But Charley, confident of the 'purity' of his own will, consequently 'feels as if she is trying to push him into a dark place from which he will never escape. He has no words to describe a sense of guilt, a conviction of sin, but he feels by nervous imagination what they are' (p. 272).

During the trial, Charley again feels that the court is trying to impose guilt on his soul. He sees the trial as an attempt 'to shame him, to drive him down into a pit of remorse and despair'. (p. 275).

He is torn between allowing himself to be shamed and resisting that temptation: 'he feels he is not really guilty at all, that Lina and the nice magistrates still don't understand the situation' (p. 275). Without either side realising it, therefore, a fusion of the two orders is being forcibly made during this trial. Charley is being forced into a 'conviction of sin', into the acceptance of moral responsibility, in the tradition of the adult world. The result of this attempt is Charley's protest in the novel, the first major act of his now 'adult' understanding. Underneath his 'violent hysterical emotion [of tears] there is a fury like steel, a deep resolute anger. It is the protest of all his honesty against a lie, and a defilement' (p. 276). The defilement is, of course, also a defilement of childhood 'innocence'; which is to say, the breaking up of the till-then coherent and integrated moral world of childhood.

This brings us to the second of the two elements which dominate the character of the change that takes place in the philosophical and moral worlds of childhood. The growth of the children's own understanding of the 'constants' of the adult world, as we should call this element, can be seen throughout the novel. At the end of his interview with Lina, Charley is 'overwhelmed' by her plea for Bessie—'a girl like poor Bessie'. (p. 272). Thinking that Charley's tears are a sign of repentance, Lina goes away 'happy', though Charley remains 'remorseful, still more confused than before' (pp. 272–3). But Charley does not accept the criteria by which the adult world is judging his conduct. Hence much as we recognise that Charley is not guilty in Lina's sense, we know however that Charley does not fully realise what in fact it means for Liz, a girl not yet fifteen, to be expecting a baby. That is to say, Charley is yet to understand the connection between moral and social order. For much as he cared for Liz, and 'planned' marrying her and taking her to 'Ammurca', he still had that adolescent response to women which did not appreciate the extent of social responsibility involved in these plans.

Charley's association with Liz began in friendly but still childlike terms. Charley was then embarrassed by Liz's presence, and Liz, in turn, was concerned for him with 'the devotion of a nurse in charge of an ill and mysterious foreign patient'. As their friendship grew, we find a combination of immature sexual and romantic tendencies in Charley's attitude, 'the feelings due to a loyal and brave supporter' (p. 69). Only much later does he come to combine into one his two feelings about Liz: that he likes her and that he likes to be close to her. But though he does not despise himself for this 'weakness', as he might have done, he resents 'any jibe which increases his discomfort as an unfair blow' (p. 124). In the same mood, he feels ashamed of the 'impulse' which carried him 'again and again' to Lizzie (p. 162). He is 'obsessed' by her, and though 'she was always in his feelings', he does not want to see her. (p. 181).

Liz, for her part, was yet to attain the maturity of sexual or romantic experience. During the mock-party at the Burls, she puts her hands on her lips and frowns at the table 'with a look probably caught from his mother or some aunt, before a party'. When she looks again at Charley, her glance 'changes into a flash from the sketch of a mature and formidable mistress, to a childish tempter full of whim and defiance'. For all that tenderness and affection, Charley and Liz have yet to comprehend the complexity of the relationship that holds them together. Liz, for one thing, cannot trust herself to the affection of 'boys', and can, in fact, only think of Charley 'with fatalist resignation, as something that has happened to her; part good, part bad, but already in the past. She does not rely upon Charley for anything, even affection. He is, after all *a boy* (p. 178).

These considerations distinguish this childhood 'affair' from the responsible romance of adulthood into which Liz's pregnancy throws them. It is the incompleteness of their process of growth that makes childhood norms so unreliable as a guide for them to use and so difficult to criticise. Beneath Miss Allchin's criticism of Charley is her instinctive awareness of the incompleteness of the children's moral 'education'. That, in fact, is the virtue of her position and it is this virtue that saves her attempt at correcting them from being 'evil'. But in even trying to correct, she makes the mistake of not distinguishing moral from social responsibility—a difficult distinction to make since morals are, in this case, contingent on social relationships. In the trial scene, Cary resolves the problem of order for adolescents in an adult world in quite definite terms, by getting the magistrates to base their decision on the reports of Lizzie's teachers and parents, her probation officer and her doctor. These reports, the novel states, half-mockingly, have 'naturally more weight than personal knowledge acquired in five minutes' examination' (p. 274). That the irony is meant to cut deep can be seen from the double-edged expansion of that process which Cary adds:

Even if any of the magistrates should realize, as probably all have done more than once, that the varieties of human character are infinite; and recollect, even in their own experience, illiterates whose judgment and wisdom made them sounder advisers, better friends, than many learned men, they have no right or justification to take notice of the fact, or time to attempt *a better acquaintance* with the child, who is, in all probability, just what she is described p. 274 (italics added).

We would be wrong, therefore, to put the blame for the irregularities in the dispensing of justice on the custodians of the forms of social order. Magistrates do not have to be bad men to judge badly. Nor is the problem simply a matter of bad laws: reliance on 'sound' private opinion is possibly more dangerous than dependence on official reports. Indeed, the novel refuses to simplify the moral and social order by staging a conflict between the forces of good and those of evil. The police officers should therefore be seen as part of this complex moral order, the agents of a system which is both necessary and defective. Similarly, though the children are heroes, they are not saints. Cary's interest, then, may be said to be in the exploration of the resulting paradox. The beauty of the novel's final scene, from this point of view, is that it brings the children to the point where they 'feel' the moral and social prerequisites of the adult world without regretting the integrity of their earlier childhood. 'It's bin so lovely,' Lizzie says at the end, 'I wish I could die' (p. 257).

We may say then that in *Charley Is My Darling*, Cary explores the nature and growth of moral consciousness in childhood, and, along with this, the nature of good and evil, as the consequences of the intrinsic nature of the world of human relationships. In *Lord of the Flies*, Golding assumes evil to be active, and he gets Simon to locate it in the children themselves. 'Maybe there is a beast . . . What I mean is—maybe it's only us. We could be sort of.'[8] Under the pressure of this assumption the activities in which the children engage become 'diabolic' actions, manifestations of an immanent purposive evil. Cary does not assume such an existence in advance of the exploration.

In Golding, the children, when denied the advantages of a civilised environment, return to a violence which exposes their inherent diabolism. In Cary, the violence of childhood is not associated with environment; it is not even proof of intrinsic evil.

When Lizzie refuses to answer to Ginger's 'good night' because he was pestering her, she realises she has hurt him. 'I do wish I'd said good night to him', Liz sighs again. 'Poor Gingurr'. With this expression of pity, the novel says,

> She seemed to be expressing an emotion much wider and much more deeply felt than a passing sympathy with the object mentioned. Children use the same tone, when, on the loss of a doll or a boat, they say: 'Poor doll, poor boat'. They do not pity the doll or the boat so much as wonder, sometimes with curiosity, sometimes fear, at the circumstances within which dolls and boats can be so helplessly smashed (p. 94).

By exploring the motives and reactions of the children, Cary tries to determine the nature of the conduct which, on the surface, would have been regarded as evidence of evil. 'A child will torture a cat or some other smaller child,' Cary says in the Preface to the novel, 'to see what will happen, both to himself and the victim, and what he feels like in the new circumstances.'[9]

The fact that the child's action is a 'moral experiment'[10] does not, of course, make its effect any less painful (or sadistic) than Golding would have shown. Nor does Cary deny that some of childhood's violent actions are 'criminal'. Cary speaks of the act 'beyond this experimental effort' which a child 'still confused and frustrated, still unable to know, once and for all, what is right and wrong, will commit'. Such an act would be a 'real crime, a spiteful cruelty'. He will 'choose some valued thing to dirty or to smash because he identifies it with a world which obstinately closes itself to his imagination'.[11] What Cary does deny, then, is not the reality of this evil, but the assumption that it exists independently of the world, that it can be identified consistently in action, expecially violent action.

In *Lord of the Flies*, the cure for Evil is the death of the beast in man:

> There were sounds coming from behind the Castle Rock. Listening carefully detaching his mind from the giving of the sea, Ralph could make out a familiar rhythm. '*Kill the beast! Cut his throat! Spill his blood!*' The tribe was dancing. Somewhere on the other side of this rocky wall there would be a dark circle, a glowing fire, and meat. They would be savoring food and the comfort of safety.[12]

Charley Is My Darling cannot seek such a cure because there is no beast, and so no *agon*. At the end of the novel, Liz and Charley question the value of the change their stay in a Reform School is expected to bring about in them.

> Lizzie clasps her hands round her mug and shakes her head.
> 'They makes you all over in they places—you come out so nobody could know you. Praps you won't even know me, Charley.'
> 'Ere, an wot about you then? You going to that rescue ome make you any different?'
> Lizzie is obviously surprised by this suggestion . . . After a moment she says, doubtfully: 'Course they couldn't'.
> 'If they do me, why not you?'
> . . . .
> 'I don't want em to— . . . I want to be like I am and I want ee to be like you are, Charl'' (p. 285).

The reform is unnecessary, first because it is already late. Charley is already on the verge of maturity: ' . . . wy don they leave us alone. We aint kids now' (pp. 285–6). It is unnecessary, secondly, because the beast to kill is the natural imagination which is not so much changed by doctrine as tamed by experience. Irritated, for example, by the knowledge that her parents will shout at her after she has done wrong, Lizzie claims that they 'don't need to shout. I know when I didn't ought to have done something' (p. 96). But this 'truth' cannot change the determinate norms of an external, comprehensible and meaningful world. 'Asylums and gaols are full of people who have forgotten or ignored them'.[13] When Charley protests against the laws of the 'grown ups' as an injustice on the young, Lizzie can see beyond their particular predicament to the larger predicament of conduct in a morally determinate world. 'A lot of kids is silly,' Liz suggests, 'they can be fair nuissance too. I suppose they got to have laws agen the bad uns' (p. 286).

This is not piety. The context in which she says it and the meaning which she implies (that Charley and herself are not among the 'bad uns') exclude piety. Cary is only letting us see Liz and Charley reach the point of adult moral responsibility. Though he protests that he will never be different—'I can't bear that' (p. 286)—Charley can also see that he is already different. '[He] opens his mouth to say once more that they will never make him different. But in the presence of Liz he is no longer a boy playing with words. He feels even a tremor of excited anticipation. He sits still and says nothing' (pp. 286–7). Accordingly, when they are interrupted by the entry of the police officer, 'their faces show no rebellious thoughts' (p. 287). The importance of *Charley Is My Darling* as a novel of childhood thus comes from Cary's ability to sustain these philosophical considerations within the framework of a frankly traditional novel. In *Charley Is My Darling*, we have the immediacy of an actual life; in Charley we have a darling who could belong to the long gallery of Cary's 'creative' characters. But out of this sheer 'complication of actual life', Cary fashions a meaning larger than both character or event.

One can show, by comparing it with Henry James' *What Maisie Knew*, exactly what kind of novel and what kind of vision Cary sought to project in *Charley Is My Darling*. 'No themes are so human,' James declared in the Preface to that novel, 'as those that reflect for us, out of the confusion of life, the close connection of bliss and bale, of the things that help with the things that hurt, so dangling before us forever that bright hard metal, of so strange an alloy, one face of which is somebody's right and ease and the other somebody's pain and wrong.'[14] He saw that he could express this theme very acutely by using as his centre of consciousness a child whose role it would be to 'live with all intensity and perplexity and felicity in its terribly mixed little world' 'bringing people together who would be at least more correctly separate'. But though the centre of consciousness was to be his young child, preferably a young girl ('my light vessel of consciousness, swaying in such a draught, couldn't with verisimilitude be a rude little boy'),[15] the values of which she was to judge would most of them be beyond her full comprehension. For out of what this 'wondering witness materially and inevitably saw' there was 'a great deal' which she 'either couldn't understand at all or would quite misunderstand'.[16] This limitation James explains by claiming that 'small children have many more perceptions than they have terms to translate them; their vision is at any moment much richer, their apprehension even constantly stronger, than their prompt, their at all producible, vocabulary'.[17]

These considerations give a definite orientation to James' treatment of innocence in the novel. They enable him to put a child's mind beside a morally and socially sophisticated adult world, allowing the innocence (not naivety) of the child to shape our response to the elaborate schemings of the adult actors. Thus, for example, Maisie's 'ignorance of what she was to be saved from',

James tells us in the novel, 'didn't diminish the pleasure of the thought that Miss Overmore was saving her. It served to make them cling together as in some wild game of "going round"'.[18] This complication produces the comedy of the novel's action, a comedy, as Leavis has put it, which 'while being so high and spirited, is at the same time, and essentially, a rendering of the pathos of Maisie's situation'.[19]

By the same token, though, it is also a comedy of high society, much in the manner of *The Spoils of Poynton* or *The Ambassadors*, with this difference that in *What Maisie Knew*, though it is Maisie's 'relation, her activity of spirit, that determines' the novelist's concern, James would 'simply take advantage of these things better than [Maisie] herself'.[20] James' comedy thus rests on juxtaposition; the moral point, however, does not. Maisie's moral judgements do, implicitly, question and criticise adult conduct, but James does not try to consolidate Maisie's several reactions into a single epistemology or principle.

It is easy then, to see how related are James' techniques and his objectives. In *Charley Is My Darling*, the question of a centre of consciousness is made irrelevant by the presence of what might be called an empathetic omniscience which gives both childhood and adulthood their due without pleading for them. In the novel, the problem is not, as it is in *What Maisie Knew*, how, as James says, the 'wondering witness'[21] shall communicate, in her own voice, the interpretation of life which she observes. Cary's omniscient voice assumes that task resolutely: the voice which tells of Charley also feels for him. Because the world of *What Maisie Knew* is an adult world, James only allows Maisie her honoured role as the mediating consciousness in order to obtain the advantage of pathos and high comedy. In *Charley Is My Darling*, the world is the world of active childhood in the first place and only thereafter that of adulthood, even though, by the nature of things, that childhood world is surrounded by adult circumstance. James had to place Maisie in such social and moral contexts as would most easily enable her to see (and allow James to dramatise) the conflict among the adults. James, further, had to lose some of the moral certainty of his story because, since the central consciousness is 'innocent' and 'inarticulate', its judgments or statements cannot be readily evaluated without some prejudice to the precious comedy of the action.[22]

In Cary, on the other hand, the presence of childhood and adulthood is no deliberate juxtaposition; or rather the juxtaposition is not significant as comedy; the adult world world serves, indeed, as a physical unit in which childhood lives, and a great part of the emphasis of the story is on the effects of this presence. As a consequence, in *Charley Is My Darling*, apart from the moral disparity which exists between the two worlds, there is no uncertainty of authorial endorsement. The subtlety is not in the juxtaposition of innocence and experience but in the tenderness of an understood childhood. James' theme required closet-drama, Cary's an outdoor escapade.

It is precisely in view of this distinction that Cary's *A House of Children*, though admired by many critics and readers as a novel of 'grave beauty and much wisdom' behind which 'may be felt a large, magnanimous and considered view of life', is nevertheless, an unphilosophical work and, from this point of view, an unrepresentative Cary novel. For the importance, ultimately, of *A House of Children* is not in its vision, its examination of the limits of order, but in the evocation of a mood, 'the mood of childhood', as Enid Starkie called it,[23] or the 'sudden sense of glory which, however intermittently, illuminates every childhood at some time',[24] to quote Walter Allen. In short, *A House of Children* does not compel any intellectual meaning beyond the evocation; it does not demonstrate any 'meaning' not already implicit in the nature of the mood it evokes of life 'in our own tribe, among its ideas, its loves and wars; and the tribes of other children'.[25] Ending also, as it does, on a half-ironic note rejecting its own efforts at evocation, *A House of Children* does indeed show an awareness of its limitations. 'My epic, as I saw it last, in an old exercise book, when I cleared the attic, stopped in the middle of a line and had drawn over it, in blue pencil, little crude sketches of diving men. Yet the quality of our living experience could be translated into the experience of poetry which people would not read. They prefer, I suppose, to live it, if they live, in any true sense of the word, real lives' (p. 127). The reality of actual and present existence is, in other words, often preferred to the artistic ('epic') recollection of it, since that recollection cannot help being either irrelevant or superfluous. In saying, then, that *A House of Children* has no vision, it is not being suggested (as some have argued) that a 'retrospective idyll, even when it is perfect, amounts to little more than a superior form of play'.[26] That would be to judge childhood itself rather than a novel about it. It is rather that what *A House of Children* finally says is what it begins by assuming, 'that even a small child records experience from both sides of its being, in its senses and in its imagination, which can remain separate and yet react upon each other'.[27]

It is important to specify the exact context of this remark. Cary was speaking in his Preface in general philosophical terms of the connection between childhood, childhood memories and the artistic recreation of those memories. No doubt, he argued, 'it was because of this fear and glory' in the incidents of childhood, that 'the event was fixed for ever'.

> But as I say, the sensation that remains does not belong to the picture. It is confused and, as it were, inadequate even to itself, to my own feelings about it. A critic, a philosopher, objects to splitting up the world, that I must have worked on the impression as well as the picture. But I don't feel it so. I feel the impression as something that came from outside and still stands to be examined . . . Our immediate experience is of a split between mind and body, spirit and flesh, the creative imagination and the material it works upon (p. vi).

Cary's problem can be illustrated from an incident early in the novel, when the narrator recalls an exchange with his playmate, 'the red-cheeked boy' who told him that 'jumping about with a lot of kids was silly'.

> I stared at him in open-mouthed surprise for some seconds. But during all this time, the change, which may be described as a kind of crystallization in the chaotic whirl of my brain, was in rapid progress . . . It was not till the crystallization was finished and I had a clear, sharp-edged knowledge, both feeling and idea, of the new situation, that I answered. I stopped jumping about, screwed my face in an expression similar to the red-cheeked boy's (pp. 55–6).

We can thus see from this passage as well as from the tone of his Preface, that Cary was interested in this particular reaction because of the 'confirmation' it gave to his idea of childhood experience. And, in a sense, it does. 'Small children are thought happy, but for most of the time they do not even live consciously, they exist; they drift through sensations as a pantomime fairy passes through coloured veils and changing lights' (p. 1); 'for children life seems endless, and they do not know that a grief has no cure' (p. 58);

'children love beauty but don't notice it' (p. 188); 'we sought glory, but not our own exclusively; we wanted to be part of a glorious existence' (p. 195). There is however, no further conclusion which it is possible to make from that insight. This is not because such an insight would be a profitless one but because in the novel the 'recollection' excludes the intellectual and narrative structures which Cary used successfully in his other novels to give meaning to insight. The philosopher and the artist are, as it were, kept firmly apart. In the words of Cary's Preface, 'it is the philosopher's job to explain this state of affairs, as it is a writer's, as writer, to explore and describe, as exactly as he can, the experience which the philosopher (as artist in the creation of rational wholes) can use for his raw material' (p. vii). And the effect of this attitude is that the novelist becomes a chronicler without being also an interpreter; that the artist ceases to be, in himself, an unacknowledged philosopher.

At one level this separation is the result of the plotlessness of *A House of Children*, the absence of a strong narrative outline, which as an analogue to the patterns of a fable, could perhaps give the various moments or episodes of Cary's recollection a simple, but nevertheless permanent, character. The narrative outline of *Charley Is My Darling* is strong enough to sustain the moral and intellectual evaluation of Charley's career. The absence of a strong and directed storyline—a plot, in other words—denies *A House of Children* t' t kind of meaning or significance which, as Aristotle as well as other readers demand, becomes any narrative that claims to have a beginning, a middle and an end. There is, accordingly, more eventfulness than interrelated action in *A House of Children*, an eventfulness which is all the more disturbing because it does not finally lead to growth or at least development.[28]

This absence of meaning has its own importance. It makes it necessary for us to question the general assumption that it is Cary's first-person narrative voice, as such, which is primarily responsible for the success of his best fiction. *A House of Children* is, indeed, a first-person narrative. It is consistent in its point of view, sincere in its revelation of feeling, and convincing in its evocation of 'the very sense of childhood' (p. 1). Like *To Be A Pilgrim*, it is a recollection of the past; like *Charley Is My Darling*, it is a novel of childhood. Unlike *To Be A Pilgrim*, however, its present is ahistorical and undefined. Its narrator is not, for example, a man moulded by the past which he recalls. There is none of the wisdom such as we will find in *To Be A Pilgrim*, inferred from the recollection of childhood. Because Cary's narrator does not establish himself as a character—that is, as a being with a past and a present—his childhood ego, though not losing its intrinsic relevance, cannot command an unequivocal intellectual meaning based on the novel's action. Cary's achievement in *To Be A Pilgrim*, after all, is to be found in the intellectual control which allowed for the recall of childhood as well as a serious meditation on it in the light of the present and the future. Operating as it is shown to be on the 'actual sensations of childhood', Cary's inspiration led only too naturally to 'the clarity, the large skies, and wide sea views, which', he says, 'belong to the vision of my childhood' (pp. v, vii). The limitation of *A House of Children* compared to the other first-person narratives, therefore, is that it stops at the basic clarity.

There is, of course, the same intellectual *foundation* for *A House of Children* as there is for Cary's other novels. We have the same sense of history which we will find in *To Be A Pilgrim*, the sense of the cult of Empire, of elegant Victorianism, of anarchism in politics, bohemianism in society and pseudo-decadence in the arts.[29]

> I read now about the men of the nineties, their bohemianism and disillusionment, and their figures seem romantic. In Pinto, as I realised long afterwards, I knew one of those men, or at least one of the provincials who were affected by the same movement of the time spirit (p. 173).

There is also the same metaphysical awareness of the quality of human experience, with Little Anketel illustrating, in his small way, Cary's belief in the integrity of the individual personality.[30] Anketel is Cary's child-man of *Power in Men* who has innate 'power' and who cannot be coerced into action because all its acts are his own. This 'power' is demonstrated in a multitude of different incidents in the novel. But Cary moves from such demonstrations to general statements about the destructive character of old age—the sense one reads in their 'lines of repose' that . . . there is no time to begin again, to get things right. The greater a grown man's power of enjoyment, the stronger his faith, the deeper and more continuous his feeling of the waste of life, of happiness, of youth and love, of himself' (pp. 57–8). As in *Charley Is My Darling*, Cary deals in *A House of Children* with problems of maturity, the sense of moving from childhood to adolescence and thence to adulthood.

It surprised me to know that I was changing, but I did not pursue the subject. Though I did not notice real changes, I was accustomed to the idea that the whole world was changing all the time . . . I did not think this; I thought nothing; and it was at least a year before I began to form primitive conceptions of the world (p. 144).

In the novel, however, the child is generally unaware of the coming of adulthood, even though by act or word he has assumed its obligations. What Cary says of this process at the end of *Charley Is My Darling* is presented in an incident which is the natural conclusion to the theme and the action of the novel. Charley will be sent to the Reform School as the law requires, but this will not guarantee change. Indeed, Charley knows (and actually says so) that 'they will never make him different'.[31] Cary's argument is that Charley is already different in another sense: 'he is no longer a boy playing with words. He feels ashamed to strike attitudes'.[32] 'Why don't they leave us alone. We ain't kids now'.[33] In *A House of Children*, however, because he is not reaching out towards such a conclusion, Cary just discourses on the phenomenon. 'The only certain distinction I can find between child and maturity is that children grow in experience and look forward to novelty' (pp. 56–7).

This concern differs in manner and import from that of *To Be A Pilgrim* and *Charley Is My Darling*. In *To Be A Pilgrim*, there is the poignancy which attaches to the recollection of the past, especially because the very recollection is immediately pertinent to the condition of the narrator's peace of mind in the present. 'I may be old, but I don't belong to the past;' 'The truth is, I have always been a lover rather than a doer; I have lived in dreams rather than acts; and like all lovers, I have lived in terror of what I love.'[34] In *Charley Is My Darling*, childhood is recorded, not as illustration, but as fact. The effect of this is to give each incident or situation its own independence and to the series a thematic connection. The passage of time and the accompanying development of Charley's moral sense give these incidents their characteristic unity. In *A House of Children*, because of Cary's quite limited purpose, incident follows generalisation almost explicitly as illustration. 'I think that children rarely get a clear idea even of another child's unhappiness, unless it is made plain to them' (p. 115).

According to Cary's Preface, *A House of Children* is autobiographical. Cary tells us that for some reason he gave himself an older brother. This elder brother is 'also myself, and I suspect that I divided myself in this way because I realized by some instinct (it was certainly not by reason) that the two together as a single character would be too complex for the kind of book I needed to write'.[35] This is perhaps the best clue to the existence of the distinction which we have been making between *A House of Children* and the other novels, especially *Charley Is My Darling*. In the other first-person narratives, the complex nature of the autobiography is held together by the strong and critical personality of the narrator, who has a distinct existence in the present. In *A House of Children*, on the other hand, there is no revelation, no stocktaking—only reminiscence. The result is that the narrator is not a character in the sense that the other first-person narrators are, but a mind. The distinction between such a mind and a third person voice is almost non-existent. It would thus seem that in writing his own fictionalised autobiography, Cary could not summon up the same spirit of inquiry and pilgrimage which had made *To Be A Pilgrim* so valuable. Cary's use of himself as narrator, then, is easily seen as involving a problem parallel to that which he saw in Conrad's use of Marlow—the problem of having the story told in the first person by a fictitious character. As Cary himself said of Conrad's device, it 'seems to have all the faults and none of the merits' of the first- or the third-person narrator. 'It has only one advantage: it enables the writer to describe the narrator'.[36]

Compared to *Charley Is My Darling*, then, *A House of Children*, because it is pure evocation, is only the first step towards a moral or philosophical statement. *A House of Children*, in fact, shows the attachment to childhood and the empathetic affections out of which Cary constructed the tough-minded realism of *Charley Is My Darling*. Like *Charley Is My Darling*, it is a tender lyrical and closely observed story.[37] But, *Charley Is My Darling* goes beyond this tenderness of observation and creates an image of the moral order and the moral process and uses the story of a deliquent evacuee to trace the dawn of moral consciousness in childhood. It is difficult to state a parallel or comparable purpose behind *A House of Children*.

3 Being and Living: The Existentialist Trilogy

TO BE A PILGRIM

To Be A Pilgrim is Tom Wilcher's sustained soliloquy, meditation and commentary on the spiritual and the material aspects of his life and his times. It is true, indeed, as Andrew Wright has pointed out that the novel is an inquiry into the nature of Wilcher's pilgrimage through life,[1] but that inquiry turns out also to be a vicarious fulfilment of a long-delayed dream of the good life which the hero and narrator, admired in Lucy and Sara. 'The truth is, I have always been a lover rather than a doer; I have lived in dreams rather than acts; and like all lovers, I have lived in terror of change of what I love'.[2] The result, in Wilcher's case, is that paradoxically, the book he writes becomes a confession and a rationalisation so subtly executed that the effect is to engage the sympathy of the reader by making him realise that more is at stake in the novel than the vindication or the condemnation of the hero-narrator. In effect, *To Be A Pilgrim* becomes an attempt to explain the meaning of Wilcher's life by relating it to parallel developments in English public life and thought. Thus, the personal and the public themes of the novel are brought together, partly because of the social status of its hero and the relevance of Tolbrook Manor as a symbol of England and the past but primarily because the final meaning of both the 'apologia' and the 'confessio' required such a validation. To resolve the appearance of contradiction in Wilcher's life, the novel had to resolve a still larger problem: the problem of time.

To Be A Pilgrim calls it 'the tragedy of revolution', the fact that time and change cannot be reversed; that their effects are not merely sociological but also human and personal (p. 210). Allied with it is the 'injustice of one generation to another' which Wilcher calls the 'worst' of 'all things I find unbearable' (p. 312). One of the victims of this 'revolution' is Julie who, in her prime, was the star of tragedy. But now, in a different generation, her style has faded: 'The rich material was there, the dignity, the sincerity, but all began to seem meaningless and therefore tawdry; as palace velvets, when the palace becomes a show for trippers, begin at once to look like plush. The slender tragic actress had changed into theatrical poser' (p. 265). Every new generation creates its own heroes and heroines. In place of Julie, the new generation has Gladys, the modern girl who 'lay on Julie's sofa most of the evening, her feet in the air, her skirt to her thighs, smoking thirty cigarettes, drinking half a dozen whiskies and telling us about her boys, [and] how often they had tried to rape her . . . All this time John sat by, looking from Gladys to us with the expression of one who says, "Admire this wonder" ' (p. 265). Cary's point is that Gladys herself will sometime face a new generation that will contemplate her with distaste and incomprehension.

Because Wilcher is very acutely aware of this 'revolution', he has been described by some critics as a man who has fallen 'between two worlds and is in a strange position of advocating a life and faith that he has himself never been capable of living'.[3] His story, they say, is that of 'a figure whose life has been plagued by time and his sense of powerlessness before it'.[4] These judgments arise, naturally, from the anomalous position Wilcher is in as actor in and commentator on the world he creates; he not only provides us with the facts on which we are to base our estimate of his world and of himself, he also gives us the ideals by which we are to judge his failings and achievements in that world. Yet the positiveness of Wilcher's advocacy of life and faith, and the intellectual vigour with which he strives to understand the attributes of that life, cannot be nullified or even seriously qualified, by the fact of his own failure. The significance of Wilcher's meditations is that within each generation there are opportunities for the same fulfilment and the same frustration, the same greatness and inconsequence as Wilcher found in his own generation and in Ann's. The important thing, as the novel puts it, is to distinguish 'the grand old manner of the former age' from what is 'simply the flummery of any age' (p. 265).

This argument is the burden of Cary's title. The worst victim of this eternal and 'continuous' revolution is the non-pilgrim, the man caught between two generations. Wilcher is concerned for Ann because he fears that, like himself, she will become a failure through a neglect of that faith and that creative freedom which saved Sara and Lucy. The forms of Ann's life will be definitely different from his. Her education is already different: Freud is her Kant. But the essential problem will remain the same and the old will continue to suggest remedies which the young will reject. 'The truth', Wilcher explains, 'is not that old men are fussy but that they have learned from experience how much the young trust to luck, until some disaster falls upon them, by their own fault. And at that moment, of course, they cease to be young'. (p. 212).

Cary's point, then, is to show the many facets of this tragedy of change, to show the varying responses of men to the demands of life seen, on the one hand, as a creative and a free existence and, on the other, as bounded by the demands of order and property. It is better for the young that they do evil rather than do nothing, just as, for the old, an early death is perhaps the only way of avoiding the new and unfamiliar. Lazarus probably didn't enjoy his resurrection, Wilcher suspects, for things must have changed too much for his peace of mind (p. 215). If Wilcher judged his life mean, it is not because it was devoid of incident—the novel shows it was not—but because it was, philosophically speaking, inadequate.

This inadequacy is not in the age but in individual men and women. Though Lucy, Edward, Tom Wilcher's father and Old Jaffery belong to the past, each of them reacts differently to that same environment. There is a similar variety in the young generation. Robert, 'as one might expect in Lucy's son, had always a great disgust for what he called modern muck' (p. 48). Yet he is a 'modern', and has no particular attachments to the past. An old house like Tolbrook means nothing to him. It is 'charged with history, which reveals to man his own soul', but you cannot expect 'a boy like Robert to understand that' (p. 26). Robert can keep himself safe from the prison of both the old and the new because he is himself powerful and free. 'He's a real Protestant inside. He'd really like to make a whole new god for himself if he had the time' (p. 164). Robert's virtue is in his refusal to have roots, to be tied down—his pilgrim spirit. His mother, Lucy, had that same virtue and people called it her 'devilry'. Out of that devilry, Wilcher points out, Robert will make 'something good and noble' of his life, 'as his mother [Lucy] had done' (p. 48).

Ann is different. She is less strong, enjoys life less, and looks unprepared for the future because she has yet to learn to use the present without becoming slave to it; to inherit the past without being haunted by it. Robert has the strength to know what he wants from both past and present just as he knows what he wants from everything: 'from girls to traction engines' (p. 50). Lucy and Robert can be cruel even to the things they love; and more cruel if what they love is weak. Ann cannot even be angry. Her quiet voice is never raised 'even in anger' (p. 48). Because she lacks 'Lucy's spirit of life and joy, and confidence' (p. 52), Wilcher fears that she will suffer the same defeat and unfulfilment as himself.

For Wilcher (as well as for Cary) the pilgrim idea is not a form of anarchism, a denial of order. Indeed, though Robert was now thought of as a radical, he began as a conservative who despised what he called modern 'muck'. Lucy, also, did not think that all change was progress. 'She knew the value of order, of a routine, even in our rebellious nursery'. It was as if 'nature had taught her that it is precisely the stormiest spirit which needs, upon its roughest journey, some rule of the sea and road' (pp. 24–5). Edward, whose life Ann now thinks 'small', was considered a radical in his time; his attacks on the contemporary establishment were thought a danger to the very foundations of English life. Edward's generation, in fact, was an exciting and militant one.

> In Jubilee year the old men remembered Peel and Canning and Cobbett . . . Middle-aged men spoke of Dizzy and the New Tories; they had hunted with Trollope and Surtees; the young ones were full of Kipling and Kitchener, Lloyd George and the radical Chamberlain . . .
> On both sides it was a battle of faith. Rhodes was already looking for the reign of eternal peace and justice under the federation of imperial nations, and against him the Radicals passionately sought national freedom for all peoples. The first spoke in the name of God the law-giver, for world-wide justice and service; the second in the name of Christ the rebel, for universal love and trust; and both were filled with the sense of mission . . .
> We felt that our lives had fallen in an age of revolutions and heroic adventures (pp. 138–9).

And just as Wilcher's generation saw itself as one of heroism and adventure, so had the generation even before that. 'To Edward, and therefore to me, Gladstone was an old-fashioned Whig, and already an obstacle to progress. We condescended to him as the Grand Old Man. It was not for many years that we realized how great he had seemed to my father's generation; a prophet, a leader sent from God' (p. 124).

These examples show that the novel consistently asserts the constancy of the human element in any generation; it portrays the nature of the conflict between this human constant and the variations of time and history. It claims that the only possible way for the individual to mitigate the destructive capacity of this conflict is by the cultivation of what the novel calls the 'free' soul. Only 'free' souls can escape this conflict because only they have learned the lesson of history, the lesson of time. A free soul is a pilgrim soul. Like Lucy, it has no roots; it belongs 'with the spirit; her goods and possessions were all in her own heart and mind, her skill and courage' (p. 16). As Wilcher puts it in his letter to Sara, 'those who cling to this world', whether in its present or in its past form, 'must be dragged backwards into the womb which is also a grave'.

> We are the pilgrims who must sleep every night beneath a new sky, for either we go forward to the new camp or the whirling earth carries us backwards to one behind. There is no choice but to move, forwards or backwards. Forward to the clean hut, or backward. To the old camp, fouled every day by the passers (p. 37).

On one level, this is an argument for the cultivation of enthusiasm. Cary would seem to prefer the impulsive life of Lucy, Sara and Edward to the contemplative life of Wilcher and Ann; the religious imagination of Brown and the Benjamites to the propriety of traditional Anglicanism. In fact, however, Cary's interest is not in the act or the impulse, but in the sense of identity and of inner vitality. Cary's free souls, his 'pilgrims', are those who make full use of all their powers in a positive and integrated response to both the joys and vicissitudes of being. That this is the case we can see quite conclusively in that crucial episode in the novel of Wilcher's first confrontation with the preacher, Brown. Wilcher recalls 'the excitement of [Brown's] presence' when, for the first time, he [Wilcher] 'stood below him'.

> His short squat figure stood black against the crimson sign of the Wilcher Arms, hanging behind him. Its gilt lettering, sparkling in the sun make a kind of glory around his head and shoulders, the shoulders of a giant, or a dwarf; and the face of a prize-fighter, pug nose, jutting brows, thick swollen lips, roaring over all the noise of bullocks and sheep (p. 20).

This is, virtually, a domesticated transfiguration scene which makes Brown's physical presence hard to forget. Wilcher does not describe his own appearance during that meeting with Brown, but Sara's picture of him in *Herself Surprised* is some clue: '[Wilcher] was a little man', Sara says, 'with a bald head and round black spectacles. His nose was short, just like a baby's, and he had a long blue upper lip, like a priest'.[5] The three images are those of the scholar, the infant and the cleric; the intellectual, the childlike and the sentimental man he is throughout the novel.

Brown's hymn which is taken from Bunyan, moves Wilcher deeply:

> No foes shall stay his might,
> Though he with giants fight;
> He will make good his right
> To be a pilgrim.

'I felt my heart turn over' Wilcher admits (p. 20). But his first impulse is to escape from further contact with these sources of deep feeling. Was he not 'a clever young man who was reading Kant?' Because he knows that Brown has no arguments that will not 'fill [him] with contempt', he is reluctant to acknowledge the power of Brown's emotional preaching on him. Yet though not founded on abstract reason, the pilgrim cry demanded a response, not an evasion—which explains why Wilcher feels as though he would choke 'unless [he], too, opened [his] mouth and sang' (p. 21). Later in the novel, Wilcher will be in a position to explain the power behind Brown's simple faith which Brown was expressing: the Wilchers themselves shared in that faith, for they were 'as deep English as Bunyan himself. A Protestant people, with the revolution in their bones', the faith of Cromwell, Wyclif and Stiggins. For the present, however, Wilcher cannot understand that tradition. He cannot understand it because he 'knew nothing and nobody real, only knowledge of things. I knew no living soul (p. 21). The distinction is between 'real' knowledge and knowledge 'of things'; between knowledge which appertains only to the intellect and that which involves the whole active man. Bunyan's strength is the strength of experienced faith; Wilcher's that of impersonal faith. It is the sense of 'felt-conviction' in Bunyan rather than his logic that gives Brown's song its meaning and its force. In Wilcher's encounter with Brown, then, there is a parallel encounter between Bunyan and

Kant. Kant loses, not because he is wrong or unnecessary—he and Kierkegaard are, after all, Cary's authority for this very distinction[6]—but because Wilcher mistakes the intellect for the soul, 'idea' for 'existence'.

How can this argument be reconciled with one of the contentions of *To Be A Pilgrim* that 'man lives by his ideas' (p. 156)? By 'ideas' in that context Cary obviously means, not the constructs of pure reason which, like Kantian constructs, are merely analytical, but the systematised shape of constructive feeling. 'Ideas' in that sense are 'great' when they affect and direct the largest area of a man's whole being—what Cary calls the 'soul'. The shadow of Blake hangs over this understanding of life, and it is in the spirit of Blake's man of action that we have to understand Cary's men of feeling. Wilcher's escape from the enthusiasm of Brown is an escape from a vital aspect of himself, and a movement away from his own fulfilment. Kant loses to Bunyan, then, only because rather than welcome both, Wilcher evades Bunyan, even though he knows that, alone Kant cannot serve his life. 'I felt as if some internal Brown was trying to pop out of a dark hole in my own mind' (p. 22). The tragedy of Wilcher's life is that he never let it.[7] It is clear, then, that the philosophical argument of *To Be A Pilgrim* is founded on what Cary himself calls 'that continuous revolution' in which his characters are 'compelled, and we are compelled, to live, which is at once the field of freedom, our opportunity and our tragedy'.[8] This revolution has a more central place in *To Be A Pilgrim* than in the other novels of the trilogy. This is to be expected since Wilcher, more than the other narrators, is involved in that revolution in both personal and intellectual terms. As Cary himself admits, it would have been fatal to allow Sara to 'talk politics and art' since she would become less vivid as a character. It was the same consideration which forced him to give Jimson few political ideas. For good reason, therefore, Wilcher is the political and social philosopher of the trilogy. Hence, *To Be A Pilgrim* is a kind of an answer to the questioner of T. S. Eliot's 'East Coker' (*Collected Poems 1909–1962*).

> What was to be value of the long look forward to
> Long hoped for calm, and autumnal serenity
> And the wisdom of age? Had they deceived us
> Or deceived themselves, the quiet-voiced elders,
> Bequeathing us merely a receipt for defeat?

Wilcher's most pointed answer appears in his recollection of his own father's dying days when the old man tried to advise him and his brothers on the conduct of life, to tell them some of the wisdom of old age. 'I quickly gave him pencil and paper again. But he could not write' (p. 158). Typically Wilcher and his brothers are too occupied with other worries to listen to him. As Wilcher himself tells it:

> I tried to soothe the old man, but I could not do so. . . . But now, when I remember my father's eyes as he watched the syringe brought towards his helpless body, I feel such a pang of grief that my own heart knows the pain of death. For I know what he was saying to himself: 'Now they are putting me to sleep, because I want to tell them this thing, which only I can tell. Only a dying man, upon his death bed, can know it. And because they do not know it, they don't know its importance, they don't want to hear it' (p. 158).

This is the dilemma of the young and the old. It is now Wilcher's turn to face the same dilemma. Because he is now old, he cannot trust the young. 'Old men don't like strangers. How can they?' (p. 9). In the face of this dilemma, Wilcher preaches the crucial lesson of his novel: the virtues of the pilgrim spirit and of the humble soul. Only the pilgrim spirit can save the young as well as the old from the 'corruption of sense and the shims of fashion' (p. 276). Such humility is endless.

Because humility is the lesson of Wilcher's story, the novel begins as he attempts to assert the relevance of his past life, and to justify his desperate plan, late in life, to marry his housekeeper. He rejects the suggestion by his family that he is merely 'a foolish old man, who has fallen into the hands of a scheming woman'. In fact, he says, he is himself 'the unfaithful servant, and Sara the victim' (p. 9). For Sara is one of those people 'to whom faith is so natural that they don't know how they have it. She was a living faith' (p. 11). He sees his tragedy as comparable to that of the old woman who 'had broken all her china and torn all her clothes off and walked down a crowded street in the rain'. 'I've got legs and arms. I've got a body. I'm a human being after all. See? And off came the silk dress, the stays and the petticoats and the buttons and the strings, there she is walking down the street as naked as Eve' (pp. 309–10).

Wilcher goes on, in the novel, to relive and rethink the stages by

which he came to this condition. He argues that, at heart, he wa
attached to that worship of the free soul which served and save
Lucy and Edward so magnificently. He did not give full expression
to this attachment to creative power, or even to his plan to enter the
missionary life (p. 159), because of the need for and the lure c
temporal order:

> I felt as if the very frame of things in which I had lived so securel
> were falling apart, like broken screens; to show behind, darknes
> and chaos. Tolbrook suddenly appeared to me like a magi
> island, preserved in peace among the storms of the world only b
> a succession of miracles. As I walked through the room, the ver
> chairs and tables seemed to tremble in their silence, like do
> without a master, asking, 'What will happen to us now?' (p. 160)

That attachment became his 'curse' (p. 9). 'I told Ann Tolbroo
would kill me, and I was right. I had never had peace or comfort in
this house. I have been too fond of it' (p. 34).

In the last chapter of the novel, Tom Wilcher comes to a fina
prophetic conclusion about life, about England and about his ow
connections with both: 'The truth must be confessed, that I am a
old fossil, and that I have deceived myself about my abilities.
thought I could be an adventurer like Lucy and Edward,
missionary. I shouted the pilgrim's cry, democracy, liberty, and s
forth, but I was a pilgrim only by race' (p. 341). This confession c
personal inadequacy in the novel's last pages is something of
double reversal and at first suggests that Wilcher is reassessing hi
earlier defence and is now affirming a more personal and mor
intrinsic reason for his failure. This is not exactly the case, howeve
For the crisis of Wilcher's life is that, distracted as he says 'wit
worry', he did not till then think about the matter so self-criticall
or ask himself such soul-searching questions. In the past, he woul
get angry with his mother for being critical of Edward's politics, fo
failing to appreciate 'democracy', even though he himself did no
understand it, either. As manager of his family estate, he would loo
'resigned like a grown-up pestered by children' when asked an
question about business 'to which he had no answer'. He woul
'merely keep silence and assume a pre-occupied expression
(p. 159). Consequently, he failed to participate truly in or to eve
understand the active democratic life of Edward and Lucy: the lif
of the 'protestant' soul. 'I was a pilgrim only by race. England too

me with her on a few stages of her journey. Because she could not help it (p. 342).

Wilcher is contending, in other words, that his fitful manifestations of the individual power of action are attributable to an inherited English impulse. For Wilcher, England, as a nation, is the model of the pilgrim spirit. She wakes every day to 'fifty million strangers, to thousands of millions who beat past her, as deaf and blind as the waves. She is the true Flying Dutchman'. Lucy and Edward belong truly to her tradition. They follow her lead, 'faithful to ancient ways'; they 'spread old patched sails, to seek for something new' (p. 109). They and England are thus the 'pilgrims' of the world, and its 'scapegoat'. England is free. 'She stands always before all possibility, and that is the youth of the spirit. It is the life of the faithful who say, "I am ready. Anywhere at any time" ' (p. 342). Wilcher's novel is his exploration of this pilgrim spirit, of the blessings and the trials of the Flying Dutchman.

To Be A Pilgrim ends with the result of this exploration quietly affirmed in a final exchange between Wilcher and Ann. To Wilcher's remark that Ann takes life 'too seriously', Ann replies:

'Don't you think it is rather serious.'
'My dear child, you're not thirty yet. You have forty, forty-five years in front of you.'
'Yes' (p. 342).

This affirmation is important for Ann and Wilcher, and for the novel's meaning. We need to recall that soon after her father's death, Ann began collecting material for his biography. Among Edward's papers, Wilcher discovered a twenty-one-line poem on the nobility of life as Edward and his generation knew it: 'Not time destroys the old', Edward had written, 'but creeping spite/For all they fought for, in a bungled fight' (p. 282). Ann did not want to include this material in her book, and instead threw the pages into the wastepaper basket 'under the samples of oil cake, twine, and seed' (p. 282). The verses sounded to her as if Edward 'took it all too seriously'.

'All that old politics look small from this end of the telescope— and when politics gets to look small, it looks mean, too. But poor Daddy wasn't mean—no that's tricky.'

'My dear child, your father was a century before his time. That was his tragedy' (p. 283).

It is to this exchange that Ann and Wilcher allude in the last lines of the novel. That final 'Yes' from Ann is both a sign of her conversion and the moment of greatest understanding for Wilcher. Both consequences constitute a final vindication of the ideal of the pilgrim soul on which the thought of *To Be A Pilgrim* depends. Ann's future assures us again of the continuity of life, in spite of the limitations of the past. For Wilcher's fault was in taking the world of things too seriously; in letting anxiety over 'things' overwhelm him, in not asserting the creative and continuous adventurousness of the soul. Ann's 'Yes' at the end of the novel confirms that she will learn this lesson.

For Wilcher, this scene is crucial to the clarification of the persistent concerns of his life; namely the future of Tolbrook and its occupants. In the fresh wisdom of his last days, he discovers that if a man's ideas are mean, 'then his life shall be mean'.

> If he follow the idea of his body, then his life shall be narrow as one body's room, which is a single grave. But if he follow the ideas of his soul, which is to love and serve, then he shall join himself to the company of all lovers and all the servants of life, and his idea shall apprehend a common good (p. 151).

It is for this reason that Wilcher refuses to make a final will. 'What does it matter who gets Tolbrook . . . Blanche, Robert, and Ann would get each an equal share, which is probably a fair division. For Blanche has the best claim, Ann has the most need; and Robert is Lucy's son' (p. 341). This decision is not a surrender to the physical exhaustion of age. It is a major spiritual resolution. Wilcher himself calls it a 'triumph' because his past life was all too fruitlessly devoted to the making and unmaking of wills as if the wills, by themselves, would preserve Tolbrook and the Wilcher line.[9] Now, at his death, Wilcher makes none. He will even ask to be buried without a coffin (p. 341). His last days are so near and his education so complete that Ann (who is a doctor) does not even reprove him for breaking her instruction to lie flat and do nothing: 'in her silence it was understood between us that whether I die today or tomorrow does not matter to anybody' (p. 342). Ann's affirmation is quite appropriately tempered by the lesson of an eternally creative and

therefore unsettled world; and by the sheer weight of history. It is an
affirmation, nevertheless, of the inevitable, indestructible continuity of life, both in the Tolbrook tradition and in the larger
tradition of national and universal life. Ann will have to face her
own life and her own age with her own convictions and her own
faith or lack of it, much as Edward, Lucy and Wilcher faced theirs.
'Every age has its own nonsense' (p. 340). Wilcher's fear is that like
some of her generation, Ann will lack the necessary strength to
confront her own times by not having enough faith in herself. This
cynical world view of the young 'shocked and frightened' him. 'It
was as though the spring leaves, deliberately, for some secret and
devilish purpose, distilled poison in their own sap and withered on
the twigs'(pp. 257–8). Wilcher finds this cynicism everywhere. After
his escape from Tolbrook, he can find no true resting place or
destination in all England because all around him, he could see
nothing but a 'huge field of dark coats and white faces, corn high,
silently drinking from cups and glasses, each as solitary as a stone on
a beach' (p. 313). Chaucer's England, and Chaucer's pilgrims,
presumably had a surer sense of their place and their destination.
For, as Wilcher puts it, an English pilgrim is not a wandering jew,
'not a lost soul . . . nor a wanderer. He is not a tramp' (p. 313), as
are the forlorn young Englishmen of the world he now sees before
him.

These are lost souls who don't even know that they are lost. They
read three newspapers a day saying different things, and then
they put on their black overcoats and hats and come to some
place like this, to look at each other's hats and coats and to feel
nothing, to say nothing, to think nothing, only to wait. And all
the time, something called history is rushing to and fro and
changing the very shape of hats and coats and trousers and collars
(p. 313).

It is this vision of a 'hard and careworn' England that shakes
Wilcher finally from his deep sense of property and order into his
resolve to free himself by trying some mild recklessness. It now
dawns on him that, contrary to his earlier illusions, his death will not
be the end of Tolbrook, nor of England. He may have been the
manager of property but he is not the pillar of the world. In the past
he would 'walk upon the fields of the whole island as upon my own
carpet, and feel the same exasperation against them for being a

perpetual burden on my regard; I love the noble buildings as I loved those old chairs and tables, with anxiety and irritation. For I know very well that they are not being properly looked after' (p. 341). Now he knows that England (and Tolbrook) will somehow survive the carelessness of the present generation. 'She, poor thing, was born upon the road, and lives in such a dust of travel that she never knows where she is' (p. 342).

Wilcher's joy in England, like his joy in Tolbrook, he says, is that of a 'house of spirits, made by generations of lovers' (p. 342). Knowing no distinctions among them, between the spiritual and the material, between the form and the spirit of their love, England has renewed herself from a succession of differing caretakers. A 'new vigorous generation' of Englishmen had snatched peace from the monk 'in his sleepy routine' and made a farm shed out of his chapel and borne their 'half-pagan children in his holy cell . . . Why do I ever forget that the glory of my land is also the secret of youth, to see at every sunrise a new horizon' (p. 109). Like England, Tolbrook has taken on, and will conveniently accommodate, a variety of masters and lovers. Robert will effect changes in Tolbrook, and will destroy some of its most unique features. But because Robert is a Wilcher and a Brown (and more a Brown than a Wilcher), he will sustain and revitalise Tolbrook in his own way, in the spirit of his own generation. He will take Tolbrook back

> into history, which changed it once before from priory into farm, from farm into manor, from manor, the workshop and court of a feudal dictator, into a country house where young ladies danced and hunting men played billiards; where, at last, a new-rich gentleman spent his weekends from his office. And after that I suppose it was to have been a country hotel, where typists on holidays gaze at trees, the crops, and the farmer's men with mutual astonishment and dislike (p. 328).

Through these changes, and in spite of them, Tolbrook (so also England) asserts the simple faith of the people who sustained it—the 'sense of the common English, in a thousand generations', 'a wisdom and a faith so close to death and life that we could not tell what part of it was God's and what was man's' (p. 328). This larger meaning is as central to the purpose of *To Be A Pilgrim* as the personal story of Wilcher's life. *To Be A Pilgrim* thus speaks of and to a larger world.

HERSELF SURPRISED

Herself Surprised is best read after *To Be A Pilgrim*, for it is in the latter novel that the significance of Sara's story is clarified, and its larger proportions outlined. That significance is, of course, also implicit in *Herself Surprised*. But it is not till *To Be A Pilgrim* that its inevitability and its seriousness are assured. *To Be A Pilgrim* makes claims for Sara without substantiating them with the details of the life on which they were founded; *Herself Surprised* makes no claims for Sara but documents the facts and motives of the life on which Wilcher had depended for his convictions. In *Herself Surprised*, Sara sees herself merely as a fumbling, flighty woman, and a good cook. In *To Be A Pilgrim*, Wilcher speaks of her as his saviour, the catalyst for his spiritual awakening and his moral wisdom. It is, thus, as if *To Be A Pilgrim* was written mainly to give Sara the credit she earned without realising it. In her novel, Sara claims that the 'only thing I know is to work about a house'.[11] But she ends her novel with an affirmation of the eternity of her calling. 'A good cook will always find work, even without character, and can get a new character in twelve months, and better herself, which God helping, I shall do' (p. 220).

We know, however, that Sara is more than a good cook. In *To Be A Pilgrim*, Wilcher calls her a 'life manager' because, in an instinctive way, her sense of life answered to his description of the ideal: that desire 'to love and serve' in such a way that one can 'join [oneself] to the company of all lovers and the servants of life' and thereby 'apprehend the common good'.[12] Her attachment to people and to things is not that of 'any connoisseur', 'collector', or 'bored millionaire' who 'when he shows off his treasures, is seeking in your praise the resurrection and the life'. Sara's appreciation of things, he says, came 'out of her generous and lavish heart. . . . She delighted in caring for them as if they had been her own'.[13] Hence Wilcher's claim in *To Be A Pilgrim* that Sara 'came to save my soul alive'.[14]

Speaking there also of the 'three great waves of passion and agitation' which marked his life, Wilcher identifies Sara with the third of these, and likens her to 'a mild English breeze' which came to rescue him from 'the stagnant lake, the rolling trees and the tropical serpents' of his middle age, thereby bringing about the promise of his later life. Sara's influence brings about a 'bright', 'smooth and fresh' Atlantic roller which, thwarted by the suspicions of his nieces, 'struck upon a sand bar and burst into foam, bubbles,

spray, and air, etc.',[15] just as it was about to come to port. To the
world outside she was nothing more than 'a fat red-faced cook of
forty-six . . . a cunning and insinuating country woman, who had
deceived two men before she swindled [Wilcher] and robbed
[him]'.[16] Wilcher's novel denies all this. 'The facts are true yet they
believe a lie'.[17] This is also the contention of Sara's story. 'It was Mrs
Loftus' evidence went against me; and she believed every word of it,
for she was always very truthful. Yet I think she was wrong' (p. 176).
It is part of Cary's strategy in *Herself Surprised* to have as narrator, a
heroine who is totally incapable of recognising her own importance;
who is so busy living and serving life; so concerned with the simple
business of being herself that she does not even speculate on the
possible significance of her various roles.

Herself Surprised is thus Sara's humble but dignified admission of
the inadequacy of her own self-knowledge. She literally saw herself
for the very first time during her honeymoon in France when
'walking to the stairs in my new hat as big as an Easter cake, and
feeling the swish of my new silk petticoats and the squeeze of my new
French stays'.

> I seemed to be looking into the next salon, and I thought: Look at
> that fat common trollop of a girl with a snub nose and the shiny
> cheeks, jumping out of her skin to be in a Paris hat . . . What
> a shame to expose herself like that–and her nation–to these
> foreigners.
> But in the same flash I saw that it was me. It stopped me dead
> with a blow. I knew I was not a beauty, but still that hour I had
> not seen myself with the world's eyes (p. 10).

Sara was 'humble enough' to think that she did not deserve Matt.
But the fact that this well-to-do-man—'a gentleman and rich'—
took to her and proposed marriage to her—'an ordinary country
girl neither plain nor pretty'—encouraged her to think herself
better than she was. As she writes her story at the end, however, she
comes to see how wrong she was in these assumptions. For Matt is,
in fact, a very reserved and weak man, and Sara's mistaken notions
of masculine aggressiveness only lead, as she admits, to 'great harm'.
Even so, Sara never gets to hate or pity herself. Because she has her
own kind of pride in her own being, she learns to live with her
common look and her Paris hat. 'I kept the hat, and if people looked

at me I thought: If I am a body then it can't be helped, for I can't help myself' (p. 10).

During her trial, she is finally faced with her past life, in a wealth of detail and circumstance which surprises her enough to evoke the laughter that offended her trial judge. 'At first I could not believe I was anything like the woman they made me out to be' (p. 9). What Sara lacked was knowledge of herself as the world saw her. ' "Know thyself," the chaplain says, and it is true that I never knew myself till now. Yet I thought I knew myself very well' (pp. 9–10). The process of Sara's futile attempt to 'know' her public self continues throughout her novel. She returns to it at the end of the novel, dedicating herself to the task of learning from the 'errors' of her past life, 'now that I know [my flesh] better' (p. 220). Sara's search for self-knowledge thus begins and ends the novel, and serves as a framework though an ironic one, for the themes of the novel, and those that link it with *To Be A Pilgrim* and *The Horse's Mouth*.

As her story shows, though she does not intend it to, Sara is a symbol of eternal womanhood at the service of all life. Cary himself says that he 'designed Sara as an inveterate nest-builder and I don't think you could imagine anyone further than that from Defoe's old bawd'.[18] Indeed it might be said that by linking the theme of *Herself Surprised* intimately with the central theme of the trilogy, and by exploiting the novel's adventurousness for larger and unexpected meanings, Cary is in effect modifying both the eighteenth-century female archetype and the picaresque form which also fascinated that century. Within the chronology of Sara's narrative, Cary places a logic of associations determined by two thematic principles: the fact of Sara's delight in and service of life, and the need to correct the error in the judge's (and the public's) evaluation of Sara's life. This combination of a strong narrative line and a logic of themes leads to a novel of argument, a philosophical novel. Sara's novel is thus both a rationalisation of her conduct and an indictment of herself. She is not sufficiently intellectually aware of the meaning of her life to be able to construct an adequate spiritual autobiography. At the same time, she knows enough of herself and of human nature to suspect that a confession, if not circumspect, only serves to overwhelm the conscience either with its pride or its humility. There are, she says, 'as many traps in humility as pride, and . . . the Devil's best hook was baited with confession. For I had found out even as a child that a quick confession could save me a slapping and a bad conscience too, and so, back to the jam' (p.194).

Sara does not question society's moral order in any fundamental way, but, accepting it, rather wonders at her own flagrant and constant disregard of it. We must not, therefore, read this as an inadvertent consequence of what has been called Cary's own moral largesse. Sara's 'sexual generosity', Bloom states, 'is as casuistic as it is bountiful, yet it has a distressingly plausible unavoidability about it as well'.[19] That plausibility is, in fact, its truth. In *Art and Reality*, Cary held that the 'most important part of man's existence, that part where he most truly lives and is aware of living, lies entirely within the domain of personal feeling. Reason is used only to satisfy feeling, to build up a world in which feelings can be gratified, ambitions realized'. Men, 'live so entirely by feeling that reason has extremely small power over even our most intelligent, our geniuses like Marx and Tolstoy'.[20] Cary's Sara combines both the surprise implied in the empiricist dichotomy between intellect and will, and Cary's belief in what he calls 'what men live by'—the rules of life by which they conduct their lives.[21]

It is not implied in these remarks that the problem of the moral conscience is eliminated by Cary's philosophical assumptions: Hume himself could not eliminate it. Cary recognised that the divided personality, faced with a trying moral problem, does struggle even if only to bypass the moral order. *Herself Surprised* is important in this regard for the light it throws on how Cary deals with this situation of moral crisis for a frankly uncomprehending character such as Sara. It provides a means of understanding the conduct of characters such as Sara, during those moments when they have to make their feelings conform to the decisions of their moral intelligence. For Sara is not a consciousness in a state of flux. From the very first chapter, from the very inflections of her language, from the humour of her story, we 'sense' the kind of woman she is; and in the rest of the novel's action, we only seek for consistency and plausibility in that character whatever the variety of challenges to which it may be exposed. Instead of beginning with a character in the process of thought and following that thought in order to reveal the personality behind it, Cary finds a character after the event, and makes the character piece together for the benefit of a sceptical, hostile or sympathetic world, the forces responsible for actions originally performed in the fullness of feeling and the immediacy and the routine of everyday life. And since all explanations of past action involve rationalisation, motives that once seemed unquestionable because urged on us by the force of present exigency, lose their cogency, and can then only be defended by an insistent act of faith in them. Thus whereas, in some other novelist, the process is one of continuous *discovery*, in Cary's *Herself Surprised* the effort is at *recovery*. Where other novelists follow their characters in the private acts of thought which precede external action, Cary catches his characters after the act, and probes them to find the rationale which led to their choice.

Because Sara does not appreciate the premium at which her pilgrim ideal is held by Wilcher and by the trilogy in general, she does not offer us the intellectual vindication which *To Be A Pilgrim* provides; nor does she see the limitations of her life as they become evident to us in *The Horse's Mouth*. Accordingly, whereas Wilcher is apologetic about and subdued by his life, and Jimson is defiant and exultant in his, Sara is merely 'surprised' at herself in hers. Some critics complain that 'as readers, we are usually at a loss to decide when (Sara) is a genuine mystery to herself, impelled by deep, unsearchable springs of female energy and instinct, and when she is simply exploiting this mystery so as to excuse some rather question-able behaviour. The comedy of [*Herself Surprised*] resides largely, in this second possibility.'[22] What they are asking for is that Cary should make Sara either a tormented and harrassed heroine, or a self-indulging and immoral serving-woman. In the one case, she would be 'impelled by deep unsearchable springs of female energy'; in the other, she would be the cunning creature exploiting her own inability to understand herself for her own gratification.

Cary's very title for the novel would suggest that such moral tension as Bloom and also Karl[23] demand is inappropriate to the theme of the novel, and would indeed be antithetical to it. This is simply because Sara is a woman truly and honestly surprised at herself and surprising herself. Her surprise is in her capacity for life, and her continuous disregard of law and discretion. For a novelist like Cary to whom the hero's consciousness of himself is the principal determinant of moral action, this self-surprise is a sufficient subject because it converts the mystery of the moral conscience (which, for example, fascinated Conrad and Melville) into the ironically unconscious existentialism of Sara's story. In *Herself Surprised*, we do not have prolonged moral tension because the medium—that is, Sara's narrative voice—does not require it. Sara's dilemma is much more apparent to the reader than to herself; it is her life as immediate and uninterpreted experience that it offers us, with all the telling ironies which such an attempt involves. The distinctive feature of Cary's method is that it deliberately precludes the necessity for the expiation of guilt. It is as if Cary used the psychological realism of the Jamesian novel to bypass the intense and perplexed ritualism associated with the Conradian or the Melvillian moral crisis. *Herself Surprised* records the fluctuations of Sara's consciousness as a woman who is intellectually incapable of making a deep and systematic examination of it. Her novel retains the integrity of that limited insight, and, through the evident irony of her own unconsciousness, points to the larger moral significance of her actions.

In *Herself Surprised*, Cary's interest in Sara's moral conscience is subordinate to his interest in the integrity of Sara's total personality, and in the relevance of this integrity for the rest of the trilogy. For what is at stake in *Herself Surprised* is not morality but life. It is not with the legitimacy of a moral code, nor with the possible injustices of that code that the novel is concerned. Sara does not demand a reformed moral code; nor does Cary. What the novel does with morality is to show the 'moral' and 'immoral' propensities of human nature, and the profound and trivial reasons which shape these propensities. Sara knows that she is acting in contradiction to the moral code of her society. But she is also very much aware of the myriad reasons that induce her to break this code. She sees these deviations as 'errors', and accepts them as a consequence of her lack of self-knowledge, as her own failings. In consequence Cary's 'justification' of Sara is not achieved at the expense of morality, but over and above it because her 'service to life' required neither moral anarchism nor expiation.

Sara's devotion, then, is not only to Wilcher but to all life. For example, she appreciates the qualities which made Rozzie such a unique person. Born poor, without education or good looks, Rozzie 'had no luck and no prospects'. Yet she held to her own. 'She had such spirits and she never let anything put her down' (p. 17). Rozzie was usually on the loud side; at one time 'all in crimson and mauve'. She knew it was 'awful', but she was happy that, 'at least', it made 'a splash' (p. 83). Rozzie 'would say anything for a joke and she was free and bold' (p. 84). Even on her death, she kept up her pride: 'If I can't die happy, I won't go out howling' (p. 204). Though not as robust as Rozzie, Sara appreciated Rozzie's dedication to living: 'I don't know how it was, but to do anything with Rozzie, even to buy a packet of pins, was a living pleasure. She made the sun warmer and colours brighter and your food taste better; she made you enjoy being alive . . . If my poor Nina made me remember God and brought up my soul when it had fallen flat, Rozzie was the one to make me thank him for being alive' (p. 85).

Sara also instinctively recognises the quality of Robert's character and the truth that he will be the hope of Tolbrook. 'I really loved Bobby at eighteen,' she confesses (p. 218), attributing his occasional rudeness to an understandable youthful zest for life. 'Why should he know the pains [of old age], not only the rheumatism and the not sleeping, but the great heavy cares and the wondering' about past errors and future responsibilities (p. 177). His roughness was only the exuberance of the 'good young soul that had nothing to spend it on and did not know how to come close to those he loved except by running into them or slapping them, by hand or word, as little children do' (p. 154). He was, as Wilcher puts it, 'a true son of Lucy'.

Sara also exults in Jimson's zest for life. She is attracted to him because he 'never pestered or groaned or pitied himself' (p. 206). In spite of his age, he remained 'as spry as a boy'. He 'never seemed to flag, you could have taken him for a young boy in his first hot youth, and the fiercer he was, the gayer and the more full of ideas' (p. 98). As usual, her delight in people leads her to a determination to serve them even at her own cost. 'For cruel as [Jimson] was, he had yet a hold on me. I don't know how it is but when you've lived with a man, and cooked and cleaned for him and nursed him and been through troubles with him, he gets into your blood, whoever he is, and you can't get him out' (p. 166). In the end she is not sure whether it is because of his 'liveliness' or only because of 'the memory of old days' that she even takes her mending to the same room where he worked (p. 215). After being dismissed from Tolbrook, she goes occasionally to help Jimson and his new wife, Lizzie. 'Poor things, they could do nothing without me and they kept all the washing and mending till I came' (p. 215). It is significant that, at the very end, she still planned to pay the school bills for Jimson's son from the royalties she will receive for her 'confession', that is, form *Herself Surprised*.

Clarissa's efforts to persuade Sara to marry Wilcher derive from her recognition of these qualities. As she insists throughout the novel, the 'only way to save' Wilcher is for Sara to marry him (p. 195). This is a view which is shared by *To Be A Pilgrim*. When, in that novel, Wilcher gets Sara's letter asking him to come down to Lewisham, he calls the moment 'a resurrection'.[24] Sara's letter is a rebirth for Wilcher; it brings home to him the time of childhood when he shared the same ideals about the purpose of life with Lucy and Edward. Sara brings back that life and makes Wilcher feel again the saving grace of its ideal. Sara is able to accomplish this because, as Jimson once put it, Sara is 'a born servant in [her] soul' (p. 149). The compliment pleased Sara so much that it gave her heart a 'turn over, and I felt the true joy of my life as clear and strong as if the big round clock over the chimney were ticking inside me' (p. 149). 'Never once,' Wilcher remembered in *To Be A Pilgrim*, had Sara 'seemed to reflect on the hardness of her life [at Tolbrook] . . . She was ready to move on, at any moment, to some other billet, and to begin life again under what conditions she might find there, whatever mistress or master.'[25]

This is Wilcher's pilgrim ideal made incarnate and intuitive. This it is that makes her the Mediatrix of *To Be A Pilgrim*. In *Herself Surprised*, Sara stands on her own ground. 'If there's one thing sure in this uncertain life, it is that no one can afford to please himself. I know it may seem to pay in the beginning, but where are you in the end?—without a friend or a crust. Especially for anyone in the arts. Because an artist lives only by giving pleasure' (p. 90). Sara is that kind of artist, too, without realising it. Like Jimson, the artist to whom she is preaching, she can never learn her own lesson. Cary calls Sara 'a female artist' who composes the same work in the same style, 'but it is a style which does not go out of fashion'.[26] Like Mother Nature, Sara cannot help plying her trade, to her own loss. 'You are done for', Rozzie once told her, 'if you couldn't do without a man to fuss over.' (p. 90).

But like her namesake of the Bible, Sara had a duty to life, to bake bread for Abram's guests and be submissive to her husband, and even give herself to other men in order to serve life.[27] In Egypt (*Genesis* XII), and again in Gerar (*Genesis* XX), the Biblical Sara let herself be taken to the Pharaoh and to King Abimelech in the guise of Abram's sister, in obedience to her husband:

> When he [Abram] was about to enter Egypt he said to Sara, his wife, 'I know that you are a woman beautiful to behold;
> And when the Egyptians see you, they will say "This is his wife"; then they will kill me, but they will let you live.
> Say you are my sister, that it may go well with me because of you, and that my life may be spared on your account.'
> When Abram entered Egypt, the Egyptians saw that the woman

was very beautiful.
And when the princes of Pharaoh saw her, they praise her to
Pharaoh. And the woman was taken into Pharaoh's house.
And for her sake he dealt well with Abram.[28]

But Sarah was barren. When God promised her a child at her ripe
age of ninety-one, 'she laughed within herself, saying "After I am
waxed old, and my husband is old, shall I have pleasure" '.[29] She
was too aware of herself and of her human condition not to
appreciate the comedy of her good fortune. Her laughter, like Sara's
in *Herself Surprised*, was a healthy one.

Cary could have presented Sara's importance in insistent
symbolic terms. The parallels with the biblical Sarah could have
been exploited more explicitly; the pastoral element could have
been underlined; the theme of the eternal female could have
received greater endorsement from the author himself. The redeem-
ing role Sara plays to Matt, Wilcher and Jimson could have been
made more dramatic by the elimination of Sara's own pervading
unconsciousness. In *The Horse's Mouth*, Jimson identifies Sara with
Eve and with Blake's *femme fatale*. This identification is already
implicit in *Herself Surprised*, but Sara is incapable of seeing its
relevance. 'So I thought that when Gulley talked of going back to
Adam and Eve, he meant only to get me naked before him, making
his wish a religion' (p. 98).

Sara's importance is not given overt symbolic emphasis. This is
not because Cary is unaware of the possible advantages of such an
emphasis, nor because of his rejection allegory as such, but because
he always preferred to contain the symbolic meaning within the
limits of realistic fiction; because he always wanted a true life which
would appeal not merely to the intellect but also the feelings, or to
that combination of both which, in *Art and Reality*, he calls
'conceptual feeling'. The consequence of this appeal to a combination of intellect and feeling is that the reader is required to, and
can, deduce the intellectual implications of a fully realised life
without losing the immediacy of an intense emotional life. Hence, in
Herself Surprised, we have the materials for an intellectual and
symbolic construction as well as the everyday life from which these
materials have been derived. Sara's life is thus both commonplace
and symbolic. Her career is that of a farmer's daughter drifting from
a fortunate marriage to a series of affairs, marriages and thefts which
in turn lead to her imprisonment. Her career is at the same time that

of the 'servant of life', the saviour of men, a career more important in its implications than in itself. Sara's toils, like the toils of the great artist, and like those of the sea with which she is also in love, may seem futile, but they are toils in the service of life.

> The waves seemed to come up suddenly all glittering with hundreds and thousands, like cakes for Easter and birthdays, and try to go on forever, and only get so far and break themselves to pieces with a mournful noise, and fall back with a long sigh. It made me feel sad to see such waste of their work and to think of it going on forever, but then it was a comfort, too, to think that they would always be there, whether anyone was looking or not; such is the bounty of Providence, to pour out pleasures (p. 99).

This is Sara's kind of eternity, and the basis for Jimson's (and Cary's) plea in *The Horse's Mouth*: 'Don't you mind, Sara. Go on being Sara'.[30]

THE HORSE'S MOUTH

In the Preface to *The First Trilogy*, Joyce Cary says of the three narrators of the three novels that they 'have a book each for their stories. The trilogy was meant to be a line abreast rather than a line ahead'.[31] According to this scheme, *To Be A Pilgrim* is the intellectual centre of the trilogy. In it Cary asserts that only by cultivating the virtues of the humble and free soul can man escape the 'corruption of sense and the shims of fashion'. Through the hero, Cary is able to give pointed formulation to the intellectual premise of the whole trilogy. By this arrangement, *Herself Surprised* also serves as the trilogy's emotional centre, as the semiliterate, unaffected, sincere and female expression of the cogency and power of Wilcher's pilgrim ideal. In it, Cary uses the deliberate irony of Sara's unwitting service to life and art to affirm a valuable, even if precarious, freedom.

    The Horse's Mouth, in its turn, serves as the trilogy's existential core. Just as *To Be A Pilgrim* and *Herself Surprised* examine the themes of the pilgrim ideal and the eternity of motherhood through the simple accounts of the lives of Tom Wilcher and Sara Monday, so does *The Horse's Mouth* press both ideals to their absolute logical and philosophical limits through the deliberately facetious account of the life of the representative man-artist, Gulley Jimson. The novel tries to make a definitive statement about the virtues and the dangers attendant on both ideals. Scorning both Wilcher's effort at apologetic formulation, and Sara's at demonstration, the hero of *The Horse's Mouth* celebrates his own integrity and freedom in a world which he sees as necessarily and whimsically unjust. In so doing the novel vindicates the ideal of the redeemed and assertive self implied in Sara's life and urged in Wilcher's novel.

That Cary aimed at a definitive philosophical statement in the novel we can infer from his comments on the title of the German version of the novel—*Des Pudels Kern*; if understood as alluding to the 'Poodle's Heart, or Essence' from Goethe's *Faust*, it would mean, Cary says, 'the inner reality, the final truth' which he aimed at in the novel. This title, Cary says, 'satisfied the demands of philosophic dignity in a country [Germany] where philosophers are honoured. It also came close to my essential meaning'. The title conferred on the novel the 'status belonging to the classical reference without loss of conceptual meaning', even though, in consequence, it had to shed the 'vulgarity, the flash slang of the British, rich in savor of the race course tout and the cant of the shilling tipster.[32] Cary was all the more delighted with the German rendering since he had staked so much on the title: 'The Horse's Mouth' was to be 'part of the character of the book. It was to appear on every page and I was aiming at a high concentration'.[33]

In the novel itself, Cary puts a number of propositions to the test in an attempt to establish the dimensions of their truth. What does it mean, he asks, to be 'free' in the real world? What does it involve to be the 'pilgrim' soul? What are the consequences, in fact, of Sara's instinctive dedication to life, or of the conscious emulation of the dedication? Is there virtue in Rozzie's boundless and uncritical joy in life and her defiance of death, in Plantie's Christian optimism, in Coker's corroding stoicism? What is the relevance of Blake's cult of the creative man to the dilemmas of a vulnerable human being in the real world of real hardship? How can a Blakean Jimson both remain alive through labour for subsistence and be the free artist engaged in the labour of love and creation? How can he both have Sara's inspiration and escape Sara's domination? Or is he doomed both to immortalise her as the eternal female and destroy her as an ordinary woman because he cannot forget her as symbol and will not surrender to her womanhood?

If Blake, Sara and Wilcher do not have all the answers, will

Spinoza's injunction that we merely 'contemplate the glory of creation' save the free man? For Spinoza is the novel's alternative to Blake. To accept Spinoza would be to assume, too, that God (or Providence) is really irrelevant; that not only is man incapable of helping himself, he has no reason to expect God to help *him*. He who 'loves God' according to Spinoza, 'cannot endeavour to bring it about that God should love him in return'. For a man to desire that God should love him in return would be to desire that 'the God whom he loves should not be God'.[34] Would not the ethics of Spinoza then be just a way to evade the responsibility of the individual to provide for his own salvation: 'I know', Spinoza declared, '(and this knowledge gives me the greatest contentment and peace of mind) that all things come to pass by the power and unchangeable decree of a Being supremely perfect'.[35] If therefore one understood the 'true' causes of pain, pain would cease 'to be a passion' or 'the cause of pain'. Therefore in so far as we understand God to be the cause of pain, we rejoice'.[36]

The very first chapter of *The Horse's Mouth* explores these questions, and hints at the kind of answer which the novel finally reaches. The scene in this opening chapter shows Gulley Jimson as the 'free' man: an artist just out of prison. About him is a dismal Thames scene:

> Sun in a mist. Like an orange in a fried fish shop. All bright below. Low tide, dusty water and a crooked bar of straw, chicken boxes, dirt and oil from mud to mud. Like a viper swimming in skim milk. The old serpent, symbol of nature and love.[37]

The artist Jimson is able to make a mental picture of this uninspiring and dismal scene. His creative faculty as an artist, operating independently of his emotional state, fashions an aesthetically beautiful representation of the ugly. The question, however, is whether the artist's creation is a tribute to the Blakean world of concrete evil, of fearful symmetry, or to the Spinozan world of merely seeming ugliness.

Jimson suggests that neither the Blakean nor the Spinozan explanation can be fully right in his case. Blake suggests (in a passage which Jimson quotes) that man's five senses offer him his escape from the confinement of the flesh. Through the eyes, Blake says, 'one can look and see small portions of the eternal world'. Jimson cannot believe this literally. For one instance of this 'eternal world' is the ugly Thames before him. To see at all is to see ugliness, not eternity. Blake's creative man would thus only seem to be adorning the ugliness of the world with the beauty of his own purity. His imagination is not a magician's nor is his touch that of Midas. Artistic creativeness cannot turn the 'Thames mud' into a 'bank of nine carat gold rough from the fire' (p. 1). In his personal dilemma as a man just out of prison, Jimson the artist can turn the Thames into nine-carat gold in his imagination, but that would not save him from the fact of a dirty Thames, 'the old serpent', necessity.

Nor can it save him from his physical difficulties as a man. 'I must have been hopping up and down Greenbank Hard for half an hour grinning like a gargoyle, until the wind began to get up my trousers and down my back, and to bring me to myself as they say. Meaning my liver and lights (p. 1). Art can indeed create; it can also sublimate. If it saves, however, it does so only metaphorically. 'They say a chap just out of prison runs into the nearest cover; into some darker cover; into some dark little room, like a rabbit put up by a stoat. The sky feels too big for him' (p. 1). In other words, Necessity forces a man into the caverns of darkness from which the creative imagination, apparently, would like to save him. Blake could indeed be relied upon to save completely if only he could also save materially.

This realisation leads Jimson into the consideration of a pseudo-Spinozan view of evil. Even if evil is real, as the imagination is real, is there not a sense in which evil can be transcended, or at least obliterated, through a gesture of the mind, and thereby made virtually 'unreal'? Jimson seems attracted to some such thought. For his reaction to the oppressive force of necessity—to the sky that is 'too big for him'—is to regard its evil as unreal, and then to love it. 'I liked it. I swam in it. I couldn't take my eyes off the clouds, the water, the mud' (p. 1). In other words, Jimson chooses for the brief moment to view evil, as Spinoza would have mankind do, as part of the scheme of larger things, *sub specie aeternitatis*. Jimson can do this because the Thames, which is the occasion for his thoughts, is not only the symbol of necessity—'the old serpent'—but also that of love both divine and human. Through the contemplation of this transcendent possibility of ultimate goodness derived from immediate evil, Jimson is saved from the oppression of the ugly and the disheartening. He can accept the death of Providence by deliberately obliterating the fact of ugliness from his mind. Good can come out of evil. To be 'brought to oneself' is to know and feel the tragedy of man, to discover 'the solid hard world, good and evil. Hard as rocks and sharp as poisoned thorns'—and to know the opportunities of that condition, 'the way to make gardens' (p. 177).

These two ways of looking at the ugly world — as a subject for transcendent creativeness or as an object for transcendent contemplation—are really two alternative means to the inner freedom of man. The free man may either transcend the fact of evil by seeking to create a world of beauty out of the facts of evil or, by postulating an indifferent and unsympathetic Providence, he can take heart at the beauty and the magnificence of the universe of which he is only a puny part. Spinoza, who favoured the second alternative, hoped that his metaphysics would bring about this 'inner freedom'. 'Nature', he says, '*does not work with an end in view*', and God, who is also Nature, 'does not exist for the sake of an end', nor acts 'for the sake of an end'.[38] The inner freedom of man thus resides in the contemplation of life and in the acquiescence to the necessary fact that what is is and has to be. Being conscious of himself, of God and of things, the free man 'by a certain eternal necessity never ceases [to be free], but always possesses true acquiescence of his spirit'.[39]

Jimson's experience and his commitment to Blake, however, cannot let him acquiesce in the fact of evil. 'Anarchists who love God', Jimson complains in *The Horse's Mouth*, 'fall for Spinoza because he tells them that God doesn't love them. That is just what they need. A poke in the eye. To a real anarchist, a poke in the eye is better than a bunch of flowers. It makes him see stars' (p. 84). Jimson cannot want Spinoza. 'I haven't got any self-respect, and besides, I'm an optimist. I get a lot of fun out of fun, as well as the miseries' (p. 84). Plantie did not have such freedom. 'When you tell a man like Plantie that he isn't free except to take it as it comes, he feels free. He says, "All right, let'em all come"' (p. 84). Plantie's problems, as Jimson sees it, is his acceptance of Spinoza's equation of 'freedom' with 'contemplation' or what Spinoza called 'the intellectual love of God (Nature)'. Contemplation, Jimson argues, does not get into the heart of freedom or into the heart of reality— 'Contemplation, in fact, is ON THE OUTSIDE'.

It's not on the spot. And the truth is that Spinoza was always on the outside. He didn't understand freedom, and so he didn't understand anything. Because after all, I said to myself, with some excitement, for I saw where all this was leading to,

Freedom, to be plain, is nothing but THE INSIDE OF THE
OUTSIDE. And even a philosopher like Ben [Spinoza] can't
judge the XXX by eating pint pots. It's the wrong approach
(p. 102).[40]

Hence for Jimson to accept Spinoza would mean to despair of
himself, to negate the activity of his creativeness, to fail to find the
inside of the outside, *le tuyan increvable*,[41] the 'final truth'.

According to Jimson, Spinoza believed that 'being alive was
enough—to contemplate God's magnificence and eternity. That
was happiness. That was joy' (p. 101). Jimson disagrees. What he
wants is not contemplation, but truth. 'Hold on to that, old boy, I
said, for it's the facts of life. It's the ginger in the gingerbread. It's the
apple in the dumpling. It's the jump in the OLD MUSQUITO. It's
the kick in the old horse. It's the creation' (p. 102). By facing the
reality of life and the 'power' of creation and the created, Jimson
hoped to be able to do two things: record the fact of evil in the world
and at the same time escape the limitations of man's tragedy.

A tear is an intellectual thing. And a joy. It's wisdom in vision.
It's the prophetic eye in the loins. The passion of intelligence. Yes,
by Gee and Jay, I thought. The everlasting creation of delight.
The joy that is always new and fresh because it is created. The
revelation ever renewed, in every fall (p. 103).

Jimson thus chooses the joy of creation—also the joy of a tear—in
place of the intellectual joy of contemplation because it allows for a
critical, as opposed to an indifferent, coexistence of evil and
creativeness. 'What you get on the inside, I said to myself, is the
works,—it's SOMETHING THAT GOES ON GOING
ON . . . It's a Fall. Into the pit. The ground gives way, and down
you go head over heels. Unless, of course, you know how to fly. To
rise again on your wings'(pp. 102-3).

The Thames scene at the opening of the novel actually points to
the validity of this preference. The Thames is dirty, in a real sense:
'dusty water and a crooked bar of straw, chicken boxes, dirt and oil
from mud to mud. Like a viper swimming in skim milk'. It is also
'dirty', in the aesthetic sense, for it is denied the saving grace of the
sun which is 'in a mist'. 'Like an orange in a fried fish shop. All
bright below'. The point seems to be that only with the liberation of
this sun can the Thames ever hope to be 'freed' from the sordid

reality of its actual dirt. The Thames could become a 'bank of nine carat gold rough from the fire' if the sun would only shine on it.

Cary points to the process of this transformation of the Thames through the power of a creative sun. When the sun 'crackled into flames at the top', 'you could see crooked lines of gray, like old cracks under spring ice'. Then, the Thames changed.

> Snake broken up. Emeralds and sapphires. Water like varnish with bits of gold leaf floating thick and heavy. Gold is the metal of intellect. And all at once the sun burned through in a new place, at the side, and shot out a ray that hit the Eagle and Child (p. 2).

A bit later the creative power of the sun affirms itself even more insistently. The sun, 'all in a blaze' is beside itself with its own creativeness—'Lost its shape'. And the Thames is full of bubbles, 'every bubble flashing its own electric torch. Mist breaking into round fat shapes, china white on Dresden blue. Dutch angles by Rubens della Robbia. Big one or top curled up with her knees to her nose like the little marble woman Dobson did for Courtauld. A beauty. Made me jump to think of it' (p. 4). As if to emphasise the gap between the transforming power of the sun and that of genius, Cary follows the sun to its moment of almost divine splendour. The sun reaches the peak of its own creativeness at a level impossible to the abilities of man.

> Sun coming up along a cloud bank like clinkers. All sparks. Couldn't do it in paint. Limits of the arts. Limits of everything. Limits of my fingers which are all swole up at the joints. No fingers, no swell, no swell, no art. Old Renoir painting his red girls with his brushes strapped to his wrists (p. 19).

We can reasonably interpret this progress of the sun as representing the limits and possibilities of creative man in the real world. The actual scene remains the same. The old serpent, the old viper, remains. But it is no longer swimming in skim milk. It is revelling in splendour. The lesson seems clear: only creative power, can free man from the reality of evil. To be free is to have power. And the glory of God is the power of his creation, the 'jump in the OLD MUSQUITO'.

> The pride of the peacock is the glory of God

The lust of the goat is the bounty of God
The wrath of the lion is the wisdom of God
The nakedness of women is the work of God (p. 19).[42]

Hence, creativeness is all. Pride, lust, wrath and nakedness—are all in their different ways an expression of the Godhead and an acknowledgement of eternal limitless beauty. Hence, too, aided by the creative power of man, even the 'nakedness of these trees, pavements, houses, old Postie's red nose and white moustache' can be made into the glory, the bounty, the wisdom and the work of God. It is the sun of Blakean creativeness, not the cold stare of Spinozan contemplation, that 'brightens the world' (p. 4). Jimson can thus reflect in triumph at the transcendence of his own art.

> Tiger, tiger, burning bright. A ravening brute with a breath like a rotten corpse and septic claws. This beauty grows with cruelty . . .
> I could see old Spinoza with round spectacles and a white apron polishing a lens and looking at my tigers. On a ground of tall brown tree trunks as close together as a chestnut fence—a few tufts of green at the top. No sky. No blue, no vision. Orchids sticking out of the ground with thick stamens like lingams modeled in raw meat. Beauty, majesty, glory (p. 157).

The argument of *The Horse's Mouth* is an amplification of this reflection on the nature and the triumph of Jimson's art. The existential question which the novel proposes is based on a view of the character of the artist and his creation as asserted by Jimson. The freedom of man which the novel preaches is a larger version of the freedom of the artist implicit in Jimson's sense of his own godlike power. 'I am an artist. A son of Los (p. 97).'I am God' (p. 174). The tragedy of the human condition established in *The Horse's Mouth* is founded on the analogy of Jimson's (and Blake's) beautiful but tragic art, symbolised in the tiger and the whale. In Blake's words: 'Some sons of Los surround the passions with porches of iron and silver. Creating form and beauty around dark regions of sorrow (p. 143).

In Jimson's words: 'Tiger, tiger, burning bright. A ravening brute with a breath like a rotten corpse and septic claws. This beauty grows with cruelty'. So also does the beauty of his whale:

. . . as soon as those eyes took shape and I put in the pupils, they got me. They were so something, I don't know what. There they were, gazing at me like all the grief and glory in the world, about a yard long and a foot high; and they brought the tears to my eyes (p. 301).

These aspects of Cary's theme are comprehended in the crucial figure of 'The Fall'. In that figure, Cary holds in balance the personal, aesthetic, narrative and metaphysical elements of his subject. In one sense, for example, Jimson's calling to the profession of art is a Fall. It is fall from the innocence and the relative security of the non-creative life into the precarious life of the artist. 'If you find life a bit dull at home and want to amuse yourself', Jimson advises Nosy, the young boy who wants to be an artist, 'put a stick of dynamite in the kitchen fire, or shoot a policeman. Volunteer for a test pilot, or dive off Tower Bridge with five bobs' worth of candles in each pocket. You'd get twice as much fun [as an artist] at about one-tenth of the risk' (pp. 15–16). To Professor Alabaster, the art critic, he says the same thing: 'If [the artist] ends up in the Academy, then he ought to thank God that he escaped worse' (p. 142).

Jimson dates the moment of his fall from the day he tried to push an ink blot into the shape of a face. 'And from that moment I was done for' (p. 55). His employer also knew it: 'Tell me what's gone wrong. Never mind what it is. I'm not going to be stupid about. Is it debts? You haven't been gambling, I suppose? Is your petty cash all right? Take a couple of days off and think it over' (p. 56). Having once fallen into knowledge, Jimson can never return to in-experience. Nor can he rest content with the achievements of any period of his career as artist. He could 'turn you off a picture, all correct, in an afternoon', but it would be 'just a piece of stuff', 'lovely forms', not what 'you call a work of imagination' (p. 56). Every achievement leads him to a further fall into disaffection: 'By Gee and Jay, I said, I was dead, and I didn't know' (p. 57). This 'death' forces him to further creativeness. He recalls Blake's figure of 'a little female babe' springing from the 'fire on the hearth' and is inspired—'I felt her jump'. Creation comes again, though in the guise of destruction. 'I botched my nice architectural water colors with impressionist smudges. And I made a mess of my impressionist landscapes that I could not bear to look at them myself' (p. 57). This disaffection prepares him to appreciate Blake: 'I took Blake's Job drawings out of somebody's bookshelf and peeped into them and shut them up again. Like a chap who's fallen down in the cellar steps and knocked his skull in and opens a window too quick, on something too big' (p. 58).

But even discovering Blake (and Persian carpets) cannot save him from the consequence of his fall which is the obligation to create his own forms. Blake and the Persians were only an example. His imitations of them 'didn't belong to the world [he] lived in. A new world with a new formal character'. This brings him to his maturity as a creator of art. He comes to realise that 'the job is always to get hold of the form you need. And nothing is so coy' (p. 59). The task is that of perpetual experiment: 'Well, I suppose Cézanne did more wandering in the desert even than me—he wandered all his life'.

> The trees bring forth sweet ecstacy
> To all who in the desert roam
> Till many a city there is built
> And many a pleasant shepherd home (p. 60).

Hence the fall of man into the role of the artist can be likened to man's fall out of Eden into the role of the wanderer. Such was the consequence of Cézanne's fall. And like Cézanne, Jimson wanders on: 'I've lost sight of the maiden [of inspiration] altogether. I wander weeping far away, until some other take me in' (p. 60). This is the process of continuous creation which, we saw, Jimson described as 'SOMETHING THAT GOES ON GOING ON'.'It's not pleasure, or peace, or contemplation, or comfort, or happiness—it's a Fall' (p. 102).

The other fall in *The Horse's Mouth* is the major painting of Jimson's career, 'The Fall'. At the beginning of the novel, we are told only of sketches and scenes on this subject. Jimson returns from prison to find that 'The Living God', a part of the Fall sequence, was missing, 'with his stretchers and stiffeners'. But ideas on the Fall were taking shape in other ways. Jimson sees that the serpent 'wants to be a bit thicker'. Its tail could also conveniently be made to make 'a nice curl over the tree'. Adam is 'a bit too blue, and Eve could be redder—to bring up the blues'. Adam's 'right leg is a gift. Nobody has done that before with a leg' (p. 5). These details excite Jimson's imagination, though he does not yet have a sufficient clue to their final culmination in the picture of the Fall. 'Yes, yes, I thought, getting a bit excited, as I always do when I come back to work after a holiday, I have got something here' (p. 5). Later in the novel, we find this idea of the Fall still haunting him. Using coffee stains, he makes a shape of a man 'kneeling down like Adam'. And also Eve. 'Yes, bring his arm right out and have Eve pushing it away. Yes, have her doing the modest. Fending off the first pass. And that nice line will lie right up against the serpent—the serpent will have to come a little behind Adam and avoid two cylinders meeting in a vertical' (p. 20).

Plantie appreciated Jimson's choice of subject calling the picture 'a fine picture'. 'Great subject, the Fall' (p. 65). But Jimson himself is disturbed by it, because it possessed him completely: 'That picture was a curse to me. It left me no freedom to paint' (p. 176). Jimson's involvement in the subject of the Fall is real. He had done a more modest painting of the same subject on canvas. But during his term in prison, Mrs Coker had used it to mend a leaking roof. 'I felt,' Jimson says, 'as if the top of my skull was floating off, I was quite feeble. To lose the Fall like this suddenly; it was like being told your home and family had fallen down a hole in the ground' (p. 171). Now again, in the intoxication of his ideas of the new Fall, he is totally possessed. That intoxication leads him to define precisely what he was going to say through the painting.

> 'Yes,' I said, 'the Fall into Freedom, into the real world, among the everlasting forms, the solid. Solid as the visions of the ancient man. And that's what I'm going to do in this new Fall. Adam like a rock walking, and Eve like a mountain bringing forth with sweat like fiery lava, and the trees shall stand like souls pent up in metal; cut bronze and silver and gold'.
> 'Yes,' I said, for why shouldn't I call it the Fall. 'It might as well be that as anything else. The blue tower could be Adam and the red wave Eve, and the yellow things the serpents. Yes,' I said, 'it's going to be the Fall, only much better. Much solider. I have learnt a lot since I started the Fall and I know what was wrong with it. It was not immediate enough. It didn't hit you hard enough. It wasn't solid enough' (pp. 177 and 179).

The solidity he needed was the solidity of form and the solidity of medium. He had to use the wall, because he needed a wall. 'Walls have been my salvation, Nosy . . . Walls and losing my teeth young, which prevented me from biting bus conductors and other idealists. But especially walls' (p. 310).

There is a third Fall in *The Horse's Mouth*, a literal fall which is part of the simple plot-structure of the novel. This fall is the physical equivalent to Jimson's other fall into artistic creativeness. It is, also a fall out of artistic creativeness, because it is a fated culmination to his artistic career. Jimson knew that even if the local engineer allowed him the three weeks he needed to complete the work, the wall would have to be pulled down with the painting immediately afterwards. Yet as artist he cannot see this fact as reason not to create.

Jimson faced a similar futility on earlier occasions. He found on his return from prison that 'somebody had been shooting at the birds [in his painting] with an air gun and there was a piece about a foot square cut out of Adam's middle with a blunt knife'. Some mother 'anxious about her children' had probably done that to make Adam 'respectable'. The children, for their part, had been writing names all over Eve'. They seem, Jimson reflects, 'to have appreciated my picture a whole lot' (p. 6). His painting in the village hall at Ancombe was similarly ruined—covered over 'under four coats of whitewash' (p. 141). His picture of 'Jacob and his wives stealing away with Laban's flocks' was last seen 'covering a screen in a barber's shop—they'd cut it down a bit and given it a coat of black japan, but you could still see Leah's eyes and a bit of Rachel's left leg coming through' (p. 142). So also with his 'biggest' work, 'The Holy Innocents'. That, too, was mutilated by a Government agency that didn't like babies because they hadn't trousers on. So it said the plaster was dangerous and knocked it about a bit with hammer. And most of it fell down' (p. 142).

The difference between these cases of futility and the case of his wall painting of 'The Fall' is that the wall itself is physically unsafe for Jimson's work on it. This final impediment does not deter Jimson who even sees it as a blessing in disguise: 'Most of the roof at the end had also disappeared. Which greatly improved the lights' (p. 307). Jimson's eventual fall from that tower of creativeness is significant in that it is both a fall from grace as well as an ascension into beatitude. His descent to earth is also an ascension into heaven.

I couldn't believe it, and no doubt I was looking a little surprised with my brush in my hand, and my mouth open, because when the dust began to clear I saw through the cloud about ten thousand angels in caps, helmets, bowlers and even one top hat, sitting on walls, dustbins, gutters, roofs, window sills and other people's cabbages laughing. That's funny, I thought, they've all seen the same joke. God bless them. It must be a work of eternity, a chestnut, a horse laugh (pp. 308–9).

Jimson falls still eulogising the beauty of his artistic intuition. Because he will never again have the opportunity, he can only thank God for past opportunities. 'In form, in surface, in elasticity, in lighting, and in that indefinable something which is, as we all know, the final beauty of a wall, the very essence of its being. . . . Yes, boys, I have to thank God for that wall' (p. 310).[43] Jimson's death is a tribute to the joy of creation, the 'revelation ever renewed, in every fall' (p. 103).

A fourth Fall is developed in *The Horse's Mouth*. It is the existential version of the mythical Edenic Fall which religion uses to explain the nature of the human predicament. Jimson's picture of biblical 'Fall' aims, in fact, at representing this existential philosophy. In Jimson's mind, the mythical Fall recalls 'fire and brimstone. Blues and reds'. These, he believes, are 'symbols of something', probably 'generation'.

> Generation would do. Or a lot of little flames like men and women rushing together, burning each other up like coals. And then to carry the pattern upwards you could have white flowers, no, very pale green, moving among the stars, imagination born of love. Through generation to generation. . . . The old Adam rising to chase the blue-faced angels of Jehovah. And beget a lot of young devils on them (p. 118).

Jimson interprets this duality—red coals of hatred and greens and blues of love—as symbols of the paradox of man's fall, his fortunate fall. He calls this coexistence 'freedom'. Man's fall is thus a fall into freedom and into wisdom: 'Into the light and the fire. Every man his own candle. He sees by his own flame, burning up his own guts. Oh to hell, I said, with the meaning. What I want is those green flames on a pink sky' (p. 119).

Jimson elaborates on the nature of this predicament of man's fall. Man's freedom, he points out, is man's doom and man's hope. This fall, in keeping with traditional biblical interpretation, is for Jimson a 'discovery of the solid world, good and evil' (p. 177). But this discovery gives man power and freedom. It makes him 'free to cut his throat, if he likes'.

. . . or understand the bloody world, if he likes, and cook his breakfast with hell-fire, if he likes, and construct for himself a little heaven, all complete with a pig-faced angel and every spiritual pleasure including the joys of love; or also, of course, he can build himself a little hell full of pig-faced devils and all the material miseries including the joys of love and enjoy it in such tortures of the damned that he will want to burn himself alive . . . He's in hell, that is, real hell – material hell, nailed to the everlasting fire with a red-hot clag; and his kicks and wriggles are enough to make a cat laugh (pp. 178–9).

Jimson finds this fall re-enacted in the daily life of man. It 'happens every day. It's the old story'. Boys and girls in love are 'driven mad and go blind and deaf and see each other not as human animals with comic noses and bandy legs and voices like frogs, but as angels so full of shining goodness that like hollow turnips with candles put into them, they seem miracles of beauty'. But almost as easily they fall into hatred and 'seem to each other like devils, full of spite and cruelty' (pp. 177–8). Their fall is this liability to goodness and to spite; their hope is that they can use their 'imagination' to avoid driving 'each other mad'. Even enough 'to laugh' (p. 178).

It is in view of this interpretation of the Fall that the theme of injustice assumes a role of almost equal importance to that of the creative imagination in *The Horse's Mouth*. For one consequence of the existentialist view of man's fall is to deny him the security of Divine protection, to substitute creativeness for Providence. As a result, man learns to face the 'injustice' and 'tragedy' of the world as a permanent element of his existence, as inseparable from his freedom and power. It is this interpretation that makes Plantie and Spinoza so relevant to Cary's argument.

Injustice ('fundamental injustice') is behind all the comedy, the cynicism and the argument of the novel. Its manifestations are several. 'I put a *Times* down each leg', Jimson reports 'and when the dog nipped me, he got such a surprise that he couldn't believe his teeth. He staggered away in silence. He must have felt like a gourmet who bites on a stick of asparagus and finds it a solid drainpipe' (p. 112). On another level of injustice is Frank's case. He was having trouble with boils. 'He had a plaster on his neck and was carrying his head all on one side . . . He's about nineteen and is just getting his first real worries. The girls he fancies don't fancy him; the ones he fancied last year and doesn't fancy any more are lying in

wait for him with kisses and hatchets' (p. 49). On yet another level i
Coker's case. As a quite unattractive girl, Coker was suffering from a
natural and inescapable handicap. Willie was kind enough to love
her for a while, but he 'was a piece of luck. Due to the carols last
Christmas—in the bad light' (p. 11). Willie has soon enough ran of
with a blonde, leaving Coker with his baby:

> Coker: 'I shouldn't mind if I'd got justice.'
> Jimson: 'You can't get justice in this world. It doesn't grow in
> these parts.'
> Coker: 'You're telling me.'
> Jimson: 'It makes you laugh. . . . The damned unfairness of
> things' (pp. 89–90).

'The damned unfairness of things' is Jimson's phrase for the
fundamental injustice of existence itself. It is this injustice that
cannot be remedied, because it is not even deserved by those who
suffer from it. Conspicious among those suffering from it are the
physically deformed: 'Look out for cripples, stammerers, lame boys
and ugly girls. The army of the frontier. Battalion of the damned
Do or die. Saints or snakes' (p. 37). Among them are the 'deaf,
blind, ugly, cross-eyed, limp-legged, bulge-headed, bald and
crooked girls in the world, sitting on little white mountains and
weeping tears like broken glass tinkling in a plate. And the ground
trembled like a sleeping dog in front of the parlor fire when the bell
tolls for a funeral' (p. 13). They are the innocent girls who are 'liable
to be strangled by young devils like Rockway. Always were and
always will be' (p. 62). Also among the victims of this injustice is
Plantie himself. An old man on crutches, he is no match for the
young derelict who forcibly deprives him of his turn with the
fryingpan. The young chap snatched the fryingpan while another
'knocked his hat over his eyes, gave [Plantie] a push that sent him
flying back into the corner and said, "Go and scrape yourself, you
bum" ' (p. 130). Plantie hit the wall 'so hard that he didn't know
where he was'. He knew the injustice of it: 'The old man was
crying . . . He's got a sense of justice. Poor old chap. And he can't
get over it—not at his age' (p. 130).

Jimson's response to this injustice is as important as his documentation of it. This response is, again, founded on an analogy with the
biblical Fall, and the text that clarifies it for him is from Blake.

The angel that presided at her birth
Said, little creature, born of joy and mirth
Go love without the help of anything on earth (p. 130).

Jimson is saying, in effect, that from birth man is alone in the world
and is obliged to construct his own happiness, his joy and mirth,
'without the help of anything on earth'. The pattern of injustice in
The Horse's Mouth supports this view of man's isolated helplessness.
The pattern of responses which Jimson records helps explain his
own calculated strategy for facing the injustice of the world without
self-corroding bitterness.[44]

Jimson is explicit on the nature of this strategy.

> . . . I musn't get up a grievance. Plays the deuce. I must keep
> calm. For the fact is, IT'S WISE TO BE WISE, especially for a
> born fool.
> Anything like bad temper is bad for me. It spoils my equanimity.
> It blocks up my imagination. It makes me stupid so that I can't
> see straight . . . Cool off, I said to myself. Don't get rattled off
> your center (p. 9).

This response is in sharp contrast to that of most of the injured in the
novel. Ranken, for example, refused to pay his debts because he
'thought the whole world couldn't pay him enough to make up for
its injustice to him' (p. 163). Coker had a more spirited sense of
vengeance. When Jimson prayed God to put forgiveness in her, she
retorts: 'He couldn't do that to me. Let him try, that's all' (p. 11).
Men, she says with bitterness, 'make my guts wind. And there isn't
room' (p. 172).

Coker is, in fact, the exact opposite to Jimson in this respect. She
had 'a lot of womanliness in her nature', Jimson observes, but 'she
didn't indulge it' (p. 257). Coker's reasoning is clear: 'I feel like I
want to do murder or something, and so would you if you'd taken a
barrel full of pink pills and pints of oil and jumped off the tables and
run around carrying trunks on your head and fallen downstairs and
all for nothing' (p. 171).

> I'm not complaining. But if I should have one accident with a bus
> or a traction engine, don't let anybody send flowers. Send along a
> pick axe to bash my head in and make a good job of it. Put me in a

sausage machine and can me into cat's meat and write Bitch, second quality, on the lid (p. 172).

Jimson warns her against this self-destroying rage at life's injustice. 'Don't let it get you down, Coke. Don't get in a state. That was my trouble, getting in a state.' Coker replies: 'That's the only advantage I've got. I don't give a damn for myself . . . Give me hell. That's what I'm for' (p. 11).

This disagreement between Jimson and Coker about the proper attitude to the 'damned unfairness of things' puts the tacit disagreement between Jimson and Plantie over the same subject in proper relief, and so points to the special appropriateness of Cary's use of Spinoza as the symbol of that other attitude to metaphysical injustice. To Jimson, Blake represents his kind of man, the 'greatest Englishman who ever lived', a 'poet and painter [who] never had a chance'. Hence Jimson tries to raise a contribution for a memorial in his name. 'This memorial is for justice, that's all' (p. 14). Spinoza represents Plantie's kind of man. According to Plantie, Spinoza was 'the most independent man that ever lived, never asked for anything of anybody. He'd rather have died, and he did die. And mind you, a happy man. In the contemplation of the majesty and glory of God's being'. He was, Plantie believes, the 'happiest man that ever lived, the God drunk man' (p. 129).

The difference between Blake and Spinoza is really that one seeks positively to find a creative defence for the injustice of the world whereas the other assumes a supreme disdain for the fact of evil and injustice. The difference between Jimson and Plantie is that Jimson can escape what torments Plantie—the sense of fundamental injustice in the world. Jimson takes injustice in his stride, and lives with it: 'No fingers, no swell, no swell, no art' (p. 19). 'What I say to an artist is, WHEN YOU CAN'T PAINT—PAINT. But something else . . . It went so well that I forgot my feet, I forgot my head' (p. 86). Plantie, for his part, sought to find some rational conceptual frame for the world of injustice before him. This search is behind his sponsorship of Professor Ponting's lecture on 'Religion and Humanity' which ironically ends with the singing of a Blakean prophecy: 'Till we have built Jerusalem/In England's green and pleasant land' (p. 81).

It is the idealism of this search, however, that alienates Jimson from Plantie. For Jimson's world is irremediable; his Jerusalem is possible only in canvas and paint, or in poetry. 'Learned the good

bits of Jerusalem by heart. Nothing like poetry, when you lie awake
at night. It keeps the old brain limber. It washes away the mud and
sand that keeps up blocking up the bends' (p. 109). Creativeness,
not contemplation, is his corrective for injustice. An artist

has no right to complain of his fate. For he has great pleasures. To
start new pictures. Even the worst artist that ever was, even a one-
eyed mental deficient with the shakes in both hands who set out to
paint the chickenhouse, can enjoy the first stroke. Can think, by
God, look what I've done. A miracle. I have transformed a chunk
of wood, canvas, etc., into a spiritual fact, an eternity' (p. 174).

There can be little doubt that Cary's tribute to Jimson's view of
life is implied in the change which comes over Plantie at the end of
the novel. There, overwhelmed by the injustice of the robbers'
stealing of the paints kindly given to the needy Jimson, Plantie can
hardly speak. 'I thought perhaps he'd got over all his philosophies.
Grown out of them. He'd stopped looking for a rabbit hole and was
feeling what you might call the nature of things, at last' (p. 243). But
Plantie's sleep that night is disturbed.

Whenever I looked his way I could see his little eyes glinting as he
stared at the ceiling. But what he was thinking of, I don't know.
An old man's thoughts are an old man's secret, and no one else
would even understand them . . .
'. . . why aren't you asleep?' [Jimson asks him].
'I've had my sleep. I wondered how you were sleeping.'
'Like a top,' I said. For it saves a lot of trouble between friends to
swear that life is good, brother. It leaves more time to live
(p. 245).

'I'm an optimist', Jimson says. 'I get a lot of fun out of fun, as well as
the miseries. And so when Plantie tried to convert me to dignified
independence I quarreled with him' (p. 84). So also, when the nun
at the hospital tried to convert him to prayer and silence, he
preferred his existential joy in life.

'It's dangerous for you to talk, you're very seriously ill.' 'Not so
seriously as you're well. How don't you enjoy life, Mother. I
should laugh all round my neck at this minute if my shirt wasn't a

bit on the tight side.' 'It would be better for you to pray.' 'Sam
thing, Mother' (p. 311).

Thus, in effect, *The Horse's Mouth* is offering an existentialis
vindication of the pilgrim ideal presented intellectually in *To Be*
Pilgrim and affirmed actively in *Herself Surprised*. What is new in *Th*
Horse's Mouth, in this respect, is that Cary gives new dimensions t
the significance of Sara's life advanced by Tom Wilcher. In *To Be*
Pilgrim, Sara is without reservations 'the saviour'. She came
Wilcher says, 'to save my soul alive'. In *The Horse's Mouth*, she als
saves (or better, serves) life. But in keeping with the central motif c
the biblical Fall, she is also the tempter, the source of man's fall
Cary uses Blake to give point in *The Horse's Mouth* to these ne
aspects of Sara's importance, thereby making her both an in
dividual woman and an archetypal female. According to Blake
Woman is the natural enemy of the Man.

> She binds iron thorns around his head
> She pierces both his hands and feet
> She cuts his heart out at his side
> To make him feel both cold and heat
> Her fingers number every nerve
> Just as a miser counts his gold
> She lives upon his shrieks and cries
> And she grows young as he grows old (p. 45).

It is this notion of woman that informs Jimson's view of Sara a
the 'man-eater', 'the old boa-constrictor' (p. 28). This view must
however, be understood at its proper fundamental level. At tha
level, the destructive influence of Sara is much more than a kind o
domestic henpecking. The destruction is of another kind. Jimsor
says,

> As a Briton, I fell in love with Mrs Monday, the mother and th
> wife. I wanted to rest upon the domestic bosom. But she turnec
> into a bride and wanted to rest on mine. As an artist, I fell in lov
> with Sara, and her grand forms, but she was an artist herself, anc
> she appreciated herself so much that she couldn't bear me t
> paint anyone or anything else . . . Sara was a tyrant who tried tc
> put me in a bottle and cork me up into a woman's cup of tea
> (p. 262).

What Sara destroys through her possessiveness is masculine creativeness. 'You could never get your own way with Sara . . . and making love to Sara was a stormy joy, thunder and lightning' (p. 263). As protector, she acts to restrain the pilgrim spirit of the artist. When Jimson is 'mad to paint', she is only intent, for her part, in putting him to bed: 'It was, "Poor Gulley, don't forget the cough medicine." . . . Stirring all that fire only to cook her own pot' (p. 45). As lover, she leads him to an equally debilitating madness. 'I was always at her, one way or another. The flesh was made word; every day. Till he, that is, Gulley Jimson, became a bleeding youth. And she, that is, Sara, becomes a virgin bright' (p. 46).

Another Blakean passage indirectly celebrates Sara's generous delight in herself and in her senses:

> And this is the manner of the daughters of Albion
>   in their beauty,
> Everyone is Threefold in Head and Heart and Loins,
>   and everyone
> Has three gates into the three Heavens of Beulah
>   which shine
> Translucent in their Foreheads and their Bosoms
>   and their Loins
> Surrounded with fire unapproachable. But whom they
>   please
> They take up into their heavens in intoxicating
>   delight (p. 90).

Wilcher does not make this point directly in his novel, but we can deduce it from the distinction which he makes between Sara and Julie. In his own novel, Jimson constantly refers to this quality. He describes Sara as 'the everlasting trumpets, a challenge to battle and death' (p. 263). He speaks of her sexuality in old age as 'the last flutter of the old candle' (p. 73). 'And there she is looking at me as if she could eat me without sauce, the old crocodile' (pp. 75–6). 'Yes,' Sara herself tells Jimson, 'I always needed a man to peg me down, a real man.' It made Jimson 'tingle all over' to hear her say so; 'it made me laugh and sing in the claves of my legs. It made my toes curl and my fingers itch at the tops. It made me want to go bozo with the old rascal. What a woman' (p. 77). Thus, again, Sara emerges as the individual woman she is and at the same time represents the quintessence of the Eternal Female. 'When you knew Sara, you knew womankind, and no one who doesn't know womankind knows anything about the nature of Nature' (p. 264).

O land of Beulah
Where every female delights to give her maiden to her husband
The Female searches land and sea for gratification to the
Male genius, who in return, clothes her in gems and gold
And feeds her with the food of Eden; hence all her beauty beams
(p. 158).

Sara does search land and sea to gratify Jimson. Jimson in return makes her the model for his Eve: 'The best model I ever had . . . There was always something about Sara that made me want to hit her or love her or get her down on canvas' (p. 79). Sara thus becomes his 'everlasting Eve'. What was lacking in his earlier sketches of Eve, he realises, was 'something female . . . something from Sara' (p. 82). She is the 'old original', 'solid brass to Adam's rib' (p. 77, 24).

Accordingly two pictures of Jimson's stand out as a tribute to Sara. One is 'The Bath'. Jimson calls it a 'good sketch': 'Head bent over to the left—line of the cheek against the hair. Lips pushed out. Eyes dropped. Looking at her breasts. Serious expression. Worship' (pp. 24–5). Looking back at it, he can see it as representing more than an occasional sketch of Sara in her bath. He realises that it is 'a work of imagination'.

> And then you feel with all the women that ever lived and all the women that are ever going to live, and you feel their feeling while they are alone with themselves—in some chosen private place, bathing, drying, dressing, criticizing, touching, admiring themselves safe behind locked doors. Nothing there but women's feeling and woman's beauty and critical eye (p. 98).

The other sketch is a study for his great work, 'The Fall'. The occasion for this sketch is particularly relevant in that it shows how far Sara had become Jimson's obsession. Before him is Lady Beeder, the elegant prosperous female of the world of property. 'A perfect lady. Full of forebearance towards this nasty dirty old man with his ignorant prejudices' (p. 155). It is on this occasion, too, that Jimson quotes Blake's tribute to the Females of Beulah and their men who clothe them in gems and gold. Ignoring both Lady Beeder's invitation ('won't you have some more wine, Mr Jimson?') and her very presence, Jimson sketches a magnificent picture of Eve with Sara as his model. In that sketch he achieves his perfect vision of Eve. 'Eve. Fearful symmetry' (p. 158).

Jimson complains early in the novel of Sara's dominating influence: 'Materiality, that is, Sara, the old female nature, having attempted to button up the prophetic spirit, that is to say, Gulley Jimson, in her plackethole, got a bonk on the conk, and was reduced to her proper status, as spiritual fodder. But what fodder' (p. 46). Jimson paid her back for the service. As he passed the stone marking the grave of Rosina Balmforth, Jimson knew the final difference at death between Sara and other women: 'And I thought, who will remember Rozzie when I go. Sara is immortal. She will live in the National Galleries of the World for ever' (p. 269). It is a fitting conclusion to the careers of Gulley Jimson—the free creative man, and Sara Monday—the eternal female, that both should survive in the one work which brought them closest together. 'The world of imagination is the world of eternity' (p. 35).

4 The Politics of Order

Prisoner of Grace, Except the Lord and *Not Honour More* are usually referred to as constituting Cary's 'political' trilogy,[1] the novels in which, it is said, Cary poured a lifetime's reflection, ideas and observations concerning the working of the creative imagination in politics.[2] The difficulty in interpreting and evaluating these reflections and observations is the comprehensiveness of the term 'politics', as Cary used it. 'The difficulty of a book about politicians,' he wrote in the 1954 Preface to *Prisoner of Grace*, 'is that people will read it as a book about government.'[3] Though this distinction is a common enough one, it is especially important to Cary's purposes in the trilogy. Cary's metaphysics, as we saw, tried to explain as well as justify the world's creativeness and its continual turmoil. This metaphysics also tried to show how the world saved itself from final anarchy by its imaginative responsiveness to the need for order. The 'free man' who rebels against all restrictions to his freedom also asks, 'at least in his heart', for justice and opportunity 'which only authority [or order] can secure for him'.[4] Thus, even the anarchism of individual freedom recognises the need to negotiate with the rest of the world, to concede to necessary influence or authority, in order to secure its freedom.

Cary believed that life 'cannot avoid tension, and tragedy. They are in the nature of things'.[5] But the character of that tension can be managed; the world of men and events can be cheated into accommodating its inalienable freedom to the necessity for temporal order. Because this is a world of 'everlasting creation and therefore continuous change',[6] and because it is full of men whose whims operate with an almost 'infinite variety of particular variation',[7] great imagination and continuous adjustment are needed to govern it. The creative world cannot be ruled by edict; it can only be 'managed' into obedience. The politican, in Cary's sense of the word, is the accomplished 'manager' of men, and politics is the business of managing the relationships between men.

To understand the 'political' trilogy, then, we must recognise the breadth of Cary's definition of his key term. Politics, as he defined it, is the 'art of human relations'; and since 'all human relations require continuous adjustment',[8] they are necessarily 'political'. This breadth of significance is clearly Cary's point in stressing that he ought in the trilogy to write of 'the whole political world, not only as commonly restricted to Parliaments and congresses, but as it works in marriage and the nursery, in all human relations'.[9]

But even given that definition of 'politics', it is at first not easy to see how it can be reconciled with the narrator's explicit statement at the opening of *Prisoner of Grace* that it is simply her attempt to defend her husband's reputation against imputations and 'revelations' threatened by several people. It is difficult, that is, to see how the larger concept of politics can be developed in a narrative which so openly advertises a different purpose and a different emphasis.

The difficulty, fortunately, is overcome if we recognise that the declaration is Nina's reason for telling her story, not Cary's for making her tell it. Cary uses Nina and her declaration of intent as part of his strategy for encompassing the several aspects of his theme of politics as the management of human relationships. This is, at best, a very indirect means of dealing with his theme. That indirection is not, however, an inadvertence on Cary's part; nor, in fact, is it a departure from Cary's method in his other novels.[10] *An American Visitor*, is, on the face of it, the story of an American rover girl's adventure in Africa, and of her conflict with local British officials and businessmen. In fact, the novel only uses the occasion of the adventure to study the nature of civilisation, primitivism and change. *Charley Is My Darling* reads at first as the portrait of a highly resourceful juvenile delinquent. As we have seen, however, the novel is a study of the nature and the growth of the moral consciousness, Charley's life being an example for the study.

In *Herself Suprised*, Sara writes her book ostensibly to raise some needed money and to correct some popular misconceptions about her life with Wilcher and Jimson, particularly the verdict of the judge that she was a threat to the 'whole fabric of civilization'. She does not realise the significance of her story which Cary puts to other uses linked with the themes of the other novels of *The First Trilogy*. The meaning of her life is beyond Sara's comprehension; only in *To Be a Pilgrim* and in *The Horse's Mouth* do we realise what Cary (as opposed to Sara) meant by Sara's story. In the first of these novels, we come to see Sara as Mother Nature at the service of life; and in the other we see her as the Blakean *femme fatale*, the death-bringer to man's artistic creativeness. The simplicity of Sara's narrative and the unpretentiousness of her declared purpose in it successfully mask Cary's own reasons for writing the novel and creating Sara as its narrator. This oblique narrative mode is, naturally, more conspicuous in the first-person than in the third-person narratives, especially because two personalities are involved in first-person narration: the fictional narrator whom Carry allows every possible freedom to tell his story, and Cary himself, who builds his own meaning on the foundation of his character's argument or confession. Indeed much of the subtlety of these first-person narratives comes from Cary's ability to put his character's declared narrative purpose to his own artistic use.

This indirection of method is made even more important in the second trilogy by the scope and nature of the 'political' theme developed in it. In *To Be A Pilgrim*, Edward Wilcher defined the ideal novel of politics and described the limitations of the traditional English and French novels dealing with that subject. According to him, the traditional novel of politics never gave the reader 'the sense of limitation and confusion, of walking on a slack wire over an unseen gulf by a succession of lightning flashes'. The ideal novel of politics, Wilcher held, should show 'what a muddle and confusion [politics] is, and that it must always be a muddle and confusion where good men are wasted and destroyed simply because by luck as by a chance bullet'.[11] Some of Cary's critics have been led by this definition of the ideal political novel to assume that the indirection of method in the trilogy is Cary's way of reproducing the confusion of actual politics. One critic, for example, complains that 'to the muddle and confusion which inhere in democratic politics as a subject, Cary adds the technical and philosophical confusion that arises from three clashing first-person accounts of that subject'.[12] This complaint arises from a misunderstanding of Cary's meaning in *To Be A Pilgrim* and from a failure to appreciate the distinction which Cary would have made between the 'confusion' of actual politics and the representation of that muddle in a work of art.

Cary has clarified this purpose for us in his comments on *The Moonlight*. Every family, Cary declares, 'shows the everlasting situation of authority and freedom'.

This situation produces a great variety of tension, comic and tragic—but it is usually confused, muddled and therefore insignificant. Or if you like, it signifies only muddle. A writer for whom muddle is the chief characteristic of life would no doubt be interested in a man or woman for whom the muddle of his family relations was incurable, who was defeated by it, or grew resigned to it, or escaped from it into some bolt hole or juju. But muddle does not interest me, except as a necessary accident of life, like the weather. It is part of a background, and so I should not be concerned with a situation of muddle or a character who illustrated it.[13]

Cary's position here is so explicit as to need little amplification. Two aspects of it may nevertheless be emphasised. The first is Cary's insistence that muddle and confusion are an inevitable part of his subject, 'an everlasting situation', 'a necessary accident'. Cary would thus have to address himself in some way or other to the problems raised by this situation. The second point is more important. Cary emphasises that the confusion is only the background for his novel, not its subject. Whatever 'muddle' he needed to project in the novel would have to be introduced and explored indirectly, as an attendant aspect of a more prominent subject.

Cary asked of the ideal novel of politics that it should do for its subject what Tolstoy's *War and Peace* did for war. Cary's political trilogy also aimed at doing this, and tried to use matter-of-fact realism, the same range and variety of character, the same emphasis on the domestic side of life, and the same awareness of experience as a combination of social and private history. Cary's version of these techniques obviously differed from Tolstoy's as his detailed view of history, politics and religion did. Nevertheless, Cary's attempt to achieve the same scope of statement in his trilogy was simply to recreate the public political career of Nimmo and to provide the kind of defence Nina attempted.

As the analysis of the novels of this trilogy will show, Cary meant to present his theme in both its public and its private aspects, with the public theme taking its meaning, in the last analysis, from the conclusions derived from the private theme. This is to say that Nina's marital life and Nimmo's political career (both seen against the background of English politics and English history) are the twin subjects of *Prisoner of Grace* which celebrates Nina's being made prisoner of politics rather than Nimmo's rise and fall. If we add to this the detailed and solemn evocation (in *Except the Lord*) of the social, economic and religious movements in the life of ordinary English people, and the graphic and momentous account (in *Not*

Honour More) of the culminating crises of the ideological, political
and labour unrests of the period, we have a close parallel to the
startling revolutionary background and intense personal history of
Tolstoy's *War and Peace*, its combination of the domestic novel of
Russian gentry and the history of a war written in the style of a
conscientious chronicle. The art of the future, Tolstoy declared in
What is Art?, will be superior to that of his own generation, 'not in
the sense of having a refined and complex technique, but in the sense
of the capacity briefly, simply, and clearly to transmit, without any
superfluities, the feeling the artist has experienced and wishes to
convey'.[14] Cary's imitation of Tolstoy in his political trilogy seems
directed at achieving the same kind of superiority.

Tolstoy managed the variations of his themes of war and peace in
War and Peace by alternating his emphases on them in the fifteen
'books'. There is a war in the very first paragraph of the novel but its
importance is suppressed in favour of a domestic scene of uneasy
peace. Tolstoy waits till the second book before reminding us quite
emphatically of the presence and movement of armies, and of the
peaceful countenance of war represented in the 'sanguine-looking
general past middle age'. In that book, peace, especially domestic
peace, yields to the urgency of war. And our sanguine-looking
general's 'quivering strut seemed to say that, apart from his military
interests, he had plenty of warmth in his heart for the attractions of
social life and the fair sex'.[15] In the third book, Tolstoy is able to
merge the implications of the first two books in a twin theme of war
and peace, domestic and military.

> The stretchers began to be moved. At every jolt [Prince Andrey]
> felt intolerable pain again. The fever became higher, and he fell
> into delirium. Visions of his father, his wife, his sister, his future
> son, and the tenderness he had felt for them on the night before
> the battle, the figure of that little, pretty Napoleon, and over all
> these the lofty sky, formed the chief substance of his delirious
> dreams.[16]

The purpose behind Tolstoy's variations of theme and emphasis
was, obviously, to produce a final impression of his subject and of the
historical period far richer than any personal or military history, or
even persistent moral commentary, could hope to achieve. Tolstoy's
norm was still the nineteenth-century realistic novel; the counter-
pointing of themes and the very massiveness of its details were

probably Tolstoy's only way of transcending the limitations of the conventional realistic novel in order to express a large and multi-faceted intuition.

Cary's use of the form of the 'trilogy' can be seen as a parallel attempt to express a large and complex theme in a realistic novel without the limitations of that mode. The three independent novels eliminate the cumbersome character of a single novel as massive as *War and Peace*. The autonomy of the three works also enables him to give varying emphases to different aspects of their common theme. The form of the trilogy, with its three independent narrators, frees him from the restrictiveness of a single point of view; while the integrity of each narrator eliminates the obstrusive authorial commentary and analyses which Tolstoy had been forced to use in order to underline the meaning of his realistic details.

PRISONER OF GRACE

It is best to approach an analysis of the trilogy from Cary's point of view, especially from that remark of his that the central scene of *Prisoner of Grace*—the scene that 'recorded for me an experience fundamental to the book's meaning' and the one he had to write first to be sure he could write the rest—was the railway-station scene between Chester Nimmo and Nina Woodville: 'I wrote the railway-station chapter . . . to show how the husband, by certain suggestions, makes it impossible for his wife to carry on with her elopement. She just daren't run away from him'.[17]

> . . . I was going to say that I had warned Chester against Jim, and therefore everything that had happened was his fault. But when I caught his eyes looking into mine, not fiercely any longer, but with a kind of sad wonder, I absolutely could not speak the words. 'Yes, I asked you to ask him,' he said. 'Was that wrong?' 'No, of course not; it was good of you. You have been goodness itself all along, and that's why—'
> Then there was a little pause while I was trying to find the right phrase.
> 'Why what?' Chester said.[18]

In this scene, Cary presents us with a heroine who is thoroughly aware of Nimmo's political conduct and his reasons for it, but is little tempted to counter Nimmo's double-dealing with a similar 'arte'. She is a woman who recognises that Nimmo's duplicity is not evil but devious, that his intention is not to deceive so much as to influence. Nina is precisely the kind of person least disposed to play at politics for whatever reasons, and whose intelligent understanding of the political act ultimately becomes a real liability. Nimmo deliberately plays on Nina's sense of honour. Because she knows that Nimmo is deliberately offering this code of 'honour' as a bait, she refuses to use it in her defence: for to do so would be mean and highbrow. But because Chester's question gives her some excuse, she makes the final effort and asserts her ideal of honour: 'I couldn't pretend things to you—it would be too mean'.

Nimmo refuses to respond to this answer in its general and ethical aspects. Rather he translates it into a statement of fact, and makes the fact seem less honourable than her reasoning was.

> 'So you want to go to Jim?'
> 'Don't you see I must go?'
> I was putting the emphasis on 'want'. 'Do you *want* to go to Jim or only to escape from me?'
> 'Please, Chester, don't cross-examine me—it's too late: it really is too late. You mustn't stop me now; you can't (p. 63).

Nimmo is able to break her resolution at the end, making her abjure her own code of honour, not because she thought the code irrelevant to her life, but because she wanted to establish the necessity for her conduct on grounds other than those of honour or propriety.

Nimmo leads her to this abjuration by making himself the fortunate and undeserving beneficiary of her love and kindness: 'Perhaps you haven't loved me—I couldn't expect that. The difference between us was too great—all the differences'.

> And when, horrified by this charge, I was going to protest that 'class' had nothing to do with the matter, he held up his hand and said, 'I say that only because it makes what you have done all the finer. You would not sin against love—you set yourself to be a true good wife.'
> 'But all I did was quite easy—it had nothing to do with our differences' (I did not want even to say the word class). 'Just being a wife—it's something to do. And what else could I do to fill the time?'

'There's a great difference in the way that people do their duty. You stooped to me, but you might have made it an insult' (p. 64).

Nimmo's victory over Nina is, of course, that of a strong character over a weak one. In addition, however, Nimmo's victory, as Cary presents it, is a negative one made possible by Nina's moral acquiesence to 'political' necessity. Nimmo is able to truimph over her because she is the prisoner of her own grace, because she would never be 'political' on her own account. She yields to Nimmo's persuasion precisely because she can see beyond his rhetoric and the scheming to Nimmo's purpose. When she yields to his plea, it is not out of a conviction of error or of guilt but from a sense of obligation to Nimmo's career, and to Nimmo's *self*. Nina could not decide to leave Nimmo because to do so would mean victory and even pleasure for her, but pain and spiritual defeat for Nimmo; and Nina, as Cary said of her, 'would not get pleasure by giving pain'.[19]

The bond between Nina and Nimmo then is not one of love but of politics. Nina tells us that it was 'a kind of relief' to her when the train finally left the station 'for it made a decision for me. It ended that agony' (p. 68). In fact, however, that decision had been made inevitable by Nina's recognition of the 'political' complications of her marital situation. She had realised, soon after Nimmo's dramatic departure from the station, that Nimmo simply *needed* her. Or more precisely, she saw that she owed it to him to remain his wife. As she came to phrase it later in the novel, 'I was able for the first time to see the important *fact* that if Chester lost the election I might have to blame myself for it' (p. 77). He might talk of 'the sin against love' but 'all he wants is to get into Parliament' (p. 67). That knowledge made her his prisoner: 'It did not matter what I thought of Chester and whether he was playing tricks or not, because I could not think. I only felt a fearful indignation like a violent headache and those frightened words whirling and beating everywhere and knocking fragile things down' (p. 67). Hence, when the train finally came and 'the women went out to catch it', Nina, too, 'got up with (her) bag and followed them' (p. 68). The mechanical response gives away her deepest inclinations. What she did on the railway platform was not to *decide* what to do, but to dramatise her resentment of the 'political' life which had made a prisoner of her.

Nina's loyalties in the novel, accordingly, move in two directions. One is towards Jim, towards honour, character, the ideal; the other is towards Nimmo, reality, creativeness, politics. By upbringing as

well as by family tradition, Nina belonged to Honour and to Jim; by
experience and marriage she is made aware of the limitations of
codes and ideals in a world of changing situations. Nina's growth in
the novel is her final understanding of the uneasy relationship
between the ideal and the real; and her realisation that to
compromise with the ideal is not always to be a villain, that to
pretend is not always to be dishonest.

Such an understanding is clearly implied in two minor incidents
surrounding Nina's decision not to elope. In the first incident, Nina
finds that because of the entry into the waiting room of two market
women—'They sat down opposite the door, and then recognized
Chester and nudged each other and gazed at me as if wondering
what sort of a woman had caught their great man' (p. 64), she had to
be 'political', to adjust the character of her quarrel with Chester to
suit the new circumstances. But sensing her difficulty, Nimmo
deliberately ignores her comment; in fact, he looks at her 'with that
fixity which meant he was plotting something and trying to spy out
his ground—that is the state of my mind' (p. 64).

> The women had now realized that we were having some kind of
> argument and were staring with all their eyes. The child, too (it
> was sucking a lollipop and it had half its very dirty hand in its
> mouth at the same time), was gazing at us, trying to discover
> what the women found so interesting. So I said, 'Really, Chester,
> we can't go on like this, in a waiting room, with all the world
> staring at us' (pp. 64-5).

In asking that Nimmo and herself 'pretend' to a cordiality which
they do not feel, Nina is in fact (and ironically) asking Nimmo to do
what Nimmo, in a bigger way, is also asking of her. As if to underline
the irony of Nina's position, Cary makes Nimmo jump up, kiss
Nina's cheek before walking out on her, thus turning Nina's
apparent triumph into defeat. On the one hand, Nimmo's gesture
was his way of conceding victory to Nina. By that polite and formal
farewell of a kiss, Nimmo frees her of all obligations to him. On the
other hand, Nina appears to have overplayed her advantage. Her
disregard of place and time, of the public waiting room and the
attentive women had indeed forced Nimmo to yield; but it had also
made Nina's victory 'unfair'. Nimmo *had* to leave to keep the
decorum which Nina wanted, and which she had now inadvertently
broken. The manner of Nimmo's departure is, appropriately, both

proud and humiliated. This is Nina's undoing. It makes her aware once again of the people about her. 'I kept sitting with my chin in the air, looking quite dignified (for the man was still scorning and the women were still wondering, and the child in its fascinated state actually climbing onto my lap and dribbling down my front)' (p. 67). Nina saw that by her successful gesture of independence, she had inadvertently broken the illusion of cordiality which she had sought to maintain before the strangers. 'I found myself grasping the handle of my bag as if it were the only clear sensible decision in my possession' (p. 67).

The other minor incident surrounding the station scene occurs immediately after Nina's return to Palm Cottage. There she found she had to give some explanation for her presence. She 'lied' to Aunt Latter that she was not well. This lie is double-edged. First, Nina was actually not well: 'when I went to bed I felt very ill' (p. 68). Secondly Aunt Latter who didn't believe her, nevertheless 'pretended to believe that I was really ill and even coddled me. And the reason was, of course, that she, like Chester, was in terror that I would ruin Chester's chance at Battwell' (p. 69). Nimmo himself 'perfectly, understood her feelings' and 'put it about that I was ill and treated me like a sick person' (p. 69). Nina saw through Nimmo's conduct, but she also saw that Nimmo was not trying to deceive her as to his real feelings but to 'get round' her. His smile, Nina says, was 'the kind of smile you see on a child's face when he wants to "get round" you but knows you know it' (p. 69).

The coincidence in the responses of Aunt Latter and Nimmo to Nina's lie about her illness is a revealing one, especially after the politics of the railway-station chapter. The two politicians—Nimmo and Aunt Latter—are united once again to cheat Nina of the meagre comfort of her already compromised personality. Not only has she had to defer to Nimmo's career by not leaving him; she will have to endure the general falseness of a pretended illness in order further to help that career. In either case, Nina remains the prisoner of a political exigency: 'I felt as if I were being slowly pressed to death like those wretched people who would not tell the judge whether they were guilty or not guilty' (p. 69). Nina is in this position because the manoeuvres of Nimmo and Aunt Latter having, in the circumstances, become 'noble' (p. 69), are now being used indirectly to humiliate her.

It was this idea that I had been picked out by fate for specially bad treatment that filled me with resentment. And, of course, all my anger centred on Chester. I felt for him that special hatred one feels toward people who take up a position of moral superiority and use it to domineer over one. The better they are, the more one hates them (p. 70).

It is in this way that Cary makes a 'political' issue of the marital life which Nina has to manage. This marital life is in the foreground of the action; the public life helps give it context and proportion. At the very opening of the novel, Nina tried to explain the circumstances of her marriage, and to give some account of the kind of relationship that developed between Nimmo and herself. 'And first of all,' she says, 'it is not true, as people say, that I was trapped into marriage, when I loved someone else. If there was any deceit, it was on my side' (p. 1). Nina proceeds to tell of her childhood life with Jim Latter and of the unusually intimate relationship which they shared long before she was seventeen. 'I have asked myself if [Aunt Latter] were simply indulging Jim with me, not perhaps deliberately, but from that passion for Jim which gradually took hold of her and made her rather blind to other people's dues' (p. 6). Jim was indeed Aunt Latter's 'darling'. She had 'not only great love but the deepest compassion' for Jim, and 'adored' him. When, however, Nina is pregnant by Jim (who cannot marry her without resigning from his regiment and so ruining his career), Aunt Latter begins her major political game which ends in Nina's marriage to Nimmo.

The marriage was simply and frankly a marriage of mutual convenience. Nina was never in love with Nimmo, nor even sympathetic to his political views. She knew he admired her, but this admiration only amused her: 'I was in an agony to hold my giggles' (p. 9). She thought Nimmo 'absurd' partly because she was 'used' to thinking so and partly because 'in that congested air of politics' she felt she could not 'bear to be admired even from a distance' (p. 9), and so rejected all his proposals of marriage and told him 'quite reasonably and politely' that she was sorry but she could only be his friend (p. 9).

Nina's pregnancy by Jim changed this comfortable and proper decision.

I daresay plenty of girls in the same bad hole [of being unmarried mothers] make the same discovery. I mean they find that, once *in* such a fearful situation, it seems quite different and they can bear it after all. Not that it is less awful, but you simply don't have to do anything except bear it, and just by bearing it you get a special sort of power to go on; you even feel a little sorry for people who haven't been through the same awfulness and don't know what it is like (p. 11).

Nina's attitude to her pregnancy is totally unacceptable to Aunt Latter's ' "practical" point of view' (pp. 11–12). She accuses Nina of doing nothing 'as usual' about her condition 'except drift' (p. 10), and suggests marriage to Nimmo as a most convenient solution to her ward's dilemma. 'He'd thank his stars to get you in a wheel-barrow—and quite right, too. It would be the making of him—and well he knows it' (p. 12).

This marriage, then, is the beginning of Nina's political life.

I had read a great deal in French novels about the private agonies of girls married off without love and I was a little apprehensive, but I certainly felt nothing even very uncomfortable. In fact, I can't remember anything except my anxiety not to upset the little man in any way (he was obviously even more nervous than I was) and relieved that he took all the responsibility and managed so well (p. 14).

Before this, she had not realised that the situation can be managed, and that a dexterous management of them can even mitigate agonies such as the 'intolerable burden' of being married without love. Until this realisation, Nina relied on a simple, inflexible code of propriety and honour. When Aunt Latter pressed the case for a marriage to Nimmo, Nina 'asked (not bothering to say that she wouldn't marry him) if he knew about her condition'.

'Of course he knows.'
This did interest me (since Nimmo was supposed to be so respectable), and I asked what he said. But Aunt grew furious again and said only, 'He's not a fool, and you can thank God for it; and keep quiet and let him do the same' (p. 13).

Nina had to shed the quixotism of her inflexible code and and accept the *mutual* advantages of a marriage to Nimmo: Nina 'can thank God for it', and so 'let (Nimmo) do the same'.

In an earlier scene with Jim, Nina herself had 'felt' but not

understood the limitations of the code. Jim had swum 'among the
biggest waves' in an effort to humour his pride and to spite Nina who
(being healthier) had fared much better in an earlier attempt in less
dangerous waters. Nina 'hated' Jim all day for his conduct because
she saw that Jim had no reason to undertake the suicidal swim other
than 'to show how brave' he was (p. 4). 'I was so enraged against
Jim . . . that I could have been quite glad if I had fallen off the cliff
on the way up and killed myself' (p. 5). Nina was not in a position,
at that time, to fully appreciate the implications of her dissatisfac-
tion with Jim's idea of honour. There was, she says, a 'heavy mass of
tangled feelings which surrounded me and tied me in on all sides'
(p. 5). She had not yet understood the need for 'politics' as an
antidote to impractical idealism and to Jim's kind of quixotism.
'At ten years old,' as Jim attests in his own novel, Nina 'didn't laugh
at an idea because it was true or fine. It was only after thirty years of
Nimmo and London society, she found anything comic in a word
like duty and could use it to make a fool of her husband,[20] Faced,
however, with her pregnancy by a man who (for 'good' reasons)
could not then marry her, and with the fact of a 'respectable'
Nimmo willing and eager to marry her for his own political reasons,
Nina was shocked into a new understanding. She came to see that
Aunt Latter's scheming was not a way of 'sacrificing' her to
Chester's career, but was aimed at doing her some 'good' as well. In
a 'strange "philosophic" mood' induced by her pregnancy and by
the amorality of Nimmo's and Aunt Latter's conduct, she reflected
on 'how interesting and different the world was on the inside'
(p. 13). This is the first aspect of her new understanding.

The second is her realisation that Aunt Latter's 'stern training in
manners' had its positive and creditable side. Aunt Latter's
'politicking' made Nina aware of the positive role of 'manners' in
human relationships: 'Politeness itself makes a situation which is
very like affection and much more manageable' (p. 14). Nimmo, as
politician, already knew the importance of manners. By being
'enormously considerate' to Nina, he made it easier for her to 'get
on' with him. Nina discovers that Nimmo was 'like another woman
in his tact; I mean, in feeling what I really wanted and arranging
that I should have it, without spoiling it, perhaps for ever, by
bringing it out into the open and pulling it all out of shape in a
contest of manners which would have been, of course, a special
danger to us when we were both so anxious to be "nice"' (p. 14).
The crucial phrase is 'contest of manners'. Nina understood the

political necessity behind Nimmo's conduct but was not ready (by temperament and upbringing) to accept it. The tensions, concessions and adjustments of her thirty years with Nimmo are the inevitable consequence of her special predicament—the predicament of one who understood what she could not accept.

Cary tells us that he began the second attempt at writing *Prisoner of Grace* in the third person and found that 'the scene at the railway station would not come through'.[21] He then tried a first-person narrator—a retired civil servant devoted to Nina, and a brother of Aunt Latter. But in the telling 'everything was falsified and cheapened, the acuteness of the observer only emphasized his lack of real understanding'.[22] Then, 'those brackets' occurred to him. 'Nina, I said, is essentially a woman who can understand another's point of view, she has to be so to tell her story.' By means of these brackets, Cary was able to change the character of Nina from the 'mean', 'small' and 'unreliable witness' of his first draft to the 'trustworthy' but 'brackety mind' of the finished novel. Without that change, Cary remarks in a fine perceptive phrase, the book would have become 'an essay in the cynical'.[23]

Nina had to be trustworthy because her attitude to the political life of the novel, as we have just pointed out, was both critical and sympathetic. She accepted the ideal of conduct founded on honour and truth and placed these above convenience and policy. 'What is incredible in a person you respect is not that they do something evil (which might be an impulse) but that they should plan it coldly and brazenly. That seems like an unnatural thing, as if the walls of some peaceful room should dissolve away and show a landscape of fire and ash' (p. 205). At the same time, she saw the need for policy, or unorthodox idealism.[24] The popular morality which deprecates 'policy' as an instrument of order depended on the misleading notion that life can at any time be described as 'ordinary' and therefore in no need of management. Against the background of international confusion, especially war, domestic life may not seem to be particularly in need of management. But as Nina found out, to say that 'ordinary life had to go on in an ordinary way' in times of crisis and after them was to say that a boat 'needs the same handling whether it is passing over five feet of water in peaceful estuary or over five miles in the middle of the Atlantic' (p. 201). Life, even obviously non-political life, needed management. People who want 'only ordinary peace and quiet' are asking for a 'great deal'. 'For the ordinary thing is more like a violent argument about the right road

in a runaway coach galloping downhill in a fog. If no one drives
(and *chooses* a road) everything and everyone, including the horses,
will crash' (p. 195).

This is Nina's new understanding of the necessity and inevitability of politics and political conduct. Nina had thought that
by leaving Nimmo she would escape from 'an atmosphere so thick
with suspicion and heavy with moral pressure that [she] could
scarcely breathe' (p. 96). For the same reason she had gone out
occasionally with Sir Robert: 'Bob was as clear as glass—he had no
tricks whatever' (p. 96). But she found at the end of her novel that
breaking from Nimmo had not changed the 'political' character of
the world.

> So that the life which was going to be so simple and restful, my
> 'retirement from politics', is more difficult and complicated than
> ever, and also, of course, more 'political'. I have to consider every
> word I say and everything I do. The tension is like a perpetual
> crisis (p. 301).

Nina's last thoughts on her life with Chester Nimmo and Jim are,
quite appropriately, political. That Cary returns to these thoughts
at the very end of the novel is indicative of the importance he
attached to Nina's married life as a central image of politics for the
trilogy. By her marriage to Nimmo, Nina bound herself to a
contract which made claims on her outside those of love. Though
she knew she belonged to Jim 'forever', she could not disregard her
obligations to that other contract. 'It's a duty', Nimmo reminded
her at the station.

> 'A duty to keep me even if I don't want to stay . . .'
> 'No, I mean a duty to our marriage, which has been so fruitful in
> results—in our work together' (p. 65).

In their situation, he explained, 'it was impossible to decide only on
personal grounds, because there was nothing to take hold of' (p. 65).

So, also, at the very end of her novel, Nina returns to the duties
imposed on her by her understanding of Nimmo's attachment to the
results of his political life. To turn Chester out would be to commit 'a
mean crime against something bigger than love'.—'I should despise
myself, which is, I suppose, what Chester means when he says that
such and such a "poor devil" is "damned". And I am terrified of

"damnation", for it would destroy my happiness and all the joy of my life, and Jim can only shoot me dead (p. 301).

To underline this structural and thematic emphasis on Nina's management of her marriage is not to detract from the importance of Nimmo's political career as a subject of interest in itself. It is rather to define in what sense that career is made significant for Cary's specific argument in his novel. For Cary used his study of Nina's marriage to illuminate the problems and resolutions of the public career. Cary wanted to tell Nimmo's story through a woman 'whose marriage needs a great deal of management' precisely because such a woman alone could appreciate the peculiar difficulties of the 'political' life. There was 'between Chester and myself', Nina relates, 'a situation'.

I mean, an unusual tension. There is, I suppose, always a 'situation' between husband and wife (unless I have been 'corrupted' by living so long in a political atmosphere; I should suppose there is a situation between everybody) and 'relations' which need the equivalent of 'understandings' and 'spheres of influence' (p. 213).

Nina is not simply transferring terms from the public to the domestic domain. She is, as it were, tracing the terms back to their origins. Cary is using her to restate the insistent thought of the novel that human relationships especially marital ones, are the original and incomparable model for the nature of all other relationships, including the so-called political ones.

EXCEPT THE LORD

If we see the form of the trilogy as indicating not merely three different points of views (as held by the narrators) but three related ways of looking at the same subject; if, in other words, we do not regard the distinctiveness of point of view in the three novels as representing unreconciled points of view but as three aspects of a single vision, we place ourselves in a position to appreciate Cary's sudden shift of emphasis from the domestic and public scene in *Prisoner of Grace* to the religious, social and familial concerns of *Except the Lord*. Obviously, there is a direct connection between the immediate subject of *Except the Lord* and the character of its narrator.

There is, however, a deeper and more important significance in the novel linking it with the trilogy as a whole. *Except the Lord* provides us with an account of Nimmo's early life. It also establishes the 'political' character of soul and household by which both the personal character of Nimmo and the political and social upheavals of the generation are to be shaped. In this sense, *Except the Lord* explains the heart and soul of Chester Nimmo and his England. It provides a spiritual background without which the activity of *Prisoner of Grace* and the commotion and bitterness of *Not Honour More* become meaningless. The political antagonism between Nimmo and Jim Latter cannot be fully understood or judged without an understanding of the suffering, the heroism and the failure of ideals implied in *Except the Lord.*

Nimmo describes his life in the opening chapter of his *own book* as a tragic failure, the story 'of a crime, of a soul, my own, plucked back from the very edge of frustration and despair'.[25] Later in the novel he speaks of 'that crime of which it is my purpose here to trace the source and nourishing' (p. 90). To establish this view of his life, Nimmo deliberately concentrates on his family life in order thereby to 'draw back now the curtain from my family life, sacred to memory . . . in the conviction that my story throws light upon the crisis that so fearfully shakes our whole civilization' (p. 1). The justification for this emphasis is given us late in the novel. 'This book,' Nimmo says,

> is not the history of political events but of a boy's mind and soul, of one who came so near perdition that his escape still seems to him like a miracle. And if perdition is a word that makes you smile, a preacher's word out of date even among preachers, I must urge that I use it in a strict sense, for one who is lost. In those days I was indeed lost, and each time I seemed to find the path again it was merely another by-track in a maze of bewilderment (p. 234).

It is evident from this formulation that Nimmo is seeking to treat the political theme in his novel on a level much higher than Nina's in *Prisoner of Grace*, and to devote his attention to the spiritual implications of both his career and that phase of English history. In *Prisoner of Grace*, we recall, Nina describes Nimmo in his defeat as very much like a man 'who comes out of a desperate battle for his very life and the life of his country, to find himself badgered by a rowd of mean creatures who hate him for the most trivial reasons—uch as having to pay more for tobacco'.[26]

Nimmo, for his part, does not take up this view of his career. He noves away from the view of the politician as a public figure or as a amily man to that of a politician as a soul, and the account of his life s a spiritual autobiography. Nimmo's father 'never lost his temper' vith his children and never beat them, but rather infused a 'fear of ;od' in them. That 'fear of God'—'something quite different and ar deeper than alarm'—provided Nimmo with one instance of deal conduct which had no reference to the actual, the momentary r the expedient. 'One does not fear God because he is terrible, but ecause he is literally the soul of goodness and truth, because to do im wrong is to do wrong to some mysterious part of oneself, and one oes not know exactly what the consequences may be' (p. 47).

The vision of order in *Except the Lord* is, accordingly, not domestic r temporal, as in *Prisoner of Grace* and *Not Honour More*, but spiritual. t points to the dilemma of a mere mortal seeking in various ideal nd ignoble ways to make the world a better and happier place. The lilemma, as the novel puts it, is that of knowing which is 'nearer the ruth of existence, the man who says, "I must consider my affairs in he world as if I was going to live in (the world) for ever", or the one vho says, "I must not forget that I am going to die and I shan't be ble to choose the day"' (p. 150). In this context, then, the spiritual haracter of Nimmo's career is to be found in the paradox that Nimmo's aroused sense of social injustice combined with his Christian fervour and reformist zeal to produce a character who eemed for a long while to forget that he was a mere mortal. Nimmo loes not realise this 'for many years', till 'the sudden reminder of nortality came to me, in my own life, at a very late date with the tunning force of a bolt from heaven, showing me at long last the pits ff my feet' (p. 150). Forced back into himself and to a recognition of he limits of political action, Nimmo is shocked back from the llusions of his earlier idealism to what he calls 'the appalling light, he challenging brutality of truth' (p. 150). That truth is the burden f *Except the Lord*: an acknowledgement of the tragic limitations of all eformist zeal, the very impossibility of a millennium on earth.

Nimmo grew up under a Christian father who had also hoped to nake the world a thoroughly happy place; but Nimmo came early o see the ultimate futility of that enterprise. A local drunk, for xample, would demand money from Nimmo's father in the name f Jesus: 'You set up for a Christian and let a man go to hell for ten shillings' (p. 2). This is moral blackmail: 'You prefer Christ, therefore you have no right to refuse anything' (p. 3). In this particular case, moreover, Nimmo's father knows that the drunk would buy more drink with whatever money is given to him and beat up his miserable wife. In other words, his Christian charity is likely to do more harm than good. The truth which Nimmo learns from this single event is that charity is not enough; that only social reform can save good men from blackmail, that the poor must be saved from having to depend on charity.

> God forbid [Nimmo says] that I should libel my countrymen, as good and true a people as exist anywhere, I am not describing faults of a character but of circumstances—the poverty that deprives, the crowding that degrades, the tensions that wear the nerves. How many gentle considerate souls were tortured day and night by the innocent exuberance of neighbours deaf to noise and blind to dirt' (p. 22).

On another occasion, Nimmo sees the relevance of this 'truth' in the performance of *Maria Marten* at the Lilmouth Great Fair. Nimmo, still a young boy, attends this performance under the influence of what he describes as a 'mysterious passion' which had seized him some days before 'to see an actor' (p. 79). He went to the performance with the habits of thought of his evangelical background, expecting the theatre to be a 'temple of lies where men and women practised feigning as an art, to deceive and confuse honest souls' (p. 83). His mood is that of a crisis—a crisis, he says, 'of conscience' in which 'fear and appetite divide the human soul so completely that there is no central point of reflection; there is no directing will within the person, and he has become a mere toy of events' (p. 83). The effect of the play which was 'sordid enough', according to Nimmo, is to draw his attention to the 'cruelest kind of wrong inflicted by the rich upon the poor', to emphasise the 'virtue, innocence and helplessness of the poor, the abandoned cruelty, the heartless indulgence of the rich' (p. 87). It fanned a feeling in him for which 'hatred' would be 'far too mild a term'. That feeling 'would not have been satisfied merely to kill. I longed to see [the exploiter of the poor] torn to pieces, to be tortured to death' (p. 88). The experience of this performance was 'decisive' in Nimmo's life. 'I have heard it said that man's first experience in the theatre opens a new world to him—it would be better to say that it destroys the old one. That half-hour in the booth at Lilmouth . . . was a decisive event in my life' (p. 88).

There are two aspects to this event. The first is this evidence of Nimmo's consciousness of class-conflict. Maria Marten thus represents the poor, and becomes an 'epitome of helpless innocence and simplicity' (p. 89). Similarly Corder, the rich man, becomes a 'common type of the village blackguard' (p. 87). Secondly, Nimmo was both repelled and impressed by the power of the popular theatre to influence people. In the recollection of old age, Nimmo still felt 'in [his] old nerves the vehement tremor of that night'.

> Is it that impersonation by itself has some secret and immemorial power over the growing spirit—some primitive urge older perhaps than humanity itself? I could not take my eyes off these strange creatures as they passed mincing, hobbling, and strutting across the boards, and disappeared again into the tent. My eyes followed them to the last coquettish flick of Maria's skirt, the last whirl of Corder's spurred heel (p. 79).

This fascination of the theatre becomes particularly important to the young Nimmo because the theatre did represent both truth and falsehood. In a sense, of course, everybody knew that the play—any play—was 'a made-up thing' (p. 88). Yet Nimmo wondered that Corder or 'any human being' could commit the villainy of murdering Maria 'and stand there before a crowd of his fellows and own it—act it' (p. 89). 'When in his soliloquies at the front of the stage, his eyes, roving over the audience, seemed to meet mine, they sent forth an indescribable thrill—it seemed that something flashed from the very centre of evil into my deepest soul (p. 89).

Hence Nimmo is fascinated not by 'the power and evil of the villain',[27] but the power of the *actor playing the villain*. He is influenced not by the crime but by the actor's temerity in admitting it 'before a crowd of his fellows'. This, in fact, is the background for Nimmo's subsequent reference to Lucifer. When Nimmo's father read Milton to his children, he would warn them against the 'charm of that evil'. 'I agreed with my father', Nimmo records, that the charm of the devil would lead to 'the absolute government of cruel and lustful egotism'. But 'Satan still carried an irresistible appeal' (p. 90). This appeal lay not so much in violence and crime but in its show of defiance: 'Some tincture of Lucifer who took upon himself all guilt and defied the very lightnings of Heaven' (p. 90). In

Corder, 'that cut-throat of a booth drama', Nimmo found 'the villain, the devil—and the hero' (pp. 90, 91).

These two insights—the class conflict, and the Satanic confidence of the hero—lead Nimmo to feel not only the injustice of the rich against the poor but the attraction of power and defiance for those who dare to use it for whatever purpose. 'Let us confess it, power itself has a fascination for the young soul in its weakness and dependence' (p. 90). What Nimmo, the 'simple, untutored son of the moors', got from the performance of *Maria Marten*, was both novel recognition of the hypnotic influence of power and the moral urge to help change the injustice of the world: on a third occasion Nimmo comes to see another aspect of this truth. The occasion is the political rally conducted by Dr Lanza. The importance of this rally derives directly from some of the implications of Nimmo's worship of the satanic actor in the performance of *Maria Marten*. Long after the performance, Nimmo 'still quivered to the mysterious power of the action' (p. 95). Nimmo called this power 'evil', and 'dreaded' it. Nevertheless he saw that it had much in common with that other power which he had seen also exercised by his father—'the spell of the orator'. 'And this was a power that could be achieved by anyone with the will and a voice, anyone capable of learning this art of stringing words together in poetic form, and striking the right attitudes' (p. 95).

Nimmo's awareness of the power of the word does not quite bring him to what he called 'my moment of illumination'. He had lived with inequality all his life and so could not immediately see how he could combine awareness of injustice with the glorious (even if potentially satanic) power of oratory. For him 'the cruelty of social injustice was swallowed up in a vaster, more dramatic, more immediate fatefulness of life itself, of arbitrary death' (p. 96). This readiness to espouse social action, and Nimmo's deep appreciation of the power of oratory explain the effect of Dr Lanza's lecture on the young Nimmo.

> What was my surprise when there sprang to the front of the platform a small fair man who, without any preliminary text, declared that for him there were no churches, no creeds, but only mankind and the soul. Even more startling to me than this unconventional beginning was the man's fervour, his dramatic gestures, the play of his voice, the indescribable spell of the true orator (p. 130).

Lanza's oratory, like Corder's acting, reached out into Nimmo's soul. Lanza's meaning, Nimmo says, 'entered into the chaos of my mind like fire and light—to sweep away the ruins of betrayed confidence, and show among the dark, still firm and fair, the roads of an ancient and noble and to my surprise, a familiar city. It was as though the order, the direction which I had needed so desperately had been all this time concealed within my own breast' (pp. 130–1). Lanza's message, in particular had a double interest. It held out hope of a means for social redress and expressed belief in the inner goodness of man. An anarchist in the tradition of Proudhon and Bakunin, Lanza held 'government and property to be the source of all evil' (p. 131). As a proto-Tolstoian nihilist, he also spoke of 'love, that family love which guarded over all childhood the love of fathers and mothers for their children, of brothers and sisters for each other' (p. 131). The one emphasis appealed to Nimmo's latent interest in social reform; the other spoke to his own family experience, to 'what was familiar to me as bread', 'an experience as deep and strong and true as it is universal' (p. 131). Cary follows this insight with a scene in which Nimmo records his first meeting with Nina. The scene is, in fact, an indirect but very pertinent comment on the very foundations of Lanza's political and moral philosophy. Nimmo is very much aware of the disparity between his station in life and that of the Latter-Slapton's. It is during this visit that Nimmo meets the young Nina Woodville whose 'splendid and curious glance', immediately reminded him of Lanza's oratory and its power. That gaze, he perceived, had 'candour and confidence' which did not arise from the 'arrogance of class' but from the 'frankness of childhood, of a soul fearless of man, because innocent of evil' (p. 134).[28] Thus, almost by accident, this childhood innocence which totally avoids class prejudices 'soothes' Nimmo's feelings and makes his meeting with Aunt Latter a fruitful one. 'I might say that to the chance entry of that child I owe all the achievement in the world for which, rightly or wrongly, I have received honour' (p. 134).

This conclusion is intimately linked with the reason for Lanza's influence on Nimmo. For although Nimmo did not have 'that other experience so necessary to judge the immediate practicality of a political programme', and lacked the 'realisation of the conflicts that arise actually from the good will in different persons having different temperaments, of the complication in all human affairs, of the place of evil in every society' (p. 135), he nevertheless could accept Lanza's thesis with confidence because it appealed to what

he knew to be 'true' 'the memory of my own childhood'. He could
thus draw from it, as the novel puts it, 'a conclusion so simple that it
seemed to place instantly within my hands a key to unlock all
problems' (p. 136). The irony in that sweeping conclusion is Cary's
not Nimmo's. Nimmo would eventually come to see his own
limitations and the impossibility of 'unlocking all the problems of
life'. But he never disowns the conviction that led him to it. But Cary
does succeed in forcing Nimmo, through that phrase, to blame
himself for falling prey to what should have been an obvious
quixotism. Cary's irony is, nevertheless, a measured one; its purpose
is to point out Nimmo's conversion to the necessity for an active
political life as opposed to the ideal Christian goodness his father
practised. In this instant, Nimmo suddenly 'discovers' a way of
redressing the injustice of the world and of applying the power of the
orator or the actor-hero to the service (so he believes) of mankind,
his new God (p. 136): 'I felt, in short, that violent agitation which
renders it almost impossible for those who have suffered such a
revolution to sit still'. Nimmo himself called this change 'a
conversion', perhaps because it had all the manifestations of the
religious conversion, 'like those converts I had heard so often cry
and groan in my father's services' (p.137).

How does Cary mean us to judge this 'conversion'? First, and
obviously, Cary is not claiming that Lanza's doctrine is the ideal.
According to Nimmo's account, Lanza's nihilism had already led to
'a long series of bomb outrages and assassinations' (p. 130). There
can, therefore, be no question of Cary's extolling it. Even so 'when
to power is added the guilt of blood, some horror of cruelty', as
Nimmo phrases it, 'its force can be hypnotic' (p. 90).

Secondly, Cary is not claiming that Nimmo accepted Lanza's
philosophy because it was 'right' but because—and here we must
learn to take Cary's use of the word seriously—it was 'true'. The
'best arguments', Nimmo maintains after the Maria Marten
episode, can achieve nothing 'if they do not strike the time and the
heart' (p. 96). Lanza's did.

> Once I had accepted Lanza's first appeal to experience, as I did
> with instant conviction, knowing its truth, I saw rise before me an
> edifice in which every part was secured by the weight and tension
> of fact, and every proportion carried the assurance of beauty, a
> vast and lofty cathedral of the spirit, which united under one
> majestic dome both my religious intuition and those vague

political notions derived from so many sources—yes, and from all
the ambition, the resentments, of a poverty-stricken childhood
(p. 137).

There is little need to elaborate on the connection between this
argument and the sources of Cary's theory of passion, reason and
conduct, nor to repeat in detail the views of politics and of art
implied in this formulation of Nimmo's defence. For the truth which
Nimmo finds in Lanza's theories is aesthetic truth, founded on a
'first appeal to experience'. Its parts are secured by 'the weight and
tension of fact' and every proportion 'carried the assurance of
beauty'. The image is architectural, but the implication is that of
the 'system', the 'complete guide' as Cary called it in *Art and Reality*.
'Men want a guide to life as navigators want a map, so that they
shan't run on destruction before they find port'.[29] Like the systems of
Plato, Hobbes, Rousseau, Hegel, Marx or Proudhon, this 'complete
guide', though difficult in some ways, is still powerful and useful to
those who find it satisfying to their idea of the good life.

Cary's attitude to Lanza's 'guide' can therefore be expected to
parallel his view of Marx's theory which (he says in *Art and Reality*) is
'a picture of the economic world and economic history rendered
harmonious and coherent by selection of those facts or apparent
facts which fitted Marx's theory of the dialectic adapted from
Hegel. It owes its power to its simplicity'. This philosophy, Cary
further states, 'inspired the most powerful and widespread social
revolution yet seen. His book became a bible to millions who carried
out his message with the ardour of missionaries, the ardour that can
be inspired only by dogma, by the assurance of truth and the
promise of paradise'.[30] And Nimmo, like his father, sought a
millennium on earth.

Finally, Nimmo's conversion involves a change in his view of the
proper relation of methods to ends. Put simply, his conversion to
Lanza's dogma meant an acceptance of the necessity for evil in the
search for political reform. This is an important point, since we
would otherwise fail to understand how Nimmo is able to maintain
his serious dedication to the ideal of brotherhood and justice while
he engaged in the deceit and the intrigue of his active political life.
We ought to recognise this 'acceptance' of politics—this marriage of
convenience, to use a phrase from *Prisoner of Grace*—as the price he
had to pay in order to attain his goal of social justice.

But as Nimmo was to realise, and as we shall soon see implied in

the very title of this novel, ends do not always justify means. Tha
they do not is, in fact, the tragedy or 'crime' which Nimmo i
confessing in his novel. We would, nevertheless, do Nimmo doubl
wrong if we read his story as if he had not already admitted to doin;
wrong in the pursuit of policies he considered necessary and
justifiable. If Nimmo compromised the absolute ideal in his searcl
for the immediate and simple truths of social action and socia
justice, it was because he believed in that 'vision of a new world is
the making, of a world of brotherhood and peace', which Nina tell
us Nimmo called the 'Cause', the vision of a 'mass of ignorance and
folly already being attacked by the heroic pioneers of the millen
nium' (p. 143). That faith saved him from unredeemed futility a
the end of his life. 'I say that, as I lie here in my bed, an old mai
condemned to a double death, of his body and his name, I am full c
faith, of hope' (p. 265).

The pattern described by this movement from early evangelica
family life to a conversion into the revolutionary anarchism o
Proudhon and Lanza is, therefore, one of spiritual growth. But thi
'growth' does not set out to characterise the forces shaping the life o
a distinguished, though controversial, politician. Cary did no
intend any such emphasis because the history of Nimmo's soul, lik
that of Nina's marriage, is only one figure in a complex pattern
because the culminating statement which *Except the Lord* make
relates more to the nature of politics in all its aspects than to th
character of Nimmo's spiritual growth, and defines its plac
alongside the social and religious developments of his times t
provoke an insight that goes beyond the personal life or the mora
growth of Chester Nimmo.

These social and religious developments not only reinforc
Nimmo's political conversion; they point to the moral argument fo
political or social commitment. One of the most vivid aspects o
Nimmo's story in *Except the Lord*, accordingly, is the hardship whicl
his family and those around them had to endure and from whicl
some of them looked up to the Second Coming for an escape. As a
child Nimmo knew of the 'fearful insecurity' of his family. 'We knev
of losses and debts, we heard talk of eviction and felt our parents
distress' (p. 4). Local people came to Nimmo's father 'not only fo;
encouragement but to beg and borrow'; and the doctrine of the
Second Coming appealed 'strongly' to such 'lost and bewildered
souls' (p. 2).

They also knew sickness and death. His mother 'overworked a

only such woman of high standard and small resources can overwork, fell ill and slowly wasted away' (p. 7). If the family had had the money to send her abroad, she might have been saved. But religious to the last, his father looked to Providence for help: 'It is not for us to question the work of Providence, the Lord gives and He takes away. You did not earn yourself, Georgy, and you would have no right to cry if you were crooked' (p. 36). Thus because of his faith, Nimmo's father shrank from the responsibility for positive action. Even Georgina, 'though she felt so strongly the want of money which deprived her mother of her chance of life, was not embittered against those who had it'; even the local community itself 'discussed' the 'sharp practice' and 'extravagances' of the local grocer, but always 'without rancour' (p. 37).

Nimmo regarded his mother, sister, and wife as the three 'noblest' women he had ever known, and this judgment is borne out in great measure by the action of *Except the Lord* and by the interplay of the actual plight of these women—especially his mother and sister—in their common dilemma as the poor. Just as Mrs Coyte's humiliation of Nimmo's mother had made his hatred of her intense and personal ('a personal feud', (p. 37), so the death of his mother made him aware not only of his own misfortunes, but of the insecurity and the anxiety which had dogged his mother's life. Her death 'struck (the family) with the force of unexpected and overwhelming disaster'; they saw in her as she lay dying 'that anxiety which had lain upon her for years grow to agonizing intensity'. 'Who could dare to estimate the depth of her longing, the earnestness of her prayer as she looked from her death bed on our five alarmed faces and asked God to watch over us' (p. 38).

Her apprehension was that of the poor, and her family knew it as such. 'The panic in our souls', Nimmo adds, pointing to the heart of the matter, was 'the sudden knowledge of tragedy that cannot be remedied, the sense already impending over us of that new dangerous world without her love that was opening now before us like the wilderness before some band of exiles' (p. 38). In Georgina's face was 'the look of confusion', or more exactly, 'a be-wilderment . . . mixed with misgivings so deep that she did not even cry' (p. 38). Poverty thus was a source of terror, 'a terror', Nimmo says, that 'overshadowed all my childhood. For the poor, it is a fearful risk, they stand always close to the precipice' (p. 41).

The truth of this observation is illustrated in Georgina who worked for Mr G, the local pub-owner. Nimmo's father hated drink as an evil, and never thought a 'child of his should ever work in such a fly trap of Satan as an inn' (p. 54). But poverty drove Georgina to Satan. Her family 'needed the money, and there was no other employment in Shagbrook which offered itself even at half the pay' (p. 55). Her father argued that 'no one needed money earned in the service of the devil and that [they] should not starve for want of five shillings a week' (p. 55). Reality was, however, on Georgina's side. Her family *needed* the money. And need *had to* win. 'Which was wrong in this battle between daughter of twelve and father of more than fifty?' the novel asks. Both, apparently; the daughter out of a dedication to one ideal—service to her family in the *only* way open to her; and her father, too, from an ideal attachment to absolute virtue even at the cost of life.

Properly seen, then, the concern for life and survival shown by Nimmo's mother and sister point to one way of looking at the political world. To accept the job at the inn, Georgina, like Lanza and Nimmo, had to put the Cause above the Moral ideal. She had to judge the 'good' which her 'sin' would involve against the 'evil' which her goodness would perpetuate. She had to chose between the good life which man can bring about, and that which Providence will command in its own good time. By implication, *Except the Lord* is arguing for the necessity of human action aimed at ameliorating the condition in which men live.

But though the novel argues this, and pits Georgina's commitment against her father's ideal virtue, it does not intend the opposition to be an inflexible and relentless one. Therefore, the novel also shows the elder Nimmo's kind of involvement in social action. In *Except the Lord*, the elder Nimmo's major political action is, appropriately enough, a mediation; but, in the world of politics and uncertainty, even this role as mediator brings him, unexpectedly, into class and labour politics. The leaders of the Tarbiton strike had asked him, 'as a respected citizen and a man well regarded on both sides', to intervene in a dispute between the officials and dissident younger strikers and their wives. He achieved a settlement among the majority of the group, but 'a minority too excited and too prejudiced to listen to him' held out and continued to fight the police. In the resulting confusion, he was knocked down and trampled upon.

The irony of the elder Nimmo's plight is not limited to this physical injury, for we are told that 'as soon as he is recognized he is arrested, as one of the miners' leaders, and carried off to the prison nfirmary' (p. 101). He refused, 'on principle' to use the strikers' money on legal fees, even though he 'had none of his own' (p. 102). Clearly, then, the elder Nimmo could not escape 'politics' by merely being good and helpful; for even his kindly willingness to be the miners' treasurer had compromised his reputation among the enforcers of the law of the rich. It had made him so even without his becoming an active participant in the revolution. The final irony of his situation is that though he would not use union funds to defend himself, Mr Newmarch and Major Udall—one a magistrate, the other related by marriage to Lord Slapton, both of them belonging to the rich class—volunteered to arrange his defence. Because Major Udall 'belonged to the same class as the prosecutor', it was assumed very reasonably that he would have means, private and public, of putting pressure on the bench'. The world, after all, was 'a issue of private and hidden relations' (p. 102).

Given this knowledge, we can see the relevance of the elaborate description in the novel of the expectation of Christ's Second Coming, and its links with Nimmo's involvement in the Tarbiton workers' strike. One of the consequences of that involvement had been that the young Nimmo was forced out of regular schooling. His father's imprisonment also made the family's poverty even more acute: 'How often', Nimmo recollects, 'did I tumble into my bunk without supper, actually without taking off my boots, certainly without washing, and all filthy still with the mud of the fields, the dung of the yards . . . I lay dirty because to be clean required an effort so great that I could not acknowledge its necessity' (pp. 104–). At the same time, however, and perhaps because of this deprivation, Nimmo begins to think of himself as grown-up enough to choose 'what knowledge he would accept' (p. 104).

It is just at this point in the novel that Cary returns to the pub-owner, Mr G, and uses his death as an occasion to introduce an account of the expected Second Coming. Cary also uses this death and the Second Coming to give direction to Ninno's search for the knowldege 'he would accept'. Since Cary's handling of these elements is typical of his kind of allusive and unobstrusive realism, we should follow this sequence carefully.

Nimmo's father, we recall, had forbidden Georgina to work in Mr G's pub. Within the community, Mr G was regarded as a special' kind of character: 'For the view in the village was that G was G. There was good and there was bad in him and it was the business of those who had dealings with him, young or old, male or female, to reckon with both' (p. 53).

Mr G, we are further told, had 'that kind of impudence' whic[h] belongs to a character who is 'sure of his power, confident of hi[s] position', and who 'for his own glory will never admit shame' (p.54[)]. This man, then, in his prosperity and his evil, defied the very laws [of] justice as God had ordained them. If drink is evil, and defiance [of] God an even greater evil, then Mr G deserved to be punished.

Mrs G, on the other hand, was a much-respected woman. A 'ver[y] handsome woman, tall, dark, with the face of a Roman empress[',] and 'indifferent to the clamour as well as the admiration of th[e] crowd', Mrs G ruled her husband's beerhouse absolutely. 'No on[e] was heard ever to swear' in her presence, and those who 'passed onl[y] once through her bar, got from her a new impression of the dignit[y] which belongs to the morally fearless' (p. 50). In a gig acciden[t] involving husband and wife, Mr G was recovered 'unscratched[',] whereas Mrs G 'was picked up quite dead—her skull was deepl[y] fractured on a stone, the only stone, so we were told, for yards abou[t]' (p. 109). The effect of this accident is to cast doubt on elde[r] Nimmo's theory of Providential justice. 'That the respected Mrs [G] should die because the disrespected G was drunk, this was a fin[e] subject for the village philosopher' (p. 109). The accident thu[s] raised questions for which the elder Nimmo had to produce answer[s.] The congregation increased, indeed, as a result of this 'judgment' o[n] the G family. Yet most of them were 'tormented deeply an[d] anxiously by a terrible question—if a good woman could die when [a] bad man was saved, where was the justice of God, where was an[y] justice—in earth or heaven?' (p. 109).

It was to answer this question that the Second Coming becam[e] such a centre of interest in the life of the community. Havin[g] despaired of earthly social justice, they looked forward to pr[o]vidential justice, to Christ's Coming. 'My father,' Nimmo relate[s,] 'offered an answer, an answer which, so he said, and we believe[d,] was to be proved within a few weeks' (p. 109). The Second Comin[g] then, was the elder Nimmo's one hope for the amelioration of th[e] human conditon around him. There is some bizarre comedy in th[is] hope, as in the actual moment of expectation. One man who ha[d] come along without a lantern had asked the elder Nimmo why the[y] 'took all the trouble to tie up the horse, for, he said, what did [it] matter if the horse strayed at this time when the world of horses an[d] mankind was standing at this door of eternity. My father made n[o] answer to this reproach' (p. 110). Then, too, the children recognise[d] a constable, 'a man known for his rough good nature and suspected for a fondness for beer'; they had not thought he, too, 'was one of the elect' (p. 111).

These comic elements have, however, to be seen as inherent in their very hope, a hope against hope. 'Did we believe then absolutely that the world was approaching its last hour?—certainly we did not disbelieve it' (p. 110). The picture of this horde of the faithful trudging to the peak of Black Man Tor to welcome Christ is more pathetic than comic; perhaps it is even tragic, because it is also potentially a comic variant of the fabled 'army of Gideon, converging for the assault' (p. 111). Nimmo in telling his story, is aware of this comic possibility and he quite persuasively puts the 'primitive religiosity' implied in the event against its proper background of social injustice and spiritual improvement. 'Those who deride our folly and credulity might ask why that poor mother among her hungry-wasted children should not believe that if Christ truly loved the poor and the outcasts He would come again to rescue them from misery' (p. 112).

The tragedy of their first disappointment at Black Man Tor has to be understood in terms of what the people had expected from it. They looked forward to it, not only in religious excitement, but also out of a desire for justice on earth. They were seeking what the elder Nimmo believed Christ would offer—God's (not Lanza's) millennium. Their particular disappointment on that occasion did not destroy the elder Nimmo's faith because he had disagreed on the date. There was still, therefore, some hope; but how strong doubt was becoming is evident from Georgina's 'angry defiance' of 'some unseen critic', and her insistence that her 'father was right—I knew he was right' (p. 115).

The failure of even the Elder Nimmo's prediction meant, in effect, the destruction of any millenial hope that Christ himself will save the poor from poverty. Nimmo calls it a 'family disaster'; it made his father 'the laughing stock in the village' (p. 121). It had two principal effects of immediate relevance to the theme of politics and the millennium. The first is that it 'nearly abolished from [Georgina's] mind all those strong political feelings which she had so suddenly revealed . . . after the fair' (p. 121). This is not surprising, since the choice is between faith in action (even Providential action) to relieve privation on the one hand and, on the other, faith in her father as a man of integrity. Georgina chooses the latter faith. To have done otherwise would have been to disown her father in his moment of crisis, especially as that crisis was brought upon him by his faith in the possibility of justice.

On Nimmo, however, the effect was different. As we saw, he was in the frame of mind, after his father's imprisonment and the accompanying hardship, to 'decide for himself what knowledge he would accept'. This episode of the Second Coming gives him that opportunity. He sees in the failure of the Second Coming a discrediting of his father's own hopes. The Coming was after all meant to resolve the theological and social questions raised by G's accident and Mrs G's death. It failed to resolve them and consequently forced Chester Nimmo into a search for some other viable truth. At this time, we should remember, he had not yet met Dr Lanza. Accordingly, the effect of the failure of his father's expectations is to encourage the loss of faith in his father's kind of millennium. It dealt 'a mortal blow' to his faith and 'removed from me my *complete* trust in my father's wisdom and so opened the way to political agitation' (p. 121).

This fact should be borne in mind if only because Nimmo himself takes issue with those of his biographers who take no account of his 'blind leap' into political activism and see his life-story 'in three parts—that of the agitator, the preacher and the statesman each of which, they say, led naturally to the next and contained all the former'.

> The agitator who learnt the art of rabble-rousing from his father passed naturally into the revivalist preacher, the preacher with his extreme Protestant and dissenting creed naturally opposed himself to privilege and entered politics to achieve the ideal of equality (p. 100).

Nimmo rejects this interpretation of his career. He objects to the attempt to see a direct and logical progression from one phase of life to another. The facts, he admits, are 'accurate', but the 'inference is wrong'. His career, Nimmo says,

> . . . resembles rather the iron crook called by shepherds a Hampshire crook; a long strong socket and a long loop ending in a sharp backward curl. The loop begins from my poverty-stricken childhood, and curves naturally, rapidly, into the phase of agitation. But the next turn, the curl, cannot be anticipated, it

does not follow. The curve was broken when I turned back, and I became a preacher not because I had been an agitator, but because I had been brought up to evangelism (p. 101).

Obviously, then, Nimmo is introducing an element of the random and the unpredictable into what seemed to most observers a logical pattern of history. He is introducing what Cary would have called the 'human element' into an ostensibly 'mechanical'—that is, predictable—situation. The povery-stricken youth (compare Georgina and Chester) does not *necessarily* become an agitator nor the agitator inevitably a statesman. Somewhere in the process there is a 'leap', a development that could never have been foreseen. This element, the novel would thus seem to argue, confounds not only the attempt to think of a personal history as logical chapters in a career, but also the attempt to see the pattern of history as a mechanical and predictable sequence. In insisting on this interpretation of his career, Nimmo is also insisting on a similar interpretation of the course of English history and politics in his generation. *Except the Lord*, Nimmo tells us, is the 'consequence' of a sudden realisation of his own mortality, the confrontation with the 'appalling light, the challenging brutality of truth'. Nimmo's hope in writing it is that it will, 'at least' 'stand to show something too easily forgotten'. namely, 'the mystery which lies beneath all history, all politics—the mighty and everlasting pressure of the soul seeking by ways unseen, and often unsuspected, its own good, freedom and enlightenment' (p. 150).

Three points in this declaration deserve attention because they are our final clue to Cary's meaning in both the novel and the trilogy. The first is Nimmo's hope that his testament will 'stand' to enlighten the world. The hope is that of the artist who believes in intuited knowledge but who knows that it has to be 'fixed' in words or symbols for it to be communicated. In that sense, Nimmo's book, which is also Cary's novel, is attempting to 'fix' that intuition. *Except the Lord* is, thus, more than an autobiography.

Secondly, 'the mighty and everlasting pressure of the soul' is directly related to Cary's idea of 'power', 'freedom' and 'creativeness' which we have already examined. Here Cary defines this creativeness as seeking 'its own good, freedom and enlightenment'. Again, the connection between this notion of the autonomous 'good' and Cary's grounds for rejecting the absolutist political theorists is very clear. For absolutist theory would fail so long as the individual soul, under this mighty and powerful pressure, is seeking 'its own' good and enlightenment.

The third point is the most important and is indeed at the heart of Cary's meaning. Granted that every soul is under this pressure to seek its own good, what becomes of politics as the organised and essentially external means of bringing about a publicly determined or endorsed good? We have seen Cary's theoretical answer to the question in *Power in Men*, his careful attempt to define liberalism so as to reduce as much as possible the conflict between the free individual soul and the mechanical and non-creative power of the state or the political machine. During the Lilmouth Fair in *Except the Lord*, Nimmo has a chance to see the possibilities of individual freedom and mechanical control. The Shagbrook community, deeply religious, meticulous and Victorian, found in the Fair its opportunity for freedom. What was 'strange' about the Fair, Nimmo recalls, was 'the sense of lawlessness, the pushing and shouting, and yet the good behaviour of most of the people'. Even at night when 'many in both sexes were now more than half drunk', the crowd remained 'extraordinarily patient', many of the men 'were stripped to the waist', and the women 'wore a single garment' (p. 75).

The scene even led him to wonder if Bunyan 'did not take old Lilmouth for a model of his fair, for we were in actual fact of "a Blood Red colour"', covered with clouds of Devon dust' like 'the children of Israel in the desert' (p. 76). The 'freedom' of the Fair held dangers as well as promises. The 'quivering lantern, the jumping flames', Nimmo claims, 'were one with us in our moment of violent life'; and gave 'an elation to our saturnalia that would not have been kindled by frigid festoons of wattage and cold eye-buring glare of the limelight'. 'It is, I believe, no sentimental illusion that mechanism is everywhere the enemy of joy: no less than the mechanical centralism of bureaucratic Utopias is the enemy of true citizenship (p. 76). What the Lilmouth Fair represents is a general dilemma. It encouraged freedom and produced 'elation'; but its moments were those of 'violent life', and Bunyan would have decried it. It was free but potentially anarchical.

The lesson which Cary draws from all this is philosophical, not programmatic. He shows the elder Nimmo (preacher), Dr Lanza (agitator) and Nimmo himself (statesman) seeking to find a millennium where the individual would be happy and free. The elder Nimmo 'took no party sides, and that was his crime, he spoke

he truth as he saw it, and that was his danger . . . He tried to save
thers from injury, and that was his own' (p. 101). Lanza cham-
ioned violence as a means to an end of the brotherhood of all men.
Ie founded his argument and policy upon the 'intuition of human
goodness' (p. 135). But after a confrontation with Pring, Nimmo
ame to recognise the inherent defect of Lanza's anarchist rev-
lutionary policy. Pring's voice, as he interrupted Nimmo's
peech, 'expressed his hearty contempt for what he called technical
oints and those who made them'.

> But what startled me still more than this scornful attitude towards
> the whole principle, as I saw it, of our democratic and
> representative constituition was his glance at me as I attempted
> to explain my grievance. In the cold stare of his blue eyes flashed
> upon me, his expression of bored and angry contempt, I
> perceived the truth about the man; a truth I had always known
> and even gloated upon, but never applied to my own case, that no
> one on earth counted with him beside the cause (p. 260).

We are thus left with the statesman, the man able to live between
he absolute pacifism of the elder Nimmo and the inflexible
nilitancy of the Pring sect. Nimmo's father 'could not utter those
olite denials and face-saving tarradiddles' which ease situations in
olite society. For him 'such statements were merely lies and could
nly increase the evil for which already we were paying forfeit'
p. 248). Yet he would not *act* to counter evil. Leaders like Brodribb
vere citing Deuteronomy and trying to implement it: 'Thou shalt
ot oppress an hired servant that is poor and needy. At his day
hou shalt give him his hire, neither shall the sun go down upon
t . . . lest he cry against thee unto the Lord and it be sin unto
hee'.[31] Others were citing Isaiah to oppose the hardline Marxists
esponsible for the strikes and the agitation (p. 246): 'Their webs
hall not become garments, neither shall they cover themselves with
heir works: their works are works of iniquity, and the act of violence
s in their hands'. Elder Nimmo, for his part, only 'reached for his
ipe' (p. 248).

Chester Nimmo tried to combine the face-saving lies of 'polite
ociety' with the selective violence of the activists. His political
conduct in *Prisoner of Grace* is not, therefore, so much a departure
rom his ideal as a deliberate choice of means; it does not argue an
nconsistency in his character but a flexibility in his thinking about

the justification of his means. His hope was that through this manipulation of people and events he would bring about the millennium.

Cary's title for this novel is an exact statement of this conclusion 'Except the Lord build the house, their labour is but lost that built it'. The Psalmist has to be understood in context. In that context the Psalm does not ask for the abandonment of all political action but for the recognition of its limitations. The 'Lord' is the omnipotent one;[32] but, as the Second Coming episode showed, He does not intervene in the affairs of men. Omnipotence, Cary claimed in *Power in Men*, does not mean 'power to do everything', but 'power to do all that is possible'.[33] In effect, then, there will never be the ideal political act, or the ideal state. All politics, in so far as it tries to cure the world of all tension, is bound to fail.

It is with this understanding of the eternal character of political uncertainty, the fact of continual turmoil, that Nimmo's own reminiscences end: ' "Here", I said, "the story began and there it shall begin again, in the things I lived with this forgotten one, in the young cruelty of the world, in the making of souls" ' (p. 276). It is with this understanding also that we are asked to confront Jim Latter's story in *Not Honour More*. For the argument of the Psalmist which denied the possibility of Nimmo attaining his millennium through practical politics also denied the ability of the man of law to prevent the creative world from seeking its own good (however bad) or its own enlightenment (however blinding).[34] 'Except the Lord keep the city, the watchman waketh but in vain'.

NOT HONOUR MORE

The solemnity of the biblical text from which the title of *Except the Lord* is taken actually masks the trilogy's furious pessimism, and suggests, in fact, that perhaps the Lord Himself will neither build nor watch the city and that any expectation of a millennium, especially a Providential one, can only be a grand delusion.

> In a moment there were half-a-dozen of these great rays irregularly spaced, piercing far up to the small grew clouds . . which now became like jewels.
> The minister had started again to pray, but even I, as I knelt there, knew that what stood before us was not the end of the world

but a fine sunrise not uncommon at that season on the high moor. Within a few minutes the sun itself appeared upon the edge of the moor like a row of sparks on a half-quenched branch. The sword-like rays faded from the air and the clouds turned from ruby, amethyst and opal to pale gold.[35]

In returning, at end of his life, to the life of the preacher, Nimmo may be suspected of meaning to return to the hope of a divine and apocalyptic assertion of temporal order. This is not the case, however. His return to preaching was his way of acknowledging the futility of his earlier attempt to bring about order by 'political' means.

Bloom calls Nimmo's reconversion a 'recourse to God', and says that Cary 'may very well be implying a specious religious con-solation in *Except the Lord*—a renunciation of the political for the religious which grows not out of conviction, but out of disappoint-ment and pique'.[36] Cary is implying something quite different. For him, Nimmo's return to the preacher's life is a recourse to the life of the spirit, especially the spirit of love. No pique is involved. The music of the great Psalm which brought about his conversion also brought with it 'a thousand remembrances' of 'vast regions of history, of his nations's glory', as a result of which he 'felt the release of a man who becomes for that moment greater than himself'. What the Psalmist had taught him was to find some 'life of soul' which would enable him endure the inevitable futility of the world's search for permanent millennial order. Such a life would be the only possible defence against the tragedy of a world in which all 'achievements' are a 'goal, or a madhouse, self-hatred, corruption and despair'.[37]

For Nimmo to return to his father's idea of order, to substitute the millennial hopes of his father for the political dreams of his middle-age would be to replace one error with a greater one. What Nimmo learns from his career and from the knowledge of his father's failure is the realisation of the limits of all ideology and the ultimate inadequacy of political action to make the world absolutely safe from evil and injustice. We are thus reminded of the song in Cary's poem, *The Drunken Sailor*

> . . . if my chaplain, learned Saul
> Thick wrapped against Polar squall
> In proofed insensity, shall call

> This way for all,
> This way salvation, this way pass
> By Hell . . .
> Then shall my bosun Fact, a lout
> That loves to knock a man about,
> Hold against his back a knife
> That when in terror of his life
> He would believe his own false pipe
> Will jag the wind out of his tripe
> And make him dream to save his breath
> And honest faith
> That pain is pain and death is death.[38]

No ideologue can ignore this harsh truth with impunity. It is the truth of this reality that is put to the test in *Not Honour More*, a watchman's story of the watchman's failure.

It would seem only logical, after the failure of Nimmo's political manoeuverings and the failure of Lanza's political theory which encouraged this manoeuvring by promising a millennium, that the trilogy would propose an alternative model of political conduct. It would seem logical, too, for Cary to place Nimmo and Nina in sharp contrast to a man of order and integrity in order to show, by the very contrast, the tragic error of Nimmo's conduct. In choosing Jim Latter as the narrator of *Not Honour More*, therefore, Cary would seem to be providing such an alternative philosophy. In *Prisoner of Grace* we were told that Aunt Latter had a high opinion of Jim: 'he was a true Latter, which was high praise'. He also had 'character, which was higher—in fact almost the highest thing that Aunt Latter could say of a man'.[39] In *Not Honour More*, Jim himself asserts his appropriately impeccable theory *of political* conduct.

> My whole case is this, that if a man or country gives up the truth, the absolute truth, they are throwing away the anchor and drifting slowly but surely to destruction. I say nothing can save but the truth and the guts to take it. For truth will always prevail.[40]

The furious pessimism of this novel (and of the trilogy as a whole) lies in Cary's judgment of this ideal. Cary does not dispute Latter's claim that 'nothing can save but the truth and the guts to take it'. But he does show in the novel that truth alone and the guts to take it may not always save either. *Prisoner of Grace* implicitly and *Except the Lord* explicitly admired Jim Latter's idealism. 'This book would be worthless,' Nimmo said of his own book, 'if it did not show how men, especially young and ardent men as I was then, come to do evil in the name of doubtful advantage'.[41] In *Not Honour More*, though with the politician's calculated irony, he repeats his tacit sympathy with the ideal of truthfulness in politics: 'Let me say that I know how to value [Jim's] sense of honour, none better. For in my long and stormy political life, and especially in recent years, I have had too much to do with the other sort' (p. 2).

In *Not Honour More*, Cary places this ideal of truth and honour in a context of personal and political activity and tests its effectiveness as a solution to the problem of order. He does so by giving its exponent the opportunity and the responsibility to secure order according to his high-minded ideal of 'honest people' doing an 'honest job' (p. 147). In the end the ideal survives only as an ideal. But so also does 'bosun Fact' that 'loves to knock a man about'. The fundamental injustice of the world, the idea of metaphysically ordained bad luck, asserts itself again at Latter's expense, and in almost flagrant disregard of the justice due to a noble and true Englishman.

The sources of this injustice or bad luck are not difficult to find once we understand Cary's idea of a world of freedom. Cary explains the fact of injustice by recourse to his idea of a world of fixed and determinate elements on the one hand and, on the other, of a variety of independent and creative wills acting on those fixed elements of the universe. One of these fixed elements is human nature, and Jim Latter's first error is to fail to take it fully into account. In the very first chapter, he is engaged in a hopeless effort to convince the world that he shot to kill Chester Nimmo in the cause of honour rather than of jealousy. Even then, he knows that an incident involving Nimmo was bound in some ways to be political: 'For many years I have considered Nimmo and his gang of a character without the first idea of honourable conduct, public or private, and this proves it' (p. 30). Jim's problem lay in his assumption that if he publicly denounced Nimmo the domestic and political issues will be resolved in his favour. Indeed, throughout the novel, he links the public and domestic aspects of his feud with Nimmo without realising the fullest implications of this connection.

I say if a murderer should be hung, which I agree to, then men like Nimmo should be hung twice over because they don't only murder people's bodies but their souls. I say it's the Nimmo gang who have destroyed all truth and honour in the country, including the sanctity of the home and marriage so that it is nothing but a jobber's match of gimme and what do I get out of it. No confidence or faith in any man and divorces running at fifty thousand a year (p. 6).

After the murder of Nina, close to end of the novel, Latter is thoroughly dissatisfied with newspaper reports of the incident in the papers. Even though he had explained to the interviewer that he killed his wife out of honour, that 'the trouble with the country was it was run from top to botton by men without honour, men on the grab', the papers ignored this larger question and concentrated on 'a lot of stuff about my devotion to my wife and my political opinions. Nothing about honour at all' (p. 308).

Jim's attempts at distinguishing between public and private politics fail, first because his intellectual analysis and his moral earnestness would not allow him to admit that his political animosity against Nimmo was in some way shaped or strengthened by Nimmo's affair with Nina, and secondly because the assumptions on which Jim based his arguments are not so eagerly shared by his more circumspect public. In fact, the outside world admired his sense of honour, but felt that, except in special circumstances, it would be suicidal to embrace it totally. For example, the newspaperman to whom he gave his Press statement would not include its first and crucial sentence in his report.

'I thought you wanted the truth and now you cut out the only important part of it. You talk about the freedom of the Press and then you say you can't give the truth.'
'I don't tell lies.'
'You make a lie if you leave out the important fact. You make me act like a lunatic.'
'It's not me—it's the law and the boss' (pp. 33–4).

What Latter is up against is clearly something larger than personal malice. He was up against part of the persistent injustice of the world. The reporters who asked Latter hard questions and called him a Fascist, a member of 'Mussolini's racket', had no personal grudges against him. It is a part of his reluctant acknowledgment of this situation that he makes that impassioned declaration on the ethics of newspaper publishing, in which, ironically he states the case for a pragmatic approach to living in an imperfect world.

> But damn it all, I know how it comes to you. A chap gets married and has kids and he wants the money, and he says to himself, 'It may be dirty work but how am I going to stop it. Who am I to stand out?' And then he says, 'Perhaps I need not eat so much dirt as some of them, perhaps I'll be able to write honest clean stuff and nobody'll notice it.' And then he goes into the job, has another kid, and by the time he wakes up and knows that he's a bug like all the other bugs, he's so jammed up with bills and worry that he don't know how to get out (p. 38).

Jim pities those who find themselves in such dishonourable circumstances, but refuses to accept their lot for himself. His hope is that if the moral indignation of those who find themselves 'caught in this slimy web that's wound itself around everything' is combined with the chivalric zeal of people like him, they could together 'blast some way out of this mess', and after that event 'wake up in God's clean daylight again' (pp. 38–9).

This project, like Nimmo's, also promises a new Jerusalem. But, again like Nimmo's, it would be wrecked by the intractable, non-mechanical fact of human nature and human society. Two short exchanges illustrate this point. First, in a scene with the reporters. Latter finds that truth has no automatic way of 'blasting some way out of the mess' of Nimmo's devious politics.

> 'Everybody knows the truth,' I said.
> 'It's only your word against his.'
> 'And your word won't make the front page,' Scoop said. And I could see in spite of them all being so busy they were amused. I asked them what was funny in a crook getting away with all his dirty work which was a danger to them and the whole country (pp. 39–40).

In another scene, Latter comes to realise that the law, too, has no sure way of bringing this about. In an interview with his lawyer, Jim reveals his deep exasperation with this situation.

Captain Latter: 'What is the good of your precious laws if they
can't distinguish between an honest man and the biggest known
liars playing the dirtiest kind of political racket ever seen
anywhere?'
Lawyer Clin: 'I am afraid the law is human and so are juries, very
human. Not to speak of judges (pp. 209–10).

Human nature, then, is at the heart of the chronic inefficiency of
the law; this same fallible human nature is responsible for the very
turmoil which the law is instituted to check. Beneath Jim's frenzied
outbursts in the novel is his high-minded determination not to
acquiesce in this inefficiency.

'I've heard that pretty often from lawyers [that juries and judges
are "human"] but what does it mean? Simply that justice is for
the crooks and liars. Ask any policeman. And you can ask yourself
why this country is in its present state of corruption and chaos'
(p. 210).

The 'truth' he ought to have derived from these encounters is that
whether he was crook or saint, he had to use all his resources of mind
and body to circumvent the limitations of the law, that mechanical
institution administered by fallible men.

Major Brightman drew Latter's attention to this truth quite early
in the novel when he pleaded with Latter to consider his next move
'very carefully' because any 'ill-considered move might well play
further into Nimmo's hand with extremely dangerous consequences' not only to Nimmo's private interests but 'the public
welfare' (p. 47). Jim Latter stuck to the 'truth'. It is the measure of
the difference between Latter and Nimmo that final praise from
Cock-Nose went to Nimmo: 'You have to take off your hat to the old
bastard' (p. 40).

Ironically, too, Latter finds himself being removed from those
very positions of authority which would have helped him bring
order to his world. When the Strike Committee asked for an
explanation for Brightman's visit to the SS *Dantzic* contrary to
official directives on such visits Latter sends in a reply which, as he
put it, 'wasn't the usual official dodgem. It was the truth' (p. 190).
But this 'truth' not only worsens his position with the Committee; it
forces him out of the local magistracy. When, as so often, this truth
fails to bring the required order, Latter is driven to fall back on

government through armed coercion. He is like the champions of state absolutism, in hating 'disorder, folly, vanity, violence, falsehood, insecurity, and ugliness',[42] and like the military in being inflexible. Jim's ultimate recourse for the solution of political and moral disorder is the gun, used in the service of honour.

I said, there's only one way out with that kind of crook, to shoot him. He may be clever and as tricky as you like but cleverness won't stop bullets. And what else can stop him, but a bullet? . . . I've been a magistrate and I've studied law and I know how important it is to make the law respected, but if the law goes against truth, then it is worse than useless (p. 42).

In the event, Latter's use of the gun only complicates the political situation and makes it necessary for the professional 'politician' to intervene. Jim himself was somehow aware of this tendency: 'I have been a soldier and do not hesitate to say about half the patrols could be avoided by use of more political officers and attending to their advice, being the men of the spot' (p. 206). In fact, Latter's account of his part in these commotions thus becomes an unwitting documentation of the limits of force as means of government and of his incomprehension of the nature of the problem he sought to solve summarily. As a champion for the rights of the Luga people, Latter had carried his just moral concern for the colonial subjects to the impractical extent of derogating the importance of economic and political development. For this he was 'hounded' out of the colonial service. Now, as a chief constable in England, he faces a public investigation for what he thought was his sincere and diligent effort to restore honesty and integrity to English public life. In this frustrated condition, Jim finds in Sergeant Varney the lone representative of his ideal Englishman.

Sergeant Varney is the watchman, the ex-solider, the man of law. He is therefore instinctively in conflict with the anarchical element in society. This is his undoing because any conflict between the Government and the rioters (however wrong the rioters may be) comes often to be seen as one more conflict between the powerless individual and the ruthless machine of the law. Nimmo knows how to exploit this kind of sentiment:

Sergeant Varney is an enemy of the people. Old soldier—brought up to butchery. Throw him into quod. Run him in for damages.

Hold him up to public disgust and contempt. Turn on the Press gent—chew him up in best printer's ink all over the world (pp. 114–15).

Even the village people of East Tarbiton are as naturally resentful of the Specials as were the Pincomb gang. The women, in particular, feeling 'fed up because they couldn't do their shopping', take out their anger and frustration on the officers, and complain about 'the prices in the market, the rents, the state of the main Lilmouth road, and about half-time at some local works' as if the officers caused them: 'I said all this was not my fault, but she went on shrieking that she'd had enough' (p. 159). 'The crowd following me and the crowd in the road then came together, and several of the younger men took up the boy's "Bash the specials. What's he doing here? Bloody Fascist", and so on' (p. 154).

In the face of this attitude in civil society towards the military man or the man of law, Latter adopts a supreme indifference to what he comes to see as the carping opinion of lesser people. Varney becomes his hero, who because he did 'a grand job and got no pay for it', represents the 'best sort' of man—the kind that 'would be ashamed to forget an obligation. Call it pride if you like, but it's not the pride that swaggers about its dignity. Just the other way. They didn't talk about personal labour. Too big a word. But they had it strong. In their bones. I was their friend for life' (p. 111).

But the context of this noble ideal in *Not Honour More* makes it totally ineffectual. Fully before us are the people and the values Latter rejects in the politics of the time—the 'crooks' who would 'sell [their] mother's skin for the ministry of piss-pots' (p. 56); the 'politics' of those whose only honour is in being able to avoid all responsiblity: 'We're a putrid lot. Let's get together and sing unto our putrefying lord the hymn of the putrid. Don't blame anyone for anything' (p. 90). Latter's own alternative solution, however, does not even offer a negative means of blasting our way into 'God's clean daylight'. And like the elder Nimmo after the failure of the expectations of the Second Coming, and Nimmo at the collapse of his Liberal government, Latter lives to see his effort at inaugurating a millennium crumble before him. He becomes aware of the tragic collapse of his dream of an army of the righteously indignant bringing back honour and order to English political life.

Sick of the gimme game, the grab boys, the bunkum and

spoof . . . It's soaked into everything. It's crept into the last
cracks. It's a bug that floats about in the air. It's a web that's tied
up people's lives till even their private thoughts are stuck up
ready to be eaten by the spider (p. 262).

That he can sense this condition of social man without reflecting
on its possible implications for the means and the hopes of the
dedicated politician and reformer, suggests an equally disconcert-
ing element in his own conception of the code of honour; which, in
turn saves us from too readily classifying his idealism as 'simple-
minded virtue'.[43] Nimmo's god, Latter says, 'doesn't need any
principles'; he doesn't need to keep his word. A god in the love
racket, turning out hot stuff for the papers' (p. 262). The conclusion
which Latter's unswerving dedication to principle imposes on us is
that any compromise with one's opponents or enemies is 'dishonourable wangling'. There can be no *honest* wangling.

The enigmatic abridgment of the last line of Lovelace's poem to
Lucasta gives us the final clue to Cary's judgment of the crucial
element in Jim Latter's philosophy. Latter founded his ideal of
honour on the same code as is implied in Lovelace's poem—'the
most beautiful and true of all poems', as he, in fact, describes it. He
copied out extracts from it in his love letters to Nina who was also
attached to this ideal. 'At ten years,' Latter recalls, Nina 'didn't
laugh at an idea because it was true and fine. It was only after thirty
years of Nimmo and London society, she found anything comic in a
word like duty and could use it to make a fool of her husband.' After
all the experience of *Prisoner of Grace*, and the realisation that the
world looked different on the inside, Nina would bring up the poem
'simply to provoke [Latter] to some word or action that [he would]
be sorry for'.—'You could not love me, dear, so much', she once told
him when Latter wanted to get back to his police offices, 'loved you
not duty more' (p. 172).

The implication is clear. The cavalier ideal which preferred
exquisite and cultivated virtue to practical and pragmatic action
cannot help appearing ridiculous in the kind of world of 'bunkum
and spoof' which Latter had to live in. The seventeenth-century
English cavalier spirit had its place and purpose. In politics it served
the king and the traditions of the country. In romance it nurtured
that exquisiteness of sentiment and loyalty to the pledged word
which was all the more remarkable because of its precariousness, its
elegant evasions.

> Tell me not, Sweet, I am unkinde,
>   That from the Nunnerie
> Of thy chaste breast, and quiet minde
>   To Warre and Armes I flie.[44]

Even in seventeeth-century England, the limitations of the cavalier tradition were as obvious as they have today become ridiculous. Against the passionate reformist politics of the Roundheads, the Cavaliers brought their highminded but ultimately reactionary loyalty to King and Church. 'I have eaten the King's bread and served him near thirty years,' one of the Cavaliers proclaimed with pride, 'and will not do so base a thing as to forsake him; and choose rather to lose my life—which I am sure I shall do—than to preserve and defend those things which are against my conscience to preserve and defend.'[45] The pride and assurance of such sentiment were now in doubt. At ten, Nina accepted that ideal without question: 'She said she would never forget it' (p. 172). But with time she reshaped it to meet the challenges of her new situation. Latter refused to change; and instead maintained what 'as a schoolboy of fourteen' his teacher had told him Lovelace's poem meant.

The abridgment of Lovelace's line to 'Not Honour More' thus allows for two conclusions. From Latter's point of view, Honour had departed from England. England was now 'so blinded and bound, so hocussed and gammoned by the bunkum boys, the smart ones' that people would think a man 'mad' because he would not live 'like a rat' (pp. 307–8). In another sense, the phrase repudiates the Cavalier ethos for being too cavalier, in the pejorative sense of that term. The phrase would thus imply that if Latter had not loved his code of honour more, he could have done more for England and for Nina.

Cary described Latter as a 'man of honour, of duty, of service, reacting against the politician'.[46] The politician, Cary says, 'is responsible for law, for physical security, and in a world of tumult, of perpetual conflict, he has the alternatives, roughly again, of persuading people or shooting them'.[47] Latter's choice is the law of the gun. The limitations of that choice are established in a spectacular confrontation between Latter and Nimmo. Trapped in bed, in a compromising incident with Nina, Nimmo is helpless before Jim's threats. Nimmo shouts at him:

> What you are is a fool. A fool and a fool and a fool. And I've had

enough of your pistol waving. I'm sick of the whole lot of you. For God's sake make a finish. Go away—or shoot . . . Now shoot, you kept ass, you hanger-on. Shoot—shoot—shoot (p. 227).

And immediately after:

Shoot—shoot—you bloody parasite. God damn your silly soul. Shoot and give me some peace. Vindicate what you call your precious honour and go to Hell (p. 228).

Without his realising it, Jim is being 'wangled' out of his just vengeance. By the sheer agility of 'political' resourcefulness, Nimmo is able to get out of a very hopeless corner. The 'political' act triumphs over the militarist threat, and Latter's idealism fails, not because its advocate is evil, but because idealism itself is in necessary conflict with facts, that is, with life. The lesson, clearly, is that politics can only hope to ameliorate the condition of man by making the world safe from human injustice, since it is totally powerless to affect the fundamental injustice of the metaphysical order.

5 Conclusion: The 'New Determinism'

Of the recurring motifs in Joyce Cary's fiction that of childhood is perhaps the most easily noticeable. *Charley Is My Darling* and *A House of Children* are devoted entirely to the evocation and characterisation of childhood. In *Except the Lord*, Cary recreates the patterns of Chester Nimmo's childhood. In *Prisoner of Grace* he introduces us to the childhood of Nina Woodville and Jim Latter. In *To Be A Pilgrim*, we have an intense recovery of an unusual childhood, and of the memories and lessons which that childhood held for the world of the narrator's dying years.

The prominence and persistence of this motif of childhood is not accidental. In part, it owes something to Cary's own childhood memories, as he himself admits in the Preface to *A House of Children*. But its sources and Cary's attachment to the motif point to his belief in the constancy of human nature from childhood to old age. Cary defines man absolutely in terms of his capacities and his tendencies rather than of his realised characteristics. Accordingly, both the child and the man have the same *kind* of power and individuality. *Power in Men* opens with such a conviction: 'The weakest child has power and will. Its acts are its own . . . It is an independent source of energy which grows with its life and ends only with death'.[1] In *Art and Reality*, Cary makes the child the prototype of the adult man. Intuitions tend to be 'evanescent'[2] in adult life, he argues, but they are still present, very much as they are in the child, and he takes this to be the only meaning in Wordsworth's speaking of intuitions fading into the light of common day.[3] We should then conclude that Cary returns to childhood, not as an escape from the world of adulthood, but in recognition of the constancy of the primal human element in the creative man.

In addition, though, the child in Cary's fiction also stands for 'uneducated' man; that is, man before he has acquired the codes of conduct and the models of thought which are part of the established or traditional order of society. Cary takes this idea quite seriously in *Charley Is My Darling* where he explores its implications for the nature and growth of the moral consciousness. Children, he says in *Art and Reality*, 'are trying to build up, each for himself, some comprehensible idea by which to guide their conduct in such a terrifying confusion'.[4] The process of growing up accordingly becomes one of adding the more complex, intellectually controlled responses of adulthood to what Cary calls the child's 'primitive equipment of aesthetic response'.[5] At the outset, the child is 'a piece of common reality of which the differentiation is simply that of one creature from another, with different potentiality and strength, different quality, as its seed belonged to a good or bad strain, but made of the same ingredients'. It is only after it has had time to 'acquire knowledge, to reflect on it, to form ideas' that it becomes an individual in the adult sense of the word.[6]

But this distinction is only true of those *acquired* ideas which can develop, as empiricists argue, over time. In other respects, there is little difference, and the child is capable not only of feeling, but of even discerning, by 'primary intuition', 'the relations in feeling'. 'Children of a year old will react at once to a mood in their mothers, even to a mood between father and mother.' Cary calls this process 'an emotional reaction in the subconscious'.[7] Accordingly, childhood becomes important as a mirror of the primary intuitions, the primitive aesthetic responses and the creative impulses common to all human nature, qualities which are not so readily recognised in adult life because of the circumscribing elements of society, decorum, religion and politics.

The persistence of this childhood motif is also related to Cary's interest in the 'natural' innocence, and the 'natural' destructiveness of man. In Cary's view, these qualities are not contradictory; they can be reconciled at the higher level of man's moral nature. In *Charley Is My Darling*, for example, Cary draws attention to the amazing capacity of the child for doing 'evil'. In *To Be A Pilgrim* and in *Except the Lord*, children are represented as destructive (or delinquent) agents. In *Except the Lord*, in particular, the young Nimmo, son of a meticulous and upright preacher, is nevertheless charmed by the destructive power of his associate, Cran, and by the violent conduct of the actor, Corder. Nimmo 'worshipped' Cran's 'stories and his ingenious tricks', the poaching raids and big forays for apples which he organised. In the world of Nimmo's childhood, 'to defy the law was brave and free'.[8]

But, also in *Except the Lord*, Cary speaks of the 'lucid gaze' of the young Nina Woodville which was 'not only the revelation of childhood's natural innocence but of qualities unique in that child—an inborn truth—an essential generosity of affection which no cruelty of fate, no bitter experience of human perfidy, could ever tarnish'.[9] The difficulty is to reconcile this *natural* innocence (it is not just innocence) with the manifest destructiveness of childhood. Cary does not always deal with this difficulty as thoroughly as he does in *Charley Is My Darling*. In *A House of Children*, for example, he uses this destructiveness and innocence as a basis for his representation of children's response to morally uncertain situations in which the children's reaction is a kind of moral perplexity which itself presumes natural innocence. In Kantian terms, this innocence is evidence of the absence of an evil will, or, perhaps more exactly, of the absence of a positive moral will. Thus, though the conduct of the children in 'causing half a ton of soot to fall on the kitchen stove and throwing the fire into the middle of the room'[10] is deliberate and evil it is, nevertheless, not the result of a deliberately evil will. Thus, also, when the children in *A House of Children* pursue their feud with Mackee and nearly drown him, they are not actually doing evil. Their spite, the narrator tells us, 'was purely ideal'. They were, Cary says, like poor children who, seeing others better dressed, 'deliberately tear each other's clothes'.[11]

Cary thus eliminates the possible contradiction of natural innocence and natural evil by making both a product of human nature seeking its own individual fulfilment. The children of *A House of Children* know their feud 'had no support from truth or commonsense', but they also suspect that they are 'in rebellion against [their] own sense of justice and decency', like 'little anti-Christs taking a pleasure in creating injustice'.[12] Cary believed enough in the fundamental 'innocence' of the child's will to make it subsume the child's capacity for evil. Cary was also sufficiently convinced of the philosophical plausibility of this view of the child to risk the statement in *Except the Lord* that he who 'founds arguments and policy upon our intuition of human goodness' as revealed in the encounter with childhood, 'will not be disappointed'.[13]

But this persistence of the childhood motif in Cary's fiction is also a reflection of his belief that childhood is a mirror of the tragic condition of man. In *Charley Is My Darling* (and *A House of Children*), we find Cary stating the moral dilemmas of the world of childhood in terms of the dilemmas of adult life. That is, he makes his children take their ostensibly petty concerns with the same seriousness, even the tragic seriousness, characteristic of the mature world. In *Prisoner of Grace*, the young Nina and the feeble Jim are used to comment on the dangers of the idealism and quixotism of the adult world. After the swimming incident early in the novel, Jim and Nina reach a point of near-alienation and hatred: 'I could not speak to him,' Nina recalls. 'We dressed in silence, sat down shivering in our wet clothes, on separate rocks, to eat our sandwiches and went home ten yards apart. I was so enraged against Jim . . . that I should have been glad if I had fallen off the cliff on the way up and killed myself'.[14] It was not 'spite', she explains, that kept her silent; 'it was a kind of heavy mass of tangled feelings which surrounded me and tied me in on all sides, so that even if I could have spoken I should not have known where to begin'.[15] Nina's crisis has two sides. One is its intense character; the other is its perplexed nature. Both qualities are also evident in Tom Wilcher's recollections in *To Be A Pilgrim*. At one time he thought of his childhood as 'peaceful and happy'. Now, he can reflect with greater insight and so understand that it was like 'the life of little foxes, wild cats, hares, does, in their savage and enchanted world'.

> They are surrounded by marvels and enormous terrors. Their eyes and ears, their secret senses, quiver to impulses unfelt even by the vixen and doe. They dart into the earth at a stroke of fancy which, to their mother, is beyond even explanation, since she herself has lost the idea of it. They rush at each other with bared teeth; they sulk; they starve themselves; they accept; they embrace the fate of the outcast, all in the same unreflective dream.[16]

Children are 'unreflective', not in the sense that they cannot compare experiences and arrange them in meaningful (that is, functional) categories, but because they lack the convenience of those predetermined categories by means of which the adult world of civil society analyses its own confusion.

Childhood is also a mirror of the tragic condition of man because the resources at the service of childhood are as inadequate for its difficulties as are those of the adult world. In *Except the Lord*, Nimmo justifies his exclusion of dialect on the grounds that, *as children*, his sister and himself expressed in dialect exactly the same feelings and emotions for which city people use standard English. His novel, consequently, is not about classes but about a world of 'human creatures under the same sentence of life, their doom and their delight'.[17] In exactly this sense, Cary means the life of his children not to represent some exotic and merely interesting kind of life, but to reflect the same doom and delight which is part of the human condition, the 'fate of the outcast'. Children, he says in this connection, may be different in that they have 'few innate pattern of conduct'. Hence their conduct may not be as habitual as it is for the educated man. In terms, however, of the universe within which the adult man lives, the 'education' of the adult is as inconsequential as that of the child. In some ways, in fact, the child has the advantage of ignorance in the absolute sense of not knowing the limitations of his own knowledge. Having been 'educated' in the complex moral and social relationships of his world, the adult man finds it almost impossible to recover his original natural innocence without disturbing those very constants of civil and moral order which age creates. In other words, adult man retains all the potential freedom and power of the child, without the actual freedom of uncoerced, non-habitual, non-moral conduct. The adult man has to save himself by a continuous act of recreation within the bounds of a large and fixed moral universe.

A second recurrent element in Joyce Cary's fiction is the first-person *apologia*. This ought really to be distinguished from the ordinary first-person narrative and understood as a form of the Confession since Cary's trilogies could have been written in the first person without their having to take on only the form of a spiritual history. Indeed, this idea of an 'apologia' is present also in the third person narratives where Cary is constantly seeking to learn why, under a particular vision, delusion, faith or arrogance, his principal characters provoke the crises of their lives. Even in the projected novel *Easy Money*, to be written in the third person, Cary sets up two characters who provide the arguments for Lord Drummer's *apologia*. One character condemns, the other defends him, and the purpose of this strategy is to know and understand the mind and soul of this principal character.[18]

Behind the idea of an *apologia*, whether self-confessed or not, there is probably the feeling that to know all is to forgive all. But for Cary understanding rather than 'forgiveness' is the true purpose of confession. The empiricist's argument that if we knew *all* the circumstances of a character we could reasonably predict his actions assumes a constant human nature by the laws of which men invariably acted and on the basis of which all their actions—especially their wrong actions—could be understood. We may never know *why* a character chooses one ideal rather than another. But we can show how the actions of a character conform to a discernible common ideal, a metaphysical disposition which generates the interior passion for self-sustenance of which the concrete ideal is a manifestation.

Cary's *apologia* is accordingly aimed at the justification not of the particular act but of a primary impulse. A sense of tolerant understanding is implied in this attitude, and this may be another way of 'forgiving'. If so, Cary's forgiveness is aimed not so much at exonerating the individual as humanity at large. Its purpose is to point up the precariousness and the fallibility of our human condition through an identification in the *apologia*.

There would seem therefore to be more than purely technical reasons for Cary's adoption of the first-person narrative device. For the device makes it possible for the form and the spirit of the novels to coincide; for the *apologia* to be presented in person. Cary combines the aesthetic and the philosophical intentions of his art in this form, each novel, that is speaks directly from the horse's mouth. It is not accidental that Cary's best fiction is written in this style. The problem which he faced in *Castle Corner* of doing justice to his philosophical intuition about the 'springs of action' is solved, in the trilogies, by his use of the *apologia*. The *apologia* gave him the technical means to tell his story, and the medium in which the narration would be based on his philosophical assumptions.

It should be noted that though, as *apologia*, these novels plead for public understanding, they are very proud documents indeed. Sara Monday is repentant in *Herself Surprised*, but her confidence in herself and in the value of her contribution to life is unshaken. Tom Wilcher is humble in *To Be A Pilgrim* but he is not supine. Gulley Jimson in *The Horse's Mouth* is defiant because he knows the world is hostile to him. He writes his story, nevertheless, in utter disregard of the world's indifference and hostility. In *Prisoner of Grace*, Nina labours under a public misunderstanding. She, too, judges herself a kind of failure. But she has faith enough in herself and in her part in the career of Chester Nimmo to feel that the world ought also to be forgiven its inability to understand the subtleties of human life. This pride, this inner sense of innocence, is important. It is an essential part of the *apologia* itself—defence through confession of error based on a supra-conventional criterion of judgment. 'I have nothing of a saint about me,' Cardinal Newman wrote, 'and it is a severe (and salutary) mortification to be thought next door to one. I have a high view of things, but it is the consequence of education and a peculiar cast of intellect—but this is very different from *being* what I admire.'[19] Instead of being charged with evil, Cardinal Newman is 'accused' of saintliness. His 'defence' is proud in the spirit of the *apologia*. It is a revelation of the soul; it is neither defence nor self-indictment, though it partakes of both.

Without meaning to suggest a necessary connection between Cary's novels and the classic confessions or apologia, we could nevertheless point to a common element which these confessions share with Cary's work, namely the paradox of man's noble nature and his meagre abilities. Shared by these confessions and by Cary's novels is this tragic sense of man as both god and beast, divine and graceless. Man, St Augustine confessed, is 'but a tiny part' of all that God created: 'He bears about him his mortality, the evidence of his sinfulness, and the evidence that Thou [God] *dost resist the proud*: yet this tiny part of all that Thou hast created desires to praise [Him]'.[20] In *Except the Lord*, Nimmo reflects on his career and on the failures and the hopes of his political life and concludes that man 'is a mystery and his destiny is hidden in a depth of time beyond imagination'.[21] The tragedy of man thus becomes the tragedy of his very nature and the mystery of humanity also the mystery of each individual man.

Out of this combination of mystery and tragedy arises the universal expectation of sympathy for those who confess their failures and their idealisms. Such an expectation of sympathy, such an identification with defeated man, is undoubtedly implicit in the notion of a tragic catharsis, or the recognition through pity and fear of the pathos of man's worth and man's doom. It is, indeed, such a feeling of sympathy in a common predicament that gives dignity to these confessions. George Eliot, it would seem, received Newman's confession in this spirit of fellowship and shared tragedy. *Apologia Pro Vita Sua*, she wrote, 'now affects me as the revelation of a life—how different in form from one's own, yet with how close a fellowship in its needs and burthens—I mean spiritual needs and burthens'.[22] There is reason, therefore, to read Cary's *apologia* for his characters as intended to produce a parallel response in us and, beyond that, to point to the inescapably tragic spiritual condition of all humanity.

We have seen the actual forms which this human failure takes in the novels, and noted the violence, death, frustration and anxiety which are the consequences of this failure. The really significant point, however, is to see how this deep sense of failure fits into the unusually exuberant and comic action of these novels, to understand how Cary meant us to harmonise the tragedy of inner life with the outward comedy of the observed life.

There are many ways of looking at this duality. We could, for example, regard the comedy as intended to lighten the seriousness of the major theme. Such a view would, however, belie the pervasiveness of the comic manner in the novels and give the impression that the comic scenes are only used, and deliberately so, to 'punctuate' sustained serious episodes. This is clearly not the case. We could also consider the duality of comedy and tragedy as reflecting patterns in postwar British fiction. As James Hall has argued, this fiction has been able 'to absorb with some cheer the shocks that elsewhere have produced a sophisticated hell-fire-and-salvation brand of existentialism'. The British novelists of this period, he further argued, knew 'about' the Absurd 'before it became a philosophical term'. They 'speak for a precarious sanity that can face horrors and retain some self-command; they speak for the human element which does not quite accept the logic of the terrors it has proved'.[23] But this view will not differentiate between the 'absurdity' of—say, Beckett and Waugh—from the 'fearful joy' of Cary's novels.[24] And unless this differentiation is made, we will miss the important fact that Cary's characters are in conflict not with society, in the institutional sense, nor with themselves (there are few introverts in his novels) but with Existence, with the fundamental mode of all life. For this very reason, in fact, we cannot even explain Cary's comedy in terms of Dickensian comedy and pathos, since unlike Dickens, Cary never links his pathos with social satire or criticism. Concentrating on the individual soul and assuming that society (as the fixed and mechanical part of the world) will always restrict the freedom and activity of that soul, Cary can detach his pathetic scenes from specific criticisms of society in a way Dickens, for his own good reasons, never would.[25]

James Hall's statement that Cary's novels could all begin with the presumption that 'directed restlessness is the hope of the age' offers nevertheless a fruitful approach to the duality of comedy and tragedy in Cary. Hall understood Cary as saying, in effect, that 'if restlessness is really basic human nature, then people can make common cause with surprise because it is what they too seek'.[26] We have already seen Cary's metaphysical arguments in *The Horse's Mouth* and in his non-fictional prose for this view of 'restlessness'. We can still extend Hall's statement and claim that not only is it commonsense to make 'common cause with surprise', it is virtual death not to.

The seriousness of this alternative consequence is an important one. It means that the exuberance of man's conduct, his restlessness, is not only a convenient or opportune way of pleasing himself, but also an enforced activity, a gesture of survival. Cary's comedy has to be understood in this light. For him, comedy results from the action of men in response to the practical advantage of making 'common cause with surprise', and the absolute need to avoid 'death' by making such a cause. The comedy thus resides not so much in the hilarity of the act, but in the discrepancy between the mortal necessity which induces it and the assurance and sense of wellbeing which the actor derives from it.

Cary's comedy is accordingly exuberant, even ribald, but very dark. In *Prisoner of Grace*, Nina describes an occasion when 'a rather important gentleman, dressed to the nines, in the piazza, had his new top-hat blown into the lagoon'. 'I was sorry for the poor man,' Nina admits, 'because he looked so foolish, and, after all, he dressed up for some important occasion, and it is right to dress up for them.' The comedy of this scene does not lie in the social embarrassment, as it would be in a comedy of manners. The gentleman's discomfiture is spiritual and, in its own way, tragic. Chester, we are told, 'roared with laughter', and 'he laughed till he cried'. Chester recognised a fundamental injustice in the man's condition—'You must admit the gentleman was a little too pleased with himself'.[27] But Nature, in utter disregard of this mood, wrecks the man's pride in a manner beyond his powers to counteract. Obviously the comedy resides in this ability of the world to make a fool of man. By laughing to tears, Chester was also, unconsciously, recognising this dark comedy.

This comic disposition has a natural affinity with Cary's sense of tragedy already discussed. 'I had waked up to the fact,' Cary says in the Preface to *Aissa Saved*, 'that the innocent may suffer the utmost misery; that there is such a thing as bad luck'.[28] Dark comedy is a recognition of the fact of bad luck by a man who also knows the destructiveness of the world's injustice. In a true sense, the gentleman with the top hat at the piazza is suffering from the same principle of life as those many good men who are shipwrecked through no fault of their own.[29] Accordingly, there is a combination of exultant joy and deep pathos in Cary's thinking about life. It is not surprising that his chief interest, as Miss Starkie tells us, should naturally become that of 'discovering why—as he said—"all men do not cut their throats", or . . . what was their particular brand of anaesthetic, or opiate, which made bearably for them the painful operation of living'.[30] It is not fortuitous that Rozzie, the comic extravagant of *Herself Surprised*, and Pinto, the ridiculous schoolmaster of *A House of Children*, are Cary's spokesmen for the necessity of the opiate of dark comedy. 'All in crimson and mauve'—and 'awful'—Rozzie was nevertheless happy that she 'at least' made 'a splash'. 'If I can't die happy,' she says, 'I won't go out howling.'[31] 'Don't let them sit on the safety valve,' Pinto warned the narrator of *A House of Children*, 'it'll stop your engine altogether.'[32] Gulley Jimson, it need hardly be said, is the triumphant and tragic embodiment of this response to the 'painful operation of living'. As Cary says of him, Gulley Jimson 'makes a joke of life because he dare not take it seriously'.[33]

It should be possible now to give a specific definition to that 'pervading sadness' which Enid Starkie called Cary's 'real philosophy'. We should call it the 'new determinism', as a way of linking it with that determinism in Hardy and Dreiser with which Cary sympathised. By calling it 'new' we would be distinguishing its roots from the Darwinism foundations of that naturalist school. Like Hardy and Dreiser, Cary had a pessimistic view of life, a sense of futility in man's life and man's hopes. Unlike them, however, Cary founded this determinism on a metaphysical view of existence itself rather than an assumed conflict between man and nature. This difference between Darwinian and existentialist determinism eliminates the tight-lipped and heavy seriousness of both Hardy and Dreiser and allows Cary that freedom to present the comedy of life as a vital and inevitable aspect of existence. Hence his tragedies are never the product of a specific social or environmental conditions. And because, for him, environment is not the determining tragic factor, Cary can do what he claims Hardy never could do—'bear the complacency, the self-satisfaction of the world'.[34]

Cary's 'new determinism' is able to live with both the tragedy and the complacency of the world. In accommodating both, Cary is able to achieve a new kind of tragic end, the falsely-comic, tragic conclusion. In his very first novel, his heroine, Aissa, is eaten up by ants while she experiences an obviously flamboyant heavenly procession in which she and her son participate. In *An American*

Visitor, Bewsher dies as if for a joke: 'he fell on his back with a look of ludicrous amazement and indignation'. When Stoker recovers what are claimed to be Bewsher's remains, he finds a 'smashed and mummified head, a horrible object whose bare-tooth grin made even Stoker feel uncomfortable'. One femur is clearly not Bewsher's. It is 'certainly goat'.[35] In *The African Witch*, the hero Aladai dies shouting 'something', nobody knew what, about his fatherland. His followers are all killed soon after him: 'they came within twenty yards before they were disposed of'.[36] Johnson's death in *Mister Johnson* is similarly a classic case of a hero ending without fanfare. It makes Rudbeck feel 'a peculiar relief and escape, like a man who, after a severe bilious attack, has just been sick'.[37]

The same pattern appears in his major fiction. Sara Monday's death in *Herself Surprised* is as accidental as it is uncelebrated. Tom Wilcher's in *To Be A Pilgrim* is not even recorded. Gulley Jimson's fall in *The Horse's Mouth* is a hilarious catastrophe. It is the culmination of a life-long scepticism about heroism, in the world's sense of it. In the political trilogy, Nina is killed, as she feared she would be, for her devotion to Nimmo's ideal of politics; and the circumstances of her death are deliberately and mockingly chivalric. 'I said it was for her to forgive me,' Jim Latter relates, 'and I finished the thing in one stroke. She fell at once and did not struggle at all.'[38] Latter, in turn, is looked upon as 'mad' because, in his words, he 'wouldn't live like a rat'. *Not Honour More* is his statement, 'so help me God, as I hope to be hung'.[39] Nimmo, the central figure of this trilogy dies a most ignominious death. 'It is a small point,' Latter says, "but you never read anywhere that Nimmo died in a W.C. What the papers said, he was found dead at Palm Cottage after a heart attack.'[40] Cary's critics have taken the matter more seriously: 'Surely', John Telling argues, 'this is a comment by Cary on what the man [Nimmo] had come to'.[41] Against the background of Cary's other unheroic deaths, it would seem dangerous and even wrong to see this death as a comment aimed directly at Nimmo's life. By the same token, it would seem more relevant to regard it as part of Cary's image of unheroic humanity, as a comment on Man rather than on individual men. The conception of fundamental injustice in Cary's metaphysics totally excludes poetic justice.

Cary calls this new determinism the 'curse of Adam': 'You can't get away from it in this fallen world'.[42] *The Horse's Mouth* describes this curse as the 'fall into manhood, into responsibility, into sin. Into freedom. Into wisdom. Into the light and the fire'.[43] In another formulation of this idea, Cary says that man's tragedy is linked with physical and imaginative labour:

It's all work, work. The curse of Adam. But if he doesn't work, he doesn't get anything, even love. He just tumbles about in hell and bashes himself and burns himself and stabs himself. The fallen man—nobody's going to look after him. The poor bastard is free—a free and responsible citizen. The Fall into freedom.[44]

In such circumstances, what hope for order? Obviously none. What remedy? Cary returns to his metaphysics for an answer based on that idea of human progress of which Mark Schorer makes such fun. Cary's answer, Schorer says, speaking of *A Fearful Joy*, 'would seem to be that there is a hundred years of uneven history, and that, trusting to our instincts, we may certainly expect to endure a hundred more'.[45] Cary meant that and more. First, in a negative formulation, Cary argues: 'What I want to suggest is that the situation (today) is neither so bad as it looks, nor so new . . . Call this a circle, but it is not a vicious circle. It is the hope of the world'.[46] More positively, Cary restates his ideal of the creative imagination. With such an imagination, one can, like Bruno, make 'the world too wide for theologians'.[47] Villon shivered 'blue as air' as the hangman lashed him.

> And yet by genius (unearned grace)
> The grin that cricks his pain-wet face
> Makes Parliament a mummy case
> For painted dust,
> The court's expedient trust
> And law itself an epithet's grimace
> Dressed up in wig and lace
> The better to appall
> Phantoms thrown upon the wall
> Of its own terrors (p. 13).

So, too, though 'wasted' with consumption, Molière could make sport of both king and commoner.

> Consumption jeers, with bloody breath,
> I am your genius, and your death (p. 13).

Cowper whose sigh was 'fainter than the breath of wren or vole' still 'spoke lightning to the souls' (p. 19). And from 'carrion earth's black lips', out of 'death's very might', Shelley fashioned a 'living beauty'

> Whose virgin throat, quick plimming to his eye
> Promises innocent Eden, see him fly
> To throne her in the bride house of a song
> Queen of all peace, the love that knows not wrong
> Of difference or pain (pp. 21–2).

Dickens used his 'ballad' novels to break the gods

> Where knights pine to the tales
> Of new crusades and a deliverer's glory (p. 24).

Dostoievsky wept 'in his own breast' that Russia was but the idiot's kingdom. So he wrote his 'saint-king's' stories about 'an idiot tumbled in a sea of powers'.

> Who jibbers in his trance of agony
> The word of mastery
> An angel's incarnation
> To make the world one brother nation
> And God a Russia (p. 24).

Some, like Tolstoy, in desperation for man, when the world had 'shrunk to be a garden', learnt 'to grow into a monk'

> And build himself a desert where
> Cut flowers fermented into prayer
> Can bring him drunkard's powers to charm on air
> Heavenly kingdom proof against all fate (p. 29).

Cary's creative imagination is thus the will to live in spite of the world, the acceptance of life rather than the world. In his view, this is the only hope for man. In darker moments, also moments of dark comedy, Cary can relate this creativeness to the comic desperation of man. 'Haul, sing, ye fainters', Cary's sailor admonishes the crew in *The Drunken Sailor*.

> If your guts,
> Drowned in spleen against the fate
> That sends you still to navigate,
> From their worn-out moorings part,
> Sing yourselves another heart (p. 60).

Or:

> Pump, pump, ye dogs, tho' vain
> You burst your hearts, though every way is pain
> But death, my spleen shall flog you from that bed
> Where rest like hundred justice chokes in lead,
> Sing, sing, ye convicts drunk with mortal spite
> .Against immortal nothing's idiot might (p. 62).

In *The Drunken Sailor*, Cary put the 'lost souls' and 'brash swankers' of the ragged privateer to the test of an attack from a modern battleship. The privateer survives. Their 'wits were all their cash'; they were 'poets, spellbinders primed to flash'

> The tale
> That sings them into hell and out of goal (p. 5).

Like humanity they are damned to the ordeal of existing. To survive they will have to sing themselves to death—'we shall sing', they say, 'because we're damned. We take damnation for our star to light the dark' (p. 8). Cary's characters all address themselves to this universal dilemma and they succeed or fail according to their ability to confront their fate as 'damned' beings with the creative resources of the man of imagination. It is to Cary's credit as artist and thinker that his metaphysics could persist so intensely in all his work without overshadowing the immediacy of life which is, for him, the heart of fiction.

'I do not want to start by saying "This novel is a metaphysical construction based on a comprehensive idea of life" Cary told Mark Schorer, for the critics 'will stop entering into my characters' lives and instead treat the book, if they tackle it at all, as a kind of crossword puzzle—they will imagine an allegory and I detest allegory—my people are real people or they are nothing'.[48] The danger so far has been of another kind—in his critics' assuming that Cary is not seriously philosophical. 'You can depend around here on practically everyone's having read *The Horse's Mouth*,' the *Paris Review* interviewers proudly assured Cary. 'Do you think that's because it's less philosophical? Or just because it's a Penguin?'

Cary: 'The Horse's Mouth is a very heavy piece of metaphysical writing. No, they like it because it's funny. The French have detected the metaphysics and are fussing about the title . . . ,

Interviewers: 'A metaphysical work?'[49]

Notes and References

CHAPTER I

1. For critical studies of Joyce Cary's fiction, see Bibliography.
2. Enid Starkie, 'Joyce Cary: A Portrait', in *Essays by Diverse Hands, Transactions of the Royal Society of Literature*, new series XXXII (1963), 128.
3. Robert Bloom, *The Indeterminate World: A Study of the Novels of Joyce Cary* (Philadelphia, 1962), pp. viii, vii.
4. Quoted in George Steinbreacher, Jr, 'Joyce Cary: Master Novelist', *College English*, XVIII (May 1957), 389.
5. F. Copleston, *A History of Philosophy*, Vol. VI (New York, 1960), p. 392.
6. *Critique of Practical Reason and other Works on The Theory of Ethics*, translated T. K. Abbott (London, 1909), p. 191.
7. Quoted in Kenneth Burke, *A Grammer of Motives* (New York, 1945), p. 197.
8. *Art and Reality: Ways of the Creative Process* (New York, 1961), p. 20.
9. See *The Critique of Judgment*, where Kant tried to bridge the gulf between the mechanistic world of Nature as presented in physical science and the world of morality, freedom and faith. It is 'worth noting', Copleston remarks (*History of Philosophy*, Vol. V, p. 209), 'how deeply Kant was concerned with the reconciliation of the scientific outlook with that of the moral and religious man'.
10. *Writers at Work*, the *Paris Review Interviews*, edited Malcolm Cowley, (New York, 1958), pp. 61–2. In *Power in Men* (p. 20), Cary makes the same point: 'Scientists deal in abstractions. They are obliged to treat nature as a mechanism even though they assume that their own minds, which are part of nature, are not mechanical'.
11. *Writers at Work*, p. 55.
12. Ibid., p. 55.
13. Letter to Mr Hughes quoted in Charles G. Hoffmann, *Joyce Cary: The Comedy of Freedom* (Pittsburgh, 1964), p. 2.
14. 'On the Function of the Novelist', *New York Times Book Review* (30 October 1949), p. 1.
15. *Art and Reality*, pp. 42–4.
16. Walter Allen, *Joyce Cary*, rev. ed. (London, 1954), p. 8.
17. Enid Starkie, op. cit., p. 128.
18. *Tristram Shandy* (New York, 1925), p. 5.
19. John Traugott, *Tristram Shandy's World: Sterne's Philosophical Rhetoric* (Berkeley, 1954).
20. Ibid., p. xv
21. *Art and Reality*, p. 118.
22. Dorothy Van Ghent, *The English Novel: Form and Function* (New York, 1961), p. 267.

23. I use the word 'ostensible' because the intellectual quality I am speaking of i distinguishable from 'real' quality which can be present whatever the nature of the hero.

24. *Tristram Shandy*, p. 7.

25. *Except the Lord* (New York, 1962), p. 150.

26. *Castle Corner* (London, 1952), p. 6.

27. *Adam International Review*, XVIII (November–December 1959), 18.

28. See *Writers at Work*, p. 58: 'Kierkegaard states the uniqueness of the individual and I stand by that'.

29. *Adam International Review*, XVIII (November–December 1959), 18.

30. 'The Way a Novel Gets Written', *Harper's* CC (February 1950), 91.

31. Preface to *The First Trilogy* (New York, 1958), p. x.

32. Jean-Paul Sartre, *Being and Nothingness*, translated Hazel E. Barnes, (New York, 1956), p. 439.

33. *Philosophical Works*, edited T. H. Green and T. H. Grose, (Aalen [Germany], 1964), Vol. II, pp. 22–3.

34. *Art and Reality*, pp. 37–9.

35. *Writers at Work*, p. 58.

36. *Art and Reality*, pp. 37–8.

37. Bloom's title for the first chapter of his book is 'The Reluctant Sage'.

38. *Art and Reality*, p. 15.

39. Ibid., p. 27.

40. *Art and Reality*, p. 27. See Sterne's comic treatment of this point in *Tristram Shandy*, ed. cit., p. 395: 'I love the Pythagoreans for their "getting out of the body, in order to think well". No man thinks right, whilst he is in it, blinded as he must be, with his congenital humours, and drawn differently aside, as the bishop and myself have been, with too lax or too tense a fibre—Reason is, half of it, Sense; and the measure of heaven itself is but the measure of our present appetites and concoctions'.

41. *Art and Reality*, p. 44.

42. *A Treatise of Human Nature*, Book I (New York, 1962), p. 113.

43. Malcolm Forster, 'Fell of the Lion, Fleece of the Sheep', *Modern Fiction Studies*, IX (Autumn 1963), 257.

44. *The Philosophical Works*, ed. T. H. Green and T. H. Grose (Aalen [Germany], 1964), Vol. I, p. 533.

45. Ibid., Vol. I, p. 534.

46. Ibid., Vol. II, p. 189.

47. Ibid., Vol. IV, p. 78.

48. *Power in Men* (Seattle, 1963), p. 7.

49. 'Appendix', *A Treatise of Human Nature*, edited D. G. C. Macnabb (New York: Meridian Books, 1962), p. 328.

50. *Critique of Practical Reason and Other Writings in Moral Philosophy*, translated and edited L. W. Beck (Chicago, 1949), p. 276.

51. *Critique of Practical Reason and Other Works on the Theory of Ethics*, translated T. K. Abbott (London, 1909), p. 67.

52. Cf. F. Copleston, *A History of Philosophy* (London, 1960), Vol. VI, p. 333: 'Obligation, "ought", implies freedom, freedom to obey or disobey the law'.

53. *Power in Men*, p. 256.

54. Ibid., p. 255.

55. Edward Caird, *The Critical Philosophy of Kant* (Glasgow, 1909), pp. 246–7.
56. *The Indeterminate World*, p. 27.
57. *Critique of Practical Reason*, translated T. K. Abbott, p. 67; p. 73–4; 334.
58. *Power in Men*, pp. 2–3.
59. See Hazard Adams, 'Introduction', *Power in Men*, pp. x–xi.
60. Following Cary's article, 'Horror Comics' in the *Spectator* (1955) a correspondent complained that Cary's attitude was 'all too reminiscent of those "liberals" who in the last century opposed any restrictions on children's hours of work or employment in the mines and factories with just the same specious arguments' (*Spectator*, 18 March 1955), p. 320.
61. *Joyce Cary*, Cary, p. 37.
62. Ibid., p. 265.
63. Ibid., p. 266.
64. *Critique of Practical Reason*, translated T. K. Abbott, p. 122.
65. *Power in Men*, p. 7.
66. *The Case for African Freedom*, p. 131.
67. *Power in Men*, p. 1.
68. Ibid., p. 76.
69. Ibid., p. 7.
70. Ibid., p. 334.
71. Ibid., p. 40.
72. Ibid., p. 94.
73. *The Case for African Freedom*, p. 14.
74. *Power in Men*, p. 35. Elsewhere he states the same thesis with regard to economics: 'The word "economy" must not hide the reality of a social order which is not fundamentally economic. Men and women are not units in an economic structure, they are living souls who are ready often to ignore even the primary needs of their bodies for some ideal satisfaction; glory or learning, religion or beauty' (*The Case for African Freedom*, p. 132).
75. Ibid., p. 35.
76. *The Case for African Freedom*, p. 131.
77. See *Power in Men*, pp. 38–9 for the four 'systems'.
78. *Power in Men*, p. 76.
79. Ibid., p. 243.
80. 'A Note on Joyce Cary's Reputation', *MFS*, IX (Autumn 1963), 207.
81. Enid Starkie, op. cit., p. 127.
82. *Power in Men*, p. 29.
83. 'The Sources of Tension in America', *Saturday Review* (23 August 1952), p. 35.
84. References are to the Anchor edition (New York, 1961).
85. See Enid Starkie's testimony, 'Joyce Cary: A Portrait', pp. 136–7: 'Joyce Cary was a very great craftsman in fiction' and used to 'discuss the technical aspects of his art, and his way of solving the problems which arose'. But he did not lecture on this 'very often, as he much preferred to deal with philosophical and abstract themes'.
86. Leo Tolstoy, 'On Art', in *What is Art and Essays on Art*, translated Aylmer Maude (London, 1929), p. 61.
87. Ibid., p. 51, footnote 1.
88. Ibid., p. 52.
89. Ibid., p. 53.

90. 'What Is Art?' in Tolstoy, op. cit., p. 161.
91. *Art and Reality*, p. 108. Cary's papers at the Bodleian (now being re-catalogued) contains an extended essay on Tolstoy's theory of art and other evidence of his familiarity with Tolstoy's essays.
92. Ibid., pp. 103, 104.
93. 'What Is Art', in Tolstoy, op. cit., p. 123.
94. In 'On Art' (op. cit., p. 53), Tolstoy spoke of the 'capacity' of men to be 'infected' by the feelings of others, and of 'a certain hypnotism' between human spirits. These Christian and mystical qualities, he believed, made communication between artist and reader both desirable and possible.
95. *Art and Reality*, p. 20.
96. Ibid., p. 20.
97. Ibid., p. 15.
98. Ibid., pp. 17–18.
99. Ibid., p. 16.
100. Benedetto Croce, *Aesthetic*, translated Douglas Ainslie (London, 1929), p. 8.
101. Cary's summary of Croce's argument. See *Art and Reality*, p. 16.
102. *Art and Reality*, p. 17.
103. Ibid., p. 28.
104. Croce, op. cit., p. 79.
105. For Croce's anti-Kantian attitude, see his *History of Aesthetics* (London, 1929), especially chapter 8.
106. Kant, quoted in Israel Knox, *The Aesthetic Theories of Kant, Hegel and Schopenhauer* (London, 1958), p. 37.
107. Kant, in Knox, op. cit., p. 36.
108. *Art and Reality*, p. 31.
109. Ibid., p. 22.
110. Ibid., pp. 22–3. See, in addition, *Art and Reality*, p. 22: 'We are almost entirely cut off from each other in mind, entirely independent in thought, and so we have to learn everything for ourselves. Hume pointed this out in his *Enquiry Concerning Human Understanding*, published in 1748, and no philosopher since has found an adequate answer to him'.
111. *Art and Reality*, p. 24.
112. Ibid., p. 29.
113. *Critique of Practical Reason*, translated L. W. Beck (Chicago, 1949), pp. 179–180.
114. Croce, op. cit., pp. 34, 68–70.
115. *Art and Reality*, p. 29.
116. Ibid., p. 117.
117. Ibid., p. 116.
118. Ibid., p. 189.
119. Ibid., p. 89.
120. Ibid., p. 90.
121. Ibid., p. 89.
122. Ibid., p. 20.
123. Ibid., p. 190.
124. Ibid., p. 191.
125. Croce, op. cit., pp. 34–5.
126. *Art and Reality*, pp. 168, 169, 167.

127. *Art and Reality*, p. 179. Cary does not accept Kant's 'categorical imperatives'. But he follows the Kantian line in rejecting the mechanism of allegory. The correspondence between Cary's view of allegory and Coleridge's is thus significant. 'Allegory', Coleridge claimed, 'is nothing but a translation of abstract notions into a picture language which is itself nothing but an abstraction from objects of the senses'. The symbol, however, 'partakes of the reality which it renders intelligible; and while it enunciates the whole, abides itself as a living part in that unity, of which it is representative'. *Statesman's Manual*, in *Works*, edited W. G. T. Shedd I (New York, 1884), p. 437.

128. *Art and Reality*, p. 180.

129. Ibid., p. 183.

130. Ibid., p. 183.

131. Ibid., p. 190.

132. Ibid., p. 190.

133. Ibid., p. 184.

134. Ibid., p. 179.

135. Ibid., p. 179.

136. *Castle Corner*, Carfax edition (London: Michael Joseph, 1952), p. 5.

137. *Castle Corner*, pp. 6–7.

138. Ibid., p. 7.

139. Ibid., pp. 7–8.

140. Ibid., p. 6.

141. Ibid., p. 8.

142. Ibid., p. 5.

143. *Art and Reality*, pp. 155, 191.

144. Ibid., p. 156.

145. Ibid., p. 185.

146. See, however, Kenneth Hamilton, 'Boon or Thorn? Joyce Cary and Samuel Beckett on Human Life', *Dalhousie Review*, XXXVIII (Winter, 1959), 433–42. It is interesting to note that Cary has been linked with the 'religious' novelists by Douglas Stewart (*The Ark of God*, London, 1961) and with the 'tragic comedians' by James Hall (*The Tragic Comedians*, Bloomington, 1963).

CHAPTER 2

1. Preface to *Charley Is My Darling*, Signet edition (New York, 1963), p. x.

2. Ibid., p. vii.

3. *Charley Is My Darling*, Signet edition (New York, 1963), pp. 16–17. Subsequent references are to this edition and will be cited in parentheses in the text.

4. Cf. *Power in Men*, p. 155: 'Evil is real. A cancer that kills the young mother of a family is a real evil. A brute who cripples a child for life does real and irreparable evil'.

5. C. Northrop Frye, *Anatomy of Criticism* (Princeton, 1957), p. 192.

6. See, however, R. W. Noble, *Joyce Cary* (Edinburgh, 1973), p. 38: 'In Western culture the figure of the bull has usually epitomised power and ferocity. Cary's imagery of bulls associates ironically with a long tradition in art and literature, from the frescoes of ancient Crete which show aspects of the

Minoan cult of the bull, to Hemingway's preoccupation with the image of the bull in *Death in the Afternoon* (1932).'

7. *The Indeterminate World*, p. 62.
8. William Golding, *Lord of the Flies*, (New York, 1955), p. 105.
9. Preface to *Charley Is My Darling*, ed. cit., p. x.
10. Ibid., p. x.
11. Ibid., p. x.
12. *Lord of the Flies*, p. 223.
13. *Art and Reality*, p. 19.
14. Preface to *What Maisie Knew* (New York, 1908), p. viii.
15. Ibid., p. viii.
16. Ibid., pp. ix–x.
17. Ibid., p. viii.
18. *What Maisie Knew*, p. 18.
19. Quoted in M. Bewley, *The Complex Fate* (London, 1952), p. 123.
20. Preface to *What Maisie Knew*, p. x.
21. Ibid., p. ix.
22. See F. R. Leavis, '"What Maisie Knew" a Disagreement', in M. Bewley, *The Complex Fate*, p. 124.
23. Enid Starkie, 'Joyce Cary, A Portrait', *Essays By Diverse Hands, Transactions of the Royal Society of Literature*, new series xxxii (1963), p. 135.
24. Walter Allen, *Joyce Cary* (Writers and Their Work, No. 41), revised edition (London, 1954), p. 11.
25. Joyce Cary, *A House of Children*, New York; Anchor Books, 1962), p. 5. Subsequent references to this edition will be cited in parantheses in the text.
26. Bloom, *The Indeterminate World*, p. 66.
27. Preface to *A House of Children*, ed. cit., p. vii.
28. Walter O'Grady, 'On Plot in Modern fiction: Hardy, James and Conrad', in Robert M. Davis, ed. *The Novel: Modern Essays in Criticism* (New Jersey, 1969), p. 208: 'In all novels, the juxtaposition of these two states [the interior and the exterior] is the spark which sets the plot in motion. It might be said that given a certain interior state, and given a certain exterior state, it is impossible that things remain the same; the novel is the working out of the process of change'.
29. For example, pp. 25–6, 69.
30. See Anketel's refusal to join the game with the other children (p. 50).
31. *Charley Is My Darling*, ed. cit., p. 286.
32. Ibid., p. 286.
33. Ibid., pp. 285–6.
34. *To Be A Piligrim*, Carfax ed. (London, 1951), pp. 80–1, 333.
35. Preface to *A House of Children*, ed. cit., p. vii.
36. Joyce Cary, 'The Way a Novel Gets Written', *Harper's* CC (February 1950), p. 92.
37. Milton Crane, in 'Masterpiece Revived', *Chicago Sunday Tribune Magazine of Books* (24 January 1960), p. 3, says that Cary 'obviously' saw in the story of Charley 'a microcosm of the problem of anarchism, a philosophy that he viewed with mingled fascination and terror all his life'.

CHAPTER 3

1. Andrew Wright, *Joyce Cary*, p. 124.
2. *To Be A Piligrim*, Carfax edition (London, 1951), p. 333. Subsequent references are to this edition and will be cited parenthetically in the text.
3. Robert Bloom, *The Indeterminate World*, p. 95.
4. Ibid., p. 96.
5. *Herself Surprised*, Carfax edition (London, 1951), p. 142.
6. For Kant's arguments against the physico-theological, the cosmological and the ontological 'proofs' of the existence of God, see Edward Caird, *The Critical Philosophy of Kant*, Vol. II, 2nd ed. (Glasgow, 1909), p. 102. Kierkegaard pointed out the absolute paradox of all faith by showing that faith could only be irrational, a 'leap into the abyss'. 'Faith,' he claimed, 'begins where thinking leaves off' (see his *Fear and Trembling*, (Princeton, 1941), p. 78).
7. Douglas Stewart, *The Ark of God*, (London, 1961), p. 150, sees in this novel a treatment of the conflict between Ronald Knox's *Enthusiasm* and Emile Brunner's *The Misunderstanding of the Church*. 'The manifestation of the spirit beyond the walls of Rome is on too great a scale, too various, too profound, to be dismissed so easily' by *Enthusiasm*, and Brunner has 'no solution for the anarchy of sectarian enthusiasm'. Cary saw this paradox, too. His answer was Lucy—'the stormiest spirit' who realised that because of its own nature it needed 'some rule of sea and road' (*To Be A Piligrim*, p. 25).
8. *The First Triology*, (New York, 1958), p. xi.
9. According to his agent, Wilcher had seventeen completed wills from his London office, five at Lloyds Bank, seven at Westminister Bank and three at Tolbrook.
10. Cf. Joyce Cary, 'The Way A Novel Gets Written', *Harpers*, CC (February 1950), 89; 'I had to show—I had to make the reader feel—the fundamental power and drive of the Protestant tradition which is the soul of British and American democracy; to get, if possible, at the roots of that religious institution'.
11. *Herself Surprised*, Carfax edition (London, 1951), p. 75. All subsequent references are to this edition and will be cited in parentheses in the text.
12. *To Be A Piligrim*, ed. cit., p. 51.
13. Ibid., p. 36.
14. Ibid., p. 308.
15. Ibid., p. 223.
16. Ibid., p. 35.
17. Ibid., p. 25.
18. Quoted in Wright, op. cit., p. 118.
19. *The Indeterminate World*, p. 86.
20. *Art and Reality*, pp. 39, 38.
21. For the philosophical origins of this persistent Carian argument, see Hume, *Philosophical Works*, edited Green and Grose, Vol. IV, pp. 140–61. For a discussion, see John B. Stewart, *The Moral and Political Philosophy of David Hume* (New York, 1963), especially pp. 80–5.
22. *The Indeterminate World*, p. 86
23. Frederick Karl, *The Contemporary English Novel*, p. 135.
24. *To Be A Pilgrim*, p. 313.

25. Ibid., p. 130.
26. 'The Way A Novel Gets Written', *Adam International Review*, XVIII (November–December, 1950), 9.
27. This comparison was first made by Andrew Wright, *Joyce Cary*, p. 113.
28. Genesis XII, 11. 16.
29. Ibid., XVIII, 12.
30. *The Horse's Mouth* (New York: Harpers and Brothers, 1944), p. 80. Subsequent references are to this edition and will be cited in parentheses in the text.
31. *The First Triology*, (New York, 1958), p. x.
32. Ibid., pp. xii–xiii.
33. Ibid., p. xiii.
34. Quoted in F. Copleston, *A History of Philosophy*, Vol. IV (London, 1958), p. 245.
35. Letter quoted in Copleston, Vol. IV, p. 263.
36. *Ethics*, Pt. IV, proposition 18, note; quoted in Copleston, Vol IV, p. 244.
37. *The Horse's Mouth*, p. 1.
38. Spinoza, *The Road To Inner Freedom*, ed. by Dagobert D. Runes (New York, 1957), p. 79.
39. Ibid., p. 163.
40. Hazard Adams uses this passage to illustrate a different but related argument in his 'Blake and Gulley Jimson: English Symbolists', *Critique*, III (Spring–Fall, 1959), 11–12.
41. Cary suggested this as the title for the French edition of *The Horse's Mouth*. 'They say this ('the unbustable tip') unworthy of a philosophical work and too like a *roman policier*. I say *tant mieux*. But they are unconvinced'. *Writers at Work*, edited Malcolm Cowley, p. 65.
42. Page references after Blake quotations refer to *The Horse's Mouth* not to any editions of Blake's *Works*.
43. Cf., however Jimson's momentary rejection of walls: 'No more walls for me that fall down or get knocked full of holes by charwomen's brooms. Give me canvas now I can afford it . . . They can't hang walls' (p. 113).
44. See Stephen A. Shapiro, 'Leopold Bloom and Gulley Jimson: The Economics of Survival', *Twentieth Century Literature*, X (April 1964), 3–11. Shapiro bases his analysis, however, on what he calls 'Freud's fundamental assertion in *The Interpretation of Dreams*: all mental processes tend to operate to avoid pain and elicit pleasure' (p. 3). It need hardly be pointed out that Cary would have rejected this explanation outright.

CHAPTER 4

1. Andrew Wright, *Joyce Cary*, p. 137.
2. Elizabeth R. Bettman, 'Joyce Cary and the Problem of Political Morality', *Antioch Review*, XVII (Summer 1957), p. 266.
3. *Prisoner of Grace*, Carfax edition (London: Michael Joseph, 1954), p. 5.
4. *Power in Men*, pp. 37–8.
5. 'Political and Personal Morality', *Saturday Review* (31 December 1955), 35.

6. Ibid., p. 35.
7. *Art and Reality*, p. 172.
8. 'Political and Personal Morality', p. 6.
9. Quoted in Elizabeth R. Bettman, 'Joyce Cary and the Problem of Political Morality', op. cit.
10. Cf. Elizabeth M. Kerr, 'Joyce Cary's Second Trilogy', *University of Toronto Quarterly*, XXIX (April 1960): 'A decided improvement over the *First Trilogy* in which Sara's and Wilcher's narratives are well motivated but Gulley Jimson's seems lacking in plausible purpose and circumstances of writing, is the statement of a convincing purpose at the beginning of each novel which lends consistent authenticity of effect to all three first person narratives'. Giles Mitchell, in 'Joyce Cary's *Prisoner of Grace*', *MFS*, IX (Autumn 1963), p. 263, on the other hand, thinks there is 'an apparent discrepancy between Nina's stated intention and final accomplishment'.
11. *To Be A Pilgrim*, pp. 266–7.
12. Bloom, *The Indeterminate World*, p. 107.
13. 'The Way a Novel gets Written', *Adam International Review*, XVIII (November–December 1950), 3–4.
14. Tolstoy, *What is Art?* and *Essays on Art*, translated Aylmer Maude (London, 1929), p. 273.
15. *War and Peace*, translated Constance Garnett, Charleton House ed., (New York, 1930), pp. 98–9.
16. Ibid., p. 270.
17. *Art and Reality*, pp. 116, 114.
18. *Prisoner of Grace*, Universal Library ed. (New York, 1962), p. 63. Subsequent references are to this edition and will be included parenthetically in the text.
19. *Preface to Prisoner of Grace*, Carfax ed. (London, 1954), p. 6.
20. *Not Honour More*, Universal Library ed. (New York, 1963), p. 172.
21. Preface to *Prisoner of Grace*, Carfax ed., p. 7.
22. Ibid., p. 8.
23. Ibid., p. 7.
24. Nina argues for the existence of two idealisms, hers and Nimmo's in the railway-station scene—'there are principles on both sides'—*Prisoner of Grace*, p. 65.
25. *Except the Lord*, Universal Library ed. (New York, 1962), p. 1. Subsequent references are to this edition and will be cited parenthetically in the text.
26. *Prisoner of Grace*, ed. cit., p. 244.
27. *The Indeterminate World*, p. 143.
28. Cf. the image, also in *Except the Lord*, p. 20: 'I rested my very joy of rebellion in it as the puppy tugging at his mother's ear, exults in the confidence that he is not only brave but safe'.
29. *Art and Reality*, p. 37.
30. Ibid., p. 34.
31. *Deuteronomy*, XXIV, 14: quoted in *Except the Lord*, p. 234.
32. The irony of Nimmo's statesmanship was, of course, that he mistook the 'Lord' for the class title he later attained. Except Lord Nimmo build the house, his thinking went, their labour is in vain that try.
33. *Power in Men*, pp. 263–4.
34. This should correct the misreading of *Except the Lord* advanced by John

Telling, SJ in 'Joyce Cary's Moral World', *MFS*, IX (Autumn 1963), 280.

35. *Except the Lord*, ed. cit., pp. 115–6.
36. *The Indeterminate World*, p. 168.
37. *Except the Lord*, p. 273.
38. Joyce Cary, *The Drunken Sailor* (London: Michael Joseph, 1947), pp. 8–9.
39. *Prisoner of Grace*, ed. cit., p. 2.
40. *Not Honour More*, Universal Library ed. (New York, 1963), p. 32. Subsequent references to this edition will be cited in parentheses in the text.
41. *Expect the Lord*, p. 243.
42. *Power in Men*, p. 42.
43. *The Indeterminate World*, p. 195.
44. Lovelace: 'To Lucasta on Going to the Wars'.
45. Sir Edward Varney, quoted in C. H. Hartmann, *The Cavalier Spirit* (London, 1925), pp. 54–5.
46. *Writers at Work* (New York, 1958), pp. 65–6.
47. Ibid., p. 56.

CHAPTER 5

1. *Power in Men*, p. 1.
2. *Art and Reality*, p. 16.
3. Ibid., p. 16.
4. *Art and Reality*, p. 12.
5. Ibid., p. 24.
6. Ibid., p. 25.
7. Ibid., p. 28.
8. *Except the Lord*, pp. 19–20.
9. Ibid., p. 135.
10. *A House of Children*, p. 68.
11. Ibid., pp. 75, 74.
12. Ibid., p. 74. Cf. St Augustine, *Confessions*, Book II, iii; translated F. J. Sheed (New York, 1943), p. 30: 'I went headlong on my course, so blinded that I was ashamed among the other youths that my consciousness was less than theirs; I heard them boasting of their exploits, and the viler the exploits the louder the boasting; and I set about the same exploits not only for the pleasure of the act but for the pleasure of the boasting, when I lacked opportunity to equal others in vice, I invented things I had not done, lest I might be held cowardly for being innocent, or contemptible for being chaste'.
13. *Except the Lord*, p. 135.
14. Ibid., p. 5.
15. Ibid., p. 5.
16. *To Be A Pilgrim*, p. 34.
17. *Except the Lord*, p. 26.
18. Excerpts from this disputation are quoted in Charles G. Hoffmann, *The Captive and the Free*: Joyce Cary's Unfinished Trilogy', *Texas Studies in Literature and Language*, V (Spring, 1963), 19.
19. Quoted in Geoffrey Tillotson, 'Introduction', *Newman: Prose and Poetry* (London, 1957), p. 24.

20. *Confessions*, Book I, i; translated F. J. Sheed (New York, 1943), p. 3.
21. *Except the Lord*, p. 264.
22. Quoted in Tillotson, op. cit., p. 25.
23. James Hall, *The Tragic Comedians* (Bloomington, 1963), p. 5.
24. Hall does, however, point out that more than any comic contemporary' Cary comes close to 'making the miracle of ecstasy out of pain ring true', even as he recognises that the pursuit of that 'creative ecstasy is not for everybody' (ibid., p. 158). Cary saw himself as an existentialist 'in the school of Kierkegaard'—'Existentialism without a god is nonsense—it atomizes a world which is plainly a unity . . . The French seem to take me for an existentialist in Sartre's sense of the word. But I'm not. I am influenced by the solitude of men's mind, but equally by the unity of their fundamental character and feelings, their sympathies which bring them together'. *Writers at Work*, edited Malcolm Cowley (New York, 1958), pp. 57–8.
25. This, in fact, is the distinguishing factor between the pathetic comedy of the wretched Jo in Dickens' *Bleak House* and that of Charley in *Charley Is My Darling*.
26. *The Tragic Comedians*, p. 84.
27. *Prisoner of Grace*, Universal Library ed. (New York, 1962), p. 15.
28. Preface to *Aissa Saved*, Carfax ed. (London, 1952), p. 9.
29. Paraphrased from a letter by Cary quoted in Enid Starkie, op. cit., p. 127.
30. Enid Starkie, op. cit., p. 127.
31. *Herself Surprised*, Carfax ed. (London, 1951), pp. 83, 204.
32. *A House of Children*, Anchor ed. (New York, 1962), p. 68.
33. Preface to *The Horse's Mouth*, Carfax ed. (London, 1951), p. 7.
34. *Art and Reality*, p. 185.
35. *An American Visitor*, Anchor ed. (New York, 1963), p. 259.
36. *The African Witch*, pp. 293–4.
37. *Mister Johnson*, p. 248.
38. *Not Honour More*, Universal Library ed. (New York, 1963), p. 309.
39. Ibid., pp. 308, 1.
40. Ibid., p. 307. In *Charley Is My Darling* (ed. cit., p. 264) Charley locks himself in the WC and 'at once' feels 'released, as though he is out of prison. He falls back against the wall, puts his hand over his face and begins to cry, silently and desperately. An oppression is broken away from his heart, from his whole body'.
41. 'Joyce Cary's Moral World', *MFS*, IX (Autumn 1963) 283.
42. *The Horse's Mouth* (New York, 1944), p. 174.
43. Ibid., p. 119.
44. Ibid., p. 178.
45. 'The "Socially Extensive" Novel', *Adam International Review*, XVIII (November–December 1950), 32.
46. 'The Idea of Progress', *Cornhill Magazine*, CLXVII (Summer 1954), 334.
47. Joyce Cary, *The Drunken Sailor: A Ballad-Epic* (London: Michael Joseph, 1947), p. 12. Other page reference to this poem will be cited in parentheses after the text.
48. Quoted by M. M. Mahood, *Joyce Cary's Africa* (London, 1964), p. 85.
49. *Writers at Work*, edited Malcolm Cowley (New York, 1958), p. 65.

Select Bibliography

JOYCE CARY'S WRITINGS

Note: For a more complete listing, see Robert Bloom, *The Indeterminate World* (1962), pp. 101–205; M. M. Mahood, *Joyce Cary's Africa* (1964), pp. 197–200; James B. Meriwether, 'The Books of Joyce Cary: A Preliminary Bibliography of English and American Editions', *Texas Studies in English Literature and Language*, I (Summer 1965), 300–10; and Andrew Wright, 'Joyce Cary's Unpublished Work', *London Magazine*, V (January 1958), 35, 42.

Fiction: (Editions used)

Aissa Saved (1932). Carfax edition (London, 1952).
An American Visitor (1933). Carfax edition (London, 1952).
The African Witch (1936). Carfax edition (London, 1951).
Castle Corner (1938). Carfax edition (London, 1952).
Mister Johnson (1939). Carfax edition (London, 1952).
Charley Is My Darling (1940). Signet edition (New York, 1963).
A House of Children (1941). Anchor edition (New York, 1962).
Herself Surprised (1941). Carfax edition (London, 1951).
To Be A Pilgrim (1942). Carfax edition (London, 1951).
The Horse's Mouth (1944). (New York: Harper, 1944).
The First Trilogy, (New York: Harper, 1958).
The Moonlight (1946). Carfax edition (London, 1952).
A Fearful Joy (1949). Carfax edition (London, 1952).
Prisoner of Grace (1952). Universal Library edition (New York, 1962).
Except the Lord (1953). Universal Library edition (New York, 1962).
Not Honour More (1955). Universal Library edition (New York, 1963).
The Captive and the Free. Carfax edition (London, 1959).
Spring Song and Other Stories. (London: Penguin Books, 1963).

Poetry

Marching Soldier (London: Michael Joseph, 1945).
The Drunken Sailor: A Ballad-Epic (London: Michael Joseph, 1947).

Aesthetics

Art and Reality: Ways of the Creative Process, Clark Lectures, Cambridge University (1958), Anchor edition (New York, 1961).

Political and Other Writings

Power in Men (1939). Introduction by Hazard Adams, (Seattle: Washington University Press, 1963).
The Case for African Freedom and Other Writings on Africa.
(Austin, Texas, 1962). Includes *The Case for African Freedom* (London, 1941, revised and enlarged, 1944); *Britain and West Africa* (1946; republished with Appendix 1947); 'Africa Yesterday: One Ruler's Burden', which appeared originally in the *Reporter*, (15 May 1951); 'Christmas in Africa', from *Esquire*, (December 1953); 'Catching Up With History', a review of Richard Wright's *Black Power*, from the *Nation* 16 October 1954).
Memoir of the Bobotes (Austin, Texas, 1963). Introduction by James B. Meriwether.

Articles and Essays

Can Western Values Survive Without Religion', *Time and Tide* (9 July 1955), pp. 901–2.
'The Censorship Plot', *Spectator* (11 March 1955), 275–6.
'Faith in Liberty', *Time and Tide* (16 July 1955), 933–4.
'Horror Comics', *Spectator* (18 February 1955), 177.
'The Idea of Progress', *Cornhill Magazine*, CLXVII (Summer 1954), 331–7.
'My First Novel', *Listener* (16 April 1953), 637–8.
'A Novel Is a Novel', *New York Times Book Review* (30 April 1950), 1, 34. Reprinted in *Adam International Review*, XVII (November–December 1960), 1–3.

'On the Function of the Novelist', *New York Times Book Review*, (30 October 1949), 1, 52.

'Party of One', *Holiday*, XX (September 1956), 9.

'The Period Novel', *Spectator* (21 November 1952), 684.

'Political and Personal Morality', (American) *Saturday Review* (23 August 1952), 6–7, 35.

'The Way a Novel Gets Written', Harper's, CC (February 1950), 87–93; *Adam International Review*, XVIII (November–December 1950), 3, 11.

'Tolstoy's Theory of Art', *University of Edinburgh Journal*, XII (Summer 1943), 91–6.

SECONDARY MATERIAL ON JOYCE CARY

Adam International Review, XVIII (November–December 1950). The entire issue is devoted to Joyce Cary.

Adams, Hazard, 'The Three Speakers of Joyce Cary', *Modern Fiction Studies*, V (Summer 1959), 108–120.

'Blake and Gulley Jimson: English Symbolists', *Critique*, III (Spring/Fall 1959), 3–14.

'Introduction', to Joyce Cary's *Power in Men* (Seattle, 1963), vii–xlvi.

Allen, Walter, *Joyce Cary* ('Writers and Their Work' series: No. 41), revised edition (London, 1954).

Allen, Walter, 'A Flood of Memories', (A Review of *A House of Children*), *New York Times Book Review*, (4 March 1956), p. 6.

'Back to Anarchy', *New Statesman and Nation* (16 December 1933), 800–1.

Barr, Donald, 'A Careful and Profound Thinker', *Adam International Review*, XVIII (November–December 1950) 30–1.

Bellow, Saul, 'A Personal Record', (A review of *Except the Lord*) *New Republic* (24 February 1954), 20–1.

Battaglia, Francis Joseph, 'Spurious Armageddon: Joyce Cary's *Not Honour More*', *Modern Fiction Studies*, XIII (Winter 1967–68), 479–91.

Bettman, Elizabeth, R., 'Joyce Cary and the Problem of Political Morality', *Antioch Review*, XVII (Summer 1957), 266–72.

Bloom, Robert, *The Indeterminate World: A Study of the Novels of Joyce Cary* (Philadelphia, 1962).

Case, Edward, 'The Free World of Joyce Cary', *Modern Age*, III (Spring 1959), 115–24.

Cecil, Lord David, 'The Novelist at Work: A Conversation between Joyce Cary and Lord David Cecil', *Adam International Review*, XVIII (November–December 1950) 15–25.

'Cheerful Protestant', *Time*, LX (20 October 1952), 118–30.

Cohen, Nathan, 'A Conversation with Joyce Cary', *Tarmarack Review*, 3 (Spring 1957), 5–15.

Cowley, Malcolm, *Writers at Work: The Paris Review Interviews* (New York, 1958), pp. 51–67.

Crane, Milton, 'Masterpiece Revived', *Chicago Sunday Tribune Magazine of Books* (24 January 1960), 3.

Eastman, Richard M., 'Historical Grace in Cary's *A Fearful Joy*', *Novel* (Winter 1968), 150–57.

Echeruo, M. J. C., *Joyce Cary and the Novel of Africa* (London, 1973).

Faber, Kathleen R. (with M. D. Faber), 'An Important Theme of Joyce Cary's Trilogy', *Discourse*, XI (Winter 1968), 26–31.

Forster, Malcolm, 'Fell of the Lion, Fleece of the Sheep', *Modern Fiction Studies*, IX (Autumn 1963), 257–62. *Joyce Cary: A Biography* (London, 1968).

Garrett, George, 'The Major Poetry of Joyce Cary', *Modern Fiction Studies*, IX (Autumn 1963), 245–56.

Hall, James, *The Tragic Comedians: Seven Modern British Novelists* (Bloomington, 1963).

Hamilton, Kenneth, 'Boon or Thorn? Joyce Cary and Samuel Beckett on Human Life', *Dalhousie Review*, XXXVIII (Winter 1959), 433–42.

Hardy, Barbara, 'Form in Joyce Cary's Novels', *Essays in Criticism*, IV (April 1954), 180–90.

'Herself Surprised', *Times Literary Supplement* (19 September 1952) 609.

Hoffmann, Charles G., 'Joyce Cary and the Comic Mask', *Western Humanities Review*, XIII (Spring 1959), 135–42.

Hoffmann, Charles G., 'The Captive and the Free: Joyce Cary's Unfinished Trilogy', *Texas Studies in English Literature and Language*, V (Spring 1963), 17–24.

Hoffmann, Charles G., 'The Genesis and Development of Joyce Cary's First Trilogy', *PMLA*, LXXVIII (September 1963), 431–39.

Hoffmann, Charles G., ' "They Want to be Happy": Joyce Cary's Unfinished Castle Corner series', *Modern Fiction Studies*, IX

(Autumn 1963), 217–25.

Hoffmann, Charles G., *Joyce Cary: The Comedy of Freedom* (Pittsburg, 1964).

Holloway, John, 'Joyce Cary's Fiction: Modernity and Sustaining Power', *Times Literary Supplement* (7 August 1959), xiv, xv. Also as 'Joyce Cary and the Sustaining Power', in his *The Colours of Clarity: Essays on Contemporary Literature and Education* (London, 1946), pp. 52–9.

Howe, Susanne, *Novels of Empire* (New York, 1949).

Johnson, Pamela Hansford, 'Three Novelists and the Drawing of Character: C. P. Snow, Joyce Cary, and Ivy Compton-Burnett', *Essays and Studies by Members of the English Association* (1950), pp. 82–91.

Kanu, S. H., *A World of Everlasting Conflict: Joyce Cary's View of Man and Society* (Ibadan [Nigeria], 1974).

Karl, Frederick R., 'Joyce Cary: The Moralist as Novelist', *Twentieth Century Literature*, V (January 1960), 183–96.

Karl, Frederick R., *A Reader's Guide to the Contemporary English Novel* (New York, 1962).

Kerr, Elizabeth M., 'Joyce Cary's Second Trilogy', *University of Toronto Quarterly*, XXIX (April 1960), 310–25.

King, Carlyle, 'Joyce Cary and the Creative Imagination', *Tamarack Review* (Winter 1959), 39–51.

Larsen, Golden L., *The Dark Descent: Social Change and Moral Responsibility in the Novels of Joyce Cary* (London, 1965).

Lyons, Richard S., 'Narrative Method in Joyce Cary's *To Be A Pilgrim*', *Texas Studies in English Literature and Language*, VI (Summer 1964), 269–79.

Mahood, M. M., *Joyce Cary's Africa* (London, 1964).

Meriwether, James B., 'The Books of Joyce Cary: A Preliminary Bibliography of English and American Editions', *Texas Studies in English Literature and Language*, I (Summer 1959), 300–10.

Michell, Giles, 'Joyce Cary's *Prisoner of Grace*', *Modern Fiction Studies*, IX (Autumn 1963), 263–75.

Noble, R. W. *Joyce Cary* (Edinburgh, 1973).

Ryan, Marjorie, 'An Interpretation of Joyce Cary's *The Horse's Mouth*', *Critique*. II (Spring–Summer 1958) 29–38.

Salz, Paulina J., 'The Philosophical Principles in Joyce Cary's Work', *Western Humanities Review*, XX (Spring 1966), 159–65.

Schorer, Mark, 'The 'Socially Extensive' Novel', *Adam International Review*, XVIII (November–December 1950), 31–2.

Shapiro, Stephen A, 'Leopold Bloom and Gulley Jimson: The Economics of Survival', *Twentieth Century Literature*, X (April 1964), 3–11.

Starkie, Enid, 'Joyce Cary: A Portrait', *Essays by Diverse Hands*, Transactions of the Royal Society of Literature new series, XXXII (w963), 125–44.

Steinbrecher, George, Jr., 'Joyce Cary: Master Novelist', College English, XVIII (May 1957), 387–95.

Stern, James, 'Beneath the Guilt Lay Innocence', (review of *Charley Is My Darling*), *New York Times Book Review* (24 January 1960), 4.

Stevenson, Lionel, 'Joyce Cary and the Anglo-Irish Tradition', *Modern Fiction Studies*, IX (Autumn 1963), 210–16.

Stewart, Douglas, 'Joyce Cary's Protestantism', in *The Ark of God: Studies in Five Modern Novelists* (London, 1961), pp. 129–58.

Stockholder, Fred, 'The Triple Vision of Joyce Cary's First Trilogy', *Modern Fiction Studies*, IX (Autumn 1963), 231–44.

Telling, John, 'Joyce Cary's Moral World', *Modern Fiction Studies*, IX (Autumn 1963), 276–83.

Van Horn, Ruth G., 'Freedom and Imagination in the Novels of Joyce Cary', *Midwest Journal*, V (Winter 1952–53), 19–30.

Wolkenfeld, Jack, *Joyce Cary: The Developing Style* (New York, 1968).

Woodcock, George, 'Citizens of Babel: A Study of Joyce Cary', *Queens Quarterly*, LXIII (1956) 236–46.

Wright, Andrew, *Joyce Cary, A Preface to His Novels* (London 1958).

Wright Andrew, 'Joyce Cary's Unpublished Work', *London Magazine*, V (January 1958), 35–42.

Wright Andrew, 'A Note of Joyce Cary's Reputation', *Modern Fiction Studies*, IX (Autumn 1963), 207–9.

Wright Andrew, 'An Authoritative Text of *The Horse's Mouth*', *Papers of the Bibliographical Society of America*, (Second Quarter 1967).

GENERAL

Augustine, Saint, *Confessions*, translated F. J. Sheen (New York, 1943).

Baker, James V., *The Sacred River: Coleridge's Theory of the Imagination* (Louisiana State University Press, 1957).

Beebe, Maurice, *Ivory Towers and Sacred Founts* (New York, 1964).

Berdyaev, Nicolas, *The Meaning of History* (London, 1933).

Bewley, Marius, *The Complex Fate* (London, 1952).

Blotner, Joseph L., *The Political Novel* (New York, 1955).

Brunner, Heinrich Emil, *The Misunderstanding of the Church*, translated Harold Knight (London, 1952).

Burke, Kenneth, *A Grammar of Motives* (New York, 1945).

Caird, Edward, *The Critical Philosophy of Kant*, 2 Vol., 2nd edition (Glasgow, 1909).

Coleridge, S. T., 'Statesman Manual' in *Works* edited W. G. T. Shedd, I (New York, 1884).

Cook, Albert, 'The Unity of *War and Peace*', *Western Review*, XXII (Summer 1958), 243–55.

Copleston, F., *A History of Philosophy*, Vol. V: Hobbes to Hume (London, 1959); Vol. VI: Kant to Hegel (London, 1960).

Croce, Benedetto, *Aesthetic as Science of Expression and General Linguistic*, translated Douglas Ainslie (London, 1929).

Davies, J. G., *The Theology of William Blake* (Oxford, 1948).

Dickens, Charles, *Great Expectations*, Gadshill edition (London, 1898).

Dreiser, Theodore, *Sister Carrie* (New York, 1946).

Durrell, Lawrence, *Justine*, Cardinal edition (New York, 1962).

Frye, C. Northrop, *Anatomy of Criticism* (Princeton, 1957).

Glicksberg, Charles I., *The Tragic Vision in Twentieth Century Literature*, Crosscurrents series, edited Harry T. Moore (Carbondale, Southern Illinois University Press, 1963).

Goldberg, S. L., *The Classical Temper* (New York, 1961).

Golding, William, *Lord of the Flies* (New York, 1955).

Grave, S. A., *The Scottish Philosophy of Common Sense* (Oxford, 1960).

Hallett, H. F., *Aeternitas: A Spinozistic Study* (Oxford, 1930).

Handy, William J., *Kant and the Southern Critics* (Austin, Texas, 1963).

Harmann, Cyril H., *The Cavalier Spirit: Its Influence on the Life and Work of Richard Lovelace, 1618–1685* (London, 1925).

Hough, Graham, *Image and Experience* (London, 1960).

Hume, David, *The Philosophical Works*, 4 Vols. edited T. H. Green and T. H. Grose (Aalen (Germany), 1964).

Hume, David, *A Treatise of Human Nature*, Bk I, edited D. G. G. Macnabb (New York: Meridian Books, 1962).

Huxley, Aldous, *Crome Yellow* (New York, 1922).

James, Henry, *A Portrait of a Lady*, (New York: Modern Library, 1951).

James, Henry, *What Maisie Knew* (New York, 1908).

Jasper, Karl, *The Origin and Goal of History*, (New Haven, 1953).

Kant, Immanuel, *Critique of Practical Reason and Other Writings in Moral Philosophy*, translated and edited L. W. Beck (Chicago, 1949).

Kant, Immanuel, *Critique of Practical Reason and other Works on the Theory of Ethics*, translated T. K. Abbott (London, 1909).

Keats, John, *Poetical Works*, edited H. W. Garrod (London, 1939).

Kierkegaard, Sorel, *Fear and Trembling* (Princeton, 1941).

Knox, Israel, *The Aesthetic Theories of Kant, Hegel and Schopenhauer* (London, 1958).

Knox, Ronald A., *Enthusiasm* (Oxford, 1950).

Krook, Dorothy, *The Ordeal of Consciousness in Henry James* (Cambridge, 1962).

Lawrence, D. H., 'Surgery for the Novel—or a Bomb', in *Modern British Fiction*, edited Mark Schorer (New York, 1961).

McCormick, John, *Catastrophe and Imagination: An Interpretation of the Recent English and American Novel* (London, 1957).

Roubiczek, Paul, *Existentialism: For and Against* (Cambridge, 1964).

Rousseau, Jean-Jacques, *The Social Contract in Political Writings*, edited with introduction by Frederick Watkins (Edinburgh, 1953).

Russell, Bertrand, *Sceptical Essays* (New York, 1928).

Sartre, Jean-Paul, *Being and Nothingness*, translated Hazel E. Barnes (New York, 1956).

Saw, Ruth Lydia, *The Vindication of Metaphysics: A Study in the Philosophy of Spinoza* (London, 1951).

Somerset Maugham, W., *The Art of Fiction* (New York, 1925).

Spence, G. W., 'Suicide and Sacrifice in Tolstoy's Ethics', *Russian Review*, XXII April 1963), 157–67.

Spinoza, B., *Ethic of Benedict de Spinoza*, translated W. Hale White and Amelia H. Stirling (London, 1923).

Spinoza, B., *The Road to Inner Freedom*, edited with an introduction by Dagobert D. Runes (New York, 1957).

Spinoza, B., *Short Treatise on God, Man and His Well-being* (London, 1920).

Sterne, Laurence, *Tristram Shandy* (New York, 1925).

Steward, John B., *The Moral and Political Philosophy of David Hume* (New York, 1963).

Tillotson, Geoffrey, *Newman: Prose and Poetry*, Nonesuch edition (London, 1957).

Tolstoy, Leo, *What is Art and Essays on Art*, translated Aylmer Maude, Vol. XVII of *Works of Leo Tolstoy*, Tolstoy Centenary Edition (London, 1929).

Tolstoy, Leo, *War and Peace*, translated Constance Garnett, Carleton House edition (New York, 1930).

Traugott, John, *Tristram Shandy's Moral World: Sterne's Philosophical Rhetoric* (Berkeley, 1954).

Van Ghent, Dorothy, *The English Novel: Form and Function* (New York, 1961).

Index